Neurofilmology of the Moving Image

Neurofilmology of the Moving Image

Gravity and Vertigo in Contemporary Cinema

Adriano D'Aloia

Routledge
Taylor & Francis Group
LONDON AND NEW YORK

First published in 2021 by Amsterdam University Press Ltd.

Published 2025 by Routledge
4 Park Square, Milton Park, Abingdon, Oxon OX14 4RN
605 Third Avenue, New York, NY 10158

Routledge is an imprint of the Taylor & Francis Group, an informa business

ISBN: 9789463725255 (hbk)
ISBN: 9781041183518 (pbk)
ISBN: 9781003700579 (ebk)
NUR 670

Cover illustration: On the virtual set of *The Walk* (Robert Zemeckis, 2015). Courtesy of Gasper Tringale

Cover design: Coördesign, Leiden

DOI: 10.5117/9789463725255

For Product Safety Concerns and Information please contact our EU representative:
GPSR@taylorandfrancis.com
Taylor & Francis Verlag GmbH, Kaufingerstraße 24, 80331 München, Germany

To Paolo Giuseppe

Table of Contents

Acknowledgements

Some of the chapters of this book are based on the following texts that appeared as contributions in edited collections or as journal articles: 'Cinematic Empathies. Spectator Involvement in the Film Experience,' in *Kinesthetic Empathy in Creative and Cultural Practices*, edited by Matthew Reason & Dee Reynolds, 91-108 (Bristol-Chicago: Intellect, 2012); 'On Icarus' Wings. Cinematic experience of falling bodies'. *Iluminace*, 4 (2012): 81-97; 'Upside-Down Cinema. (Dis)simulation of the body in the film experience'. *Cinema: Journal of Philosophy and the Moving Image*, 3 (2012): 155-182; 'The intangible ground: A neurophenomenology of the film experience'. *Necsus. European Journal of Media Studies*, 2 (2012): 219-239; 'The Character's Body and the Viewer: Cinematic Empathy and Embodied Simulation in the Film Experience'. In *Embodied Cognition and Cinema*, edited by Maarten Coëgnarts & Peter Kravanja, 187-199 (Leuven: Leuven University Press, 2015). A different version of parts of this book appeared in Italian in my *La vertigine e il volo. L'esperienza filmica fra estetica e neuroscienze cognitive* (Roma: Ente dello Spettacolo, 2013). In every case these earlier and preparatory versions have been substantially revised, enriched, and updated in function of the whole structure of the book and of the advancements in the scientific debate.

I am indebted to many friends and colleagues who supported me in the research and writing process over the last few years. I would like to thank in particular Francesco Casetti and Ruggero Eugeni for guiding my endeavours in the study of the film experience. Over the years of preparation of the book I have encountered the generosity of many scholars who have not hesitated to provide me with illuminating advice. Thanks in particular to Jennifer Barker, Robin Curtis, Roberto Diodato, Thomas Elsaesser, Vittorio Gallese, Michele Guerra, Julian Hanich, Vinzenz Hediger, Massimo Locatelli, Carmelo Marabello, Francesco Parisi, Andrea Pinotti, Patricia Pisters, Maria Poulaki, Steven Shaviro, Vivian Sobchack, Antonio Somaini, Lesley Stern, Ed Tan, and Ian Verstegen. Special thanks to Enrico Carocci, Steffen Hven, and Michael Cramer, who read the manuscript and provided me with valuable suggestions for its improvement.

In the years it took to write this book I moved between different universities. I would like to express my thanks to all the colleagues and students I have met and with whom I have had fruitful intellectual and human exchanges at the Università Cattolica del Sacro Cuore, the Università IULM in Milan, the International Telematic University UniNettuno in Rome, and the Università della Campania "Luigi Vanvitelli" in Caserta.

Many sacrifices have been requested of my family: I give infinite thanks to my parents, wife, and kids for their support, love, and curiosity.

Bergamo, 19 March 2021

As I submitted the final version of the manuscript of this book to Amsterdam University Press I realized it would be published exactly on the twentieth anniversary of the September 11 terrorist attacks of 2001. At that time I had just entered my twenties as a student in the early years of his academic path. However dramatic those events were, 9/11 was undoubtedly *that* moment that impacted on the real *and* imaginary world in the life of a young man. Years away, I can now clearly see in the rear-view mirror how that turning point has continued—more or less subtly—to produce its long-lasting effects on my scientific attitude. The journey through the cinematic forms of *vertiginous* experiences that this book offers is indirectly indebted to an awareness of the *embodied symbolic* power of visual media I learnt on that occasion. Today, the 2020-2021 global Covid-19 pandemic seems to be *that* moment for all those students currently in their twenties. I sincerely hope that the dramatic oddity of these times will turn into a fruitful awareness for them too.

11 September 2021

I Vertigo

Towards a Neurofilmology

Abstract
The chapter 'Vertigo. Towards a Neurofilmology' offers an introduction to the book's contents and methods. The implementation of psychology of perception, philosophy of mind, and suggestions from cognitive neuroscience (in particular the role of 'mirror neurons' and the hypothesis of 'embodied simulation') has the capability to renew contemporary film theory and to reduce the distance between competing approaches (i.e. cognitivist and phenomenological film studies). 'Neurofilmology' adopts an enactive and embodied approach to cognition and provides interpretative tools for the exploration of contemporary cinema. Through a series of recurrent 'aerial motifs' in which the film character loses his/her equilibrium—acrobatics, fall, impact, overturning, and drift—the cinema offers an intense motor and emotional experience that puts the spectator's somatosensory perception in tension. At the same time, it provides compensation by adopting embodied forms of regulation of stimuli and a dynamic restoration of gravity and orientation (the so called 'disembodying-reembodying' dynamic).

Keywords: Neurofilmology, Embodied simulation, Mirror neurons, Spectator-as-organism, Enaction, Embodied cognition

While examining the dream of flight, we will find still more evidence that a psychology of the imagination cannot be developed using *static forms*. It must be based on forms that are in the process of being deformed, and a great deal of importance must be placed on the dynamic principles of deformation. The psychology of air is the least 'atomic' of the four psychologies that treat material imagination. It is essentially vectorial. Every aerial image is essentially a *future* with a vector for breaking into flight. If there is a dream that is capable of showing the vectorial nature of the psyche, it is certainly the *dream of flight*. The reason is based not so much on its imagined movement as on its inner substantial nature.

—Gaston Bachelard, *Air and Dreams* 1943 (1988, 21)

D'Aloia, A., *Neurofilmology of the Moving Image. Gravity and Vertigo in Contemporary Cinema.* Taylor & Francis Group 2021
DOI: 10.5117/9789463725255_CH01

> Our own body is in the world as the heart is in the organism: it keeps the visible spectacle constantly alive, it breathes life into it and sustains it inwardly, and with it forms a system.
>
> —Maurice Merleau-Ponty, *Phenomenology of Perception* 1945 (2002, 235)

Tension in the air

Shortly before the enigmatic finale of *Inception* (Nolan 2010), the moment arrives for the members of the idea-implanting team led by Dom Cobb to climb back up the progressive levels of dreams into which they have entered. The only way that the dreamers can be successfully awakened is through the synchronization of a series of 'kicks'. A kick consists of inducing a sensation of falling in the dreamers, a disturbance of their sense of balance that causes them to wake up. In the fourth and deepest level of dream the characters throw themselves out of a window and into the void. In the third level, the fall is brought about by the explosion and resulting collapse of the entire building the dreamers are occupying. In the second level, which unfolds in a zero-gravity setting, the floating bodies of the sleeping characters are shoved into an elevator before being flung upwards by an explosive charge, which artificially generates gravity and results in the kick being felt when the elevator's movement is abruptly halted. In the first and shallowest level, the kick corresponds to the moment when the van transporting the dreamers hits the surface of the river. Jumps into the void, falling down, floating in the absence of gravity, and violent impacts: taken in all of its variations, *Inception*'s synchronized kick is a catalogue of *corporeal imbalances*—physical states in which, in order to climb up the levels of consciousness, the dreamers voluntarily seek the sensation of dizziness.

More than a simple narrative device that is strategically used to resolve the complex asynchrony that characterizes *Inception* (and almost all of Nolan's filmography, as well as the so-called 'puzzle film' genre), the series of synchronized kicks and states of imbalance signals a more general tendency in contemporary narrative cinema, which is the fundamental issue dealt with by this book: the rise of a new model of spectatorship based on a pronounced involvement of *somatosensory perception*. Along (and only apparently in conflict) with an increasingly demanding mental effort to decipher the complexity of narration and understand the *sense* of the story, a rich array of *senses* is engaged to construct a new form of interaction between the *system of bodies* that inhabits the film experience, namely the spectator's, the character's, and the film's bodies. Far beyond the mere reception of visual and auditory stimuli, and not limited to synaesthesia, contemporary spectatorship involves forms of somatosensory perception such as proprioception (the sense of one's own body position), kinesthesis (the sense of self-movement), and equilibrioception (the sense of balance). This extended sensoriality concerns the relationship between the internal and the external environment of the spectator, one who is conceived as a living organism and who is located in an experiential space traversed by an energetic flow generated by the encounter with both the character and the film. In some precise circumstances, this encounter is destabilizing because it perturbs physical and psychical equilibrium, triggers a shock interruption in the ordinary flow of perception, and not only evokes but also provokes defamiliarization.

This is, however, only one side of the coin. The opposite side is a corresponding dynamic aimed at rebalancing and restoring the lost equilibrium, a sort of homeostatic regulation that reduces excessive stimuli and re-establishes those conditions required for a full comprehension and interiorization of the experience. What is really new is the form *comprehension*: rather than a purely mental understating, contemporary cinema offers opportunities for a bodily and immediate *grasping*, a sort of 'mind gesture' or 'thought performance' in which mind and body are not dichotomised, or in which 'high-level' cognition is the sole origin of all experience. Perception, cognition, emotion, and action are not distinct and independent layers that function or that can be observed separately; rather, they are inextricable components—intimately dependent and mutually implicated—of a single experience. To quote Nolan's latest work *Tenet* (2020): 'Don't try to understand it, feel it', as the protagonist is advised when he needs to learn how the reversed and chronologically palindromic world works and how to physically move into that world.

As I will discuss in this book, the excess of stimulation and its regulation are specific characteristics of a series of recurrent themes in Western cinema after September 9, 2001 (but which can be traced back to the last forty years). In pivotal scenes of these films, the main characters walk on a wire, fall down, hit the ground, turn upside down, or float in the void: *acrobatics*, *fall*, *impact*, *overturning*, and *drift* are the five motifs that the following chapters deal with. I have chosen the word 'motif' not only to identify a predominant feature or element that recurs often in contemporary cinema, as the term is intended in the history of art, in music, or in narrative composition, but also to establish a connection between such features and the Late Latin etymology of the word (*motivus*), which emphasizes movement, mutability, return, and dynamism. The Latin *movere* ('to move') suggests a central argument of this book, namely the fact that a film is comprehended and experienced through the sensorimotor activity of its spectator.

The five tensive motifs do not, of course, cover the totality of possibilities, nor is there any presumption of completeness behind the choice of these motifs over that of others. It is nonetheless true that these motifs were not given a priori, but rather have emerged from the analysis of key *tense* sequences from a wide sample of both 'mainstream' and *auteur* films (or, rather, Hollywoodian *auteur* films that sparked critics' interest and obtained success at the box office). By necessity, only a few cases, albeit significant ones, are explicitly cited and analysed.

Although different in many respects, these five motifs hold two fundamental aspects in common. The first is the element that constitutes the nature of the environment in which the movement takes place: air. The motifs represent different declensions and variations of the movement of the body in the aerial space: acrobatic stunts, precipitous climbs, plunges, attempts at flight, revolutions, and floating in the void. The second is the force that generates the tension that is perceived by both the character and the spectator: gravity. The specificity of the motifs resides in the nature of the forces at work within an aerial space: attractive or propulsive, vertical or horizontal, which more or less pronouncedly influencing the movement of the body in space, its expressivity, and its empathetic potential. In each case the force of gravity, that is to say the force that *directs* the movement and posture of the bodies, determines their speed and direction as a function of their weight and altitude. Taking this conception of vector as intentional force, I will consider *tension* as the structuring principle of an environment that allows for a shared experience, a space in which 'fictional' forces emerge of the surface of the screen and resonate in the spectator's physical and psychic environment. Because of their capacity to elicit *tension* (in a multiplicity of meanings that I will discuss later), I call these cinematic *topoi* 'tensive motifs'.

The spectator-as-organism

How then can the spectator experience the 'kick'? How can he share the characters' physical and psychical imbalance? How can the cinematic representation alone evoke the response of the spectator's somatosensory system? How does the spectator take part *corporeally* in the actions, motivations, and emotions of the apparently *incorporeal* cinematic bodies?

How can he find a place in the fictional spatial environment in which the characters move and act? These variations and progressive extensions of the same fundamental question should be addressed by setting up a theoretical platform capable of holding together a wide range of psychological and physiological phenomena and dynamics. In particular, interrogating the involvement of somatosensory perception and the nervous system as an innovative and specific aspect of the contemporary film experience requires conceptual tools and analytical methods that are only partially already available. Relying on the notion of *embodied cognition* and, more broadly to the paradigm of *enaction*, this book aims to fill this gap.

Since the late 1980s, modern film theory has produced accurate models for the analysis of the spectator's involvement. These models have in common a dissatisfaction with and reaction to the ideological viewpoint of the dominant film theories in the 1970s—psychoanalytical semiotics in particular—but differ in the epistemological paradigms they draw on. On the one hand, cognitivist film theory launched a project of 'rationalization' of the film experience guided by the premises of analytic philosophy. Scholars such as David Bordwell (1985; 1989), Noël Carroll (1988; 1990), Edward Branigan (1992) and others proposed to adopt and progressively developed a 'mentalistic' approach that sees the human mind as the engine of the film spectator's response. Ted Nannicelli and Paul Taberham (2014) identify the main characteristics of the cognitivist approach as follows:

> (1) a dedication to the highest standards of reasoning and evidence in film and media studies and other fields (including, but not limited to, empirical data from the natural sciences); (2) a commitment to stringent inter-theoretical criticism and debate; (3) a general focus on the mental activity of viewers as the central (but not the only) object of inquiry; and (4) an acceptance of a naturalistic perspective, broadly construed (4).

Initially focused on attention, learning, memory, problem-solving, and perception as cognitive processes functional to narrative comprehension, this approach has gradually moved its attention from 'cold' cognition (information-driven inferences) to 'hot' cognition, which gives centrality to affect-driven mental processes (Smith 1995; Grodal 1997; Tan 1999; Plantinga & Smith 1999). However, as I will discuss in the next chapter in regard to the notion of empathy, even in this second age of the history of cognitive film studies, and even if this approach emerges as a reaction to the impalpable subjectivity of psychoanalytical semiology, the physical body remains an abstract object, not involved as a site of subjectivity and as the very means of the meaning-making process.

Conversely, another pathway of the reaction to semio-psychoanalysis puts the concrete and sentient body of the spectator and the reflexivity of conscious experience at the very heart of its endeavour. Opposed to ocularcentric, disembodied, and abstract spectator-film relationships, this approach, launched and led by Vivian Sobchack (cf. 1992), revolves around the idea that the spectator is addressed not simply through visual and mental processes, but also viscerally and physically, and that the form by which the spectator experiences the film is '*without a thought*' (Sobchack 2004, 64), through the 'sensemaking' capacity of the film. Sobchack's proposal is inspired by Maurice Merleau-Ponty's (1964; 2002) *Phenomenology of Perception* and in particular by the idea that in our engagement with the world sensorial processes precedes reasoning. The French philosopher already showed a direct interest in the filmic experience mid-way through the 1940s, examining it through the prism of Gestalt psychology in his lecture 'Film and the New Psychology' (Merleau-Ponty 1968). According to Merleau-Ponty, the meaning of a film does not emerge only from narration and dialogue, but also and primarily from the perception of the behaviour of the camera and the characters. Cinema is a phenomenological art capable of demonstrating the union between mind and body, between mind and world, and the expression of one in the other. In Merleau-Ponty's chiastic perspective the perceiver is never separate from the object of perception and perception is always an embodied experience that involves the perceiver's whole body, not just their sight. This means that the relationship between the sentient subject and the perceived world, between the spectator and the film, takes shape only through the body.

It is important to clarify that by body Merleau-Ponty (like Sobchack as well as I in this book) does not mean the physiological body as an object, but rather the 'lived body'. Whereas the former is the objective body that can be observed and analysed anatomically, as well as dissected into parts, each of which are responsible for specific function, the lived body is the body in the act of perceiving or experiencing the world, one which cannot be localized in a distinct function, 'since each region plays a role only in the context of a global activity' (Merleau-Ponty 1967, 207). As Shaun Gallagher (1986) summarizes, '[i]f the objective body is that which can be perceived as an object, the lived body is that non-object involved in the perceptual process' (140). These are not two separate bodies, but one and the same; the difference is not ontological, but perceptual. In Merleau-Ponty's (2002) words, 'the objective body is not the true version of the phenomenal body, that is, the true version of the body that we live; it is indeed no more than the latter's impoverished image' (501). Rather than taking the standpoint of objective science, for which the lived body derives from the physiological body, and that of philosophy, according to which the lived body is prior and the physiological body derivative, the Merleau-Pontean perspective maintains that they are not distinguishable: physiological processes are lived (brain lesions, for example, are a disturbance of the lived body) and the lived body is physiological (when I perform an action, the body spontaneously organizes itself physiologically).

Importing the notion of lived body into her theoretical framework, Sobchack (1992) describes the film experience as the result of the sensorimotor coupling of the film's and the spectator's bodies, which are no longer conceived of as, respectively, an invisible and passive viewing subject and an equally invisible and inert entity. Rather, both are perceiving and expressive of being-in-the-world, and dynamically contribute to the general and particular meaning of the audio-visual experience. Cinema uses the *modalities of embodied existence* (vision, hearing, physical, and reflexive moment) and the *structures of direct experience* (the centrality of the body in respect to the subjective world) as the substance and structure of its own 'bodily language' (Sobchack 1992, 4-5). Like no other medium, the film not only represents but also *presents* acts of vision, listening, and movement as originary structures of existence (Sobchack 2004, 63). In Sobchack's (1992) view, not only the spectator but also the film has a body, in the sense that, although it uses linguistic and technical means, it has its own capability to express vital movements in tactile, muscular, and kinetic terms. As she concludes, '[i]ndeed, it is this mutual capacity for and possession of experience through common structures of embodied existence, through similar modes of being-in-the-world, that provide the *intersubjective* basis of objective communication' (5).

The importance and at the same time the criticality of Sobchack arduous proposal, which is indebted to Merleau-Ponty's notion of reversibility of sight (viewing-viewed) and touch (touching-touched), has to be underlined. In her own words:

> It is the expressed bodily and intentional motility of the film's viewing-view that enables us as embodied and intentional spectators to understand the visual presence of the film's body to the viewed-view we see as visibly present. We understand that world we see projected before and for us as present *to* and *for* (not merely *in*) an embodied and conscious subject other than ourselves. [...] We recognize the moving picture as the work

> of an anonymous and sign-producing bodysubject intentionally marking visible choices with the very behavior of its bodily being. However, these choices are not initiated by the movement of *our* bodies or *our* intending consciousness. They are seen and visible as the visual and physical choices of some body *other* than ourselves, some body that possesses the vision more intimately than we do, some body for whom it counts as 'mine.' That some body is the film's body, and, however anonymously, our bodies experience it as a signifying presence in the film experience (277-278).

In this sense, for example, a camera movement is not only a mechanical objectual tool of visual and kinetic perception, but the manifestation of 'a subject that sees and moves and expresses perception. It participates in the consciousness of its own animate, intentional, and embodied existence in the world' (Sobchack 1982, 327). We do not only perceive through technologies of filmmaking, but also *along with* the camera, the projector, the microphone etc., which are the organs of a very special kind of subjectivity. As Sobchack writes, in fact, 'the machine is incorporated into the human intentional act of perceiving the world' (Sobchack 1992, 184).

Although in radically different and alternative modes, both cognitivism and phenomenology of film contribute to illuminating the ways in which the spectator as a conscious subject relates to both the cinematic characters and the film as a communicative entity. However, their opposing theoretical genealogies and divergent paths led to mutually exclusive models of spectatorship. For cognitivists, the spectator performs information-driven mental processes aimed at narrative comprehension, as well as affect-driven mental processes aimed at understanding characters; for phenomenologists, the spectator is a subject that perceives synesthetically and cenesthetically and that internally coordinates his/her movements and sensoriality with those of the film, conceived as a pseudo-body that, although ontologically different from that of human beings, is capable of sensing and moving. While cognitivism entails a naturalistic theoretical approach and adopts empirically grounded methods aiming to *explain* the causal processes of the human experience, phenomenology privileges a subjectivistic first-person approach suited for the *description* of the aesthetic experience.

Although it offers a simplification of more articulated perspectives (cf. Sinnerbrink 2019), this dichotomization suggests the risk of perpetuating a sort of Cartesian dualism in film studies. Upon a deeper look, neither the cognitivist nor the phenomenological approach is dualistic: in different ways, they both see the mind and the body as part of a whole. However, they grant a precedence to one over the other. For cognitivists, the mediation of the mind prevails over the immediacy of bodily multisensory perception, and vice versa for phenomenologists. Unfortunately, both pay little attention to the interaction between the system of bodies involved in the film experience—the character's, the spectator's, and the film's—and the *systemic environment* resulting from the merging of fictional, empirical, and psychological space, in which they jointly move, act, or are simply immersed.

Against the risk of an insidious dualism and, at the same time, in an attempt to overcome the rigid opposition and irreconcilability of seeming competition between an empirical/explanatory method and a descriptive/experiential perspective, the theoretical stance adopted in this book assumes the mutual implication or unity of body and mind and the interdependence of such a *bodymind* with the experiential environment as the fundamental structure of the film experience.

As Robert Sinnerbrink (2019) remarks, and as I will discuss later in regard to the role of the study of the brain as a terrain of encounter between the mind-focused and the body-focused approaches,

> the two perspectives still remain frequently estranged from each other. Or where there is no theoretical conflict, they can remain confined within well-defined disciplinary and institutional boundaries, thus rendering the possibility of a synthetic or pluralistic approach more of a promissory note than a live possibility (1-2).

In advocating a pluralistic and 'dialectical synthetic' approach to film inquiry, Sinnerbrink sees a space for a potentially productive encounter between 'thick' phenomenological description of the cinematic aesthetic experience and empirically grounded explanatory accounts of the processes behind the spectator's cognitive activity. The combination and cooperation of perspectives that privilege, alternatively, the subjective (and empirically ungraspable) or the objective (and philosophically inconsistent) dimensions of the affective, moral, and aesthetic experience, would be extremely productive in the broader epistemological (and only apparently oxymoronic) framework of *embodied cognition*. As Sinnerbrink underlines,

> Both phenomenologists and cognitivists agree on the importance of embodied experience, contextualized or 'embedded' in sociocultural niches, mediated via technological prosthetic devices (extended), and with an emphasis on activity, interactivity, and modes of communicative and pragmatic exchange (enactive) (4).

The so-called 4Es paradigm (embodied, embedded, extended, enactive) posits that cognition and meaning emerge through the interplay of a living organism and its environment, and that perception and action (or sensory inputs and motor processes) are fundamentally inseparable. I believe, with Sinnerbrink, that this paradigm offers the opportunity to overcome a 'false and misleading dichotomy' (4).

Accordingly, in this book I take inspiration from the enactive and embodied approach to human cognition and rather than opposing the cognitivist *spectator-as-mind* and the phenomenologist *spectator-as-body* approaches, I propose to conceive of the spectator as a living and sensing organism whose experience dynamically emerges from (instead of being pre-determined by) simultaneous perceptual, cognitive, affective and sensorimotor processes, all of which are dependent on the interaction with the biological, spatial, psychological, cultural and social environment in which the experience takes place. This approach will make it possible to describe the five tensive motifs as forms of complex modulation of the perceptual, affective and cognitive activity that characterizes the interaction between the *spectator-as-organism* (D'Aloia & Eugeni 2014) and his/her experiential cinematic environment. The tensive motifs, in fact, can be thought—or, rather, directly experienced—as modes of production, maintenance, and dissipation of that sensorimotor, attentional, and emotional energy that makes the cinema an experience that reveals those tensions that presently inhabit our subjectivity and society.

Cinematic neurons

Without a doubt, cognitive neuroscience is central to the process of the epistemological and methodological reformulation of film studies. As far the enactive and embodied approach to the film experience is concerned, the relatively recent discovery of the so called 'visuomotor' or 'bimodal' neurons is particularly relevant. Beginning in the mid-1990s, a group of Italian neurophysiologists of the University of Parma led by Giacomo Rizzolatti explored several areas of macaque brains with the aid of functional neuroimaging techniques. Rizzolatti's group discovered a set of sensorimotor neurons in a sector of the monkey's premotor cortex that fire both when a subject executes an object-directed action and when the subject observes another subject executing the action, without entailing any overt motor activation on the part of the observing subject (di Pellegrino et al. 1992; Rizzolatti et al. 1996; Gallese et al. 1996; Rizzolatti, Fogassi & Gallese 2001; Rizzolatti & Craighero 2004). Neuroimaging studies indicate the existence of neurons in the human brain that display patterns of activity similar to those identified in the monkey brain. (Hari et al. 1998; Grèzes, Armony & Passingham 2003; Gallese, Keysers & Rizzolatti 2004; Rizzolatti 2005; Iacoboni 2009; Mukamel et al. 2010). These nurons, appropriately termed 'mirror neurons', activate when performing or only imagining performing a goal-directed action, as well as when the action is performed by someone else. The mirroring mechanism in our brain suggests that when we see someone carry out a goal-oriented action we automatically and unreflexively *simulate* that action or response by producing it internally without any deliberate recognition the action itself. The same is valid for the perception of emotions expressed on others' faces: the observing subject mimics the emotions at a neural and pre-reflexive level. Even in this case, the internal mimicry of the other's affective state precedes its explicit recognition. Mirror neurons are thus thought to enable an understanding of the others' actions, intentions, and emotions in an immediate form based on a sensorimotor representation that precedes and is functional to their explicit recognition (Rizzolatti & Sinigaglia 2007b; Gallese 2009b). This mechanism both guides an action and 'thinks' a potential act, so that one can 'grasp' the meaning of the received stimulus without a deliberate cognitive mediation (Rizzolatti & Sinigaglia 2007a; Iacoboni 2009; Keysers 2011; Ferrari & Rizzolatti 2015). Accordingly, it has also been suggested that the mirroring mechanism has a prominent role in evoking empathy and constitutes the neural underpinnings of the intersubjective experience (Gallese & Goldman 1998; Gallese 2001; Gallese 2003; Gallese 2005a; Gallese 2005b; Goldman 2006a; Gallese 2007; Gallese 2009a).

It must be clarified that while in the 'standard simulation' hypothesis of the Theory of Mind the subject voluntarily puts themselves in the place of the other, takes on their perspective, and reproduces, also on an imaginary level, their mental states, according to the so-called 'embodied simulation' hypothesis the understanding of the other occurs automatically and pre-reflexively and without interference or cognitive processes of an associative type thanks to a sharing of the other's intentions at the neural level. Embodied simulation thus describes human beings' tendency to take the content of the actions, emotions, and intentions of the other and 'make them their own', even in those cases in which the subject is simply observing. These new discoveries about the functioning of the brain essentially demonstrate an inextricable connection, on the neural level, between *action* and *relation*, between *movement* and *emotion*, especially—though not exclusively—when action and movement are already part of the subject's motor repertoire. While embodied simulation is more intense when, say, a dancer watches a dance performance, the neural mirroring activates also when a subject has not already experienced *exactly* the same observed action. As Marco Iacoboni (2009) remarks, '[w]e understand [...] actions because we have a template in our brains for that action, a template based on our own movements. Since different actions share similar movement properties and activate similar muscles, we don't have to be skilled athletes to 'mirror' the athletes in our brain' (5). As neurophysiologist Vittorio Gallese (2018) summarizes, '[e]mbodied simulation theory posits that the mirror mechanisms underpin mental simulation processes primarily because brain and cognitive resources typically used for one purpose are reused for another purpose' (54).

The mirroring mechanism thus enables a form of *activation* that does not involve the actual execution of action and is, rather, based on 'mere' perception. In other words, perception and action are intimately implicated; they are not governed by separate areas in the brain nor mediated by cognition. Against the classic 'sandwich' metaphor that was used to describe brain functions (cf. Hurley 2000), perception *is* action. The mirror mechanism has been found to have a role in aesthetic response to art (Freedberg & Gallese 2007; Gallese 2010) and, although it is intuitive that the mirror mechanism works better with physical co-presence, images cannot be conceived as a mere substitute. Many experiments have demonstrated that mirror neurons fire in a similar way in both naturalistic and filmed situations (Caggiano et al. 2011).

Accordingly, it can be argued that embodied simulation plays a fundamental role in the spectator's engagement with a narrative film, given that the film experience is fundamentally the perception of audio-visual contents and that narrative films present pseudo-subjectivities that perform actions and express emotions. Furthermore, 'the spatiality of the situations described in a movie, notwithstanding the space that divides the screen from the audience, can also be experienced and perceptively understood through the simulation of the motor potentialities of the actors and the movements of the camera recording them' (Gallese & Guerra 2019, 24). The embodied simulation hypothesis thus can also be applied to the understanding of the neurological dynamics that subtend film participation as a particularly intensified case of *perception-as-action* activity.

According to this hypothesis, it is reasonable to see embodied simulation as a dynamic that is also active in the case of the tensive motifs, although they are forms of bodily movements that the spectator has rarely experienced before in reality (at least without severe consequences). Even though we have never walked on a tightrope, fallen from great heights and smashed to the ground, been hung upside down, nor performed a spacewalk outside the Earth's atmosphere, we are nevertheless able to simulate those movements on the basis of the template of *somatosensory perturbation*. As part of the human sensory nervous system, the somatosensory system comprises receptors (skin, tendons, joints, viscera, etc.) and neural pathways that underlie several modalities of somatic perception of the internal environment of a living organism and its external environment. As I have anticipated, sensory modalities represented by the somatosensory system include proprioception and kinesthesis. Proprioception also has a role in maintaining balance and combines with vestibular proprioceptive and visual cues to control motor responses to changes in body position. The sense of physical imbalance that the kick induces in *Inception's* dreamers affects precisely their *equilibrioception*. Even those of us who do not suffer acrophobia have experienced vertigo, loss of equilibrium, or motion sickness, either voluntarily (for example on a roller coaster or a simulator rides in an amusement park) or involuntarily (leaning out over a balcony or at the top of a ladder). Moreover, one of the fundamental points of my argument is that the 'low features' of film style (e.g. editing, camera movement, shot size, sound) have the capability to induce somatosensory perturbation even in standard cases in which the spectator sits on a fixed seat (as opposed to the mobile seats used in the so-called 4D Cinema). This provides every human being with the 'action template' (cf. Iacoboni 2009, 5) that allows them to grasp the meaning—or, rather, the *sense*—of action via embodied simulation.

Neuroskepticism

The significance of neural correlates in the filmic experience and theory is, however, an incipient undertaking (Elliott 2010). On one front, cognitivist film theory is progressively implementing its own 'psychocinematic' project (Shimamura 2013) with aspects very close to a cognitive neuroscience of film in an attempt to integrate low-level and high-level dynamics. In a nutshell, psychocinematics seeks to understand the psychological underpinnings of cinema and our aesthetic response to films by relying on empirical research and following the Post-Theory 'manifesto' (Bordwell & Carroll 1996). Post-Theory encouraged film scholars to react to 'Grand Theory'—a culturalist and ideological approach typical of semiotics and psychoanalysis—and overcome its universalistic, generic, reductionist, intuitive, introspective, and vague speculative methods and argumentative style. Instead, film studies should be concerned with 'middle-level' theorizing and should aim towards more modest yet specific goals to be achieved through rigorous argumentation based on the reasoning of analytical philosophical. While in the cognitivist tradition the use of psychological experimental procedures is a consolidated practice for the investigation into the ways in which the film (and editing in particular) guides the spectator's attention through the use of oculometrics (Smith 2012) or 'cinemetrics' (Cutting & Candan 2015), more common is the use of already available scientific findings and experimental results to prove or improve established knowledge in the field. This is, however, a very controversial point, at least from the position expressed in the wake of Post-Theory, which sees the methodology of the natural sciences as inappropriate for the examination of the human (and humanistic) significance of film theory, criticism, and experience (Allen & Smith 1997): whereas hard science research provides explanations of the phenomena of the natural world, film studies needs philosophy for its investigation of the meaning and the significance of the subjects' intentional acts. Paradoxically, some of the cognitivist resistance to neuroscience is shared by the dominant strand of continental *film-philosophy*, which has always viewed the 'exclusive' and 'imperialist' recourse to empirical sciences in cognitive film studies with scepticism (Rodowick 2007; 2014; Buckland 2009a; Mullarkey 2009; Sinnerbrink 2011), despite these criticisms having been contested or at least counterbalanced by the claim of the prevailing role of analytic philosophy in the cognitivist approach (Slugan 2020).

In the mid-1990s, the shift of cognitive research's focus from 'cold' cognition to emotions made it more evident that the *naturalization* of the theoretical approach to film spectatorship was no longer a postponable issue. This issue, in fact, characterized cognitivism's self-reflection on its modes of research in the 2000s. As Arthur Shimamura (2013) states,

> With the advent of brain imaging techniques, particularly functional magnetic resonance imaging (fMRI), psychological science can now link mental events with brain processes. Indeed, it is now possible to have individuals watch a movie in an fMRI scanner and record the brain regions that are active during the experience. In this way, psychocinematics can connect minds, brains, and experiences as we watch movies (2).

Among the approaches that use brain imaging for the study of the spectator's response, Shimamura mentions 'neurocinematics,' a project proposed by neuropsychologist Uri Hasson, based on an experiment in which the spectators' neural responses were measured through fMRI while they were watching the same film (Hasson et al. 2008b). This experiment showed that in the case of well-structured narrative sequences (such as the first 30 minutes of Sergio Leone's *The Good, the Bad, and the Ugly*), the response was similar across different spectators, suggesting a strong '[i]ntersubjective correlation', as they called it (cf. also Hasson et al. 2008a). This seems to concretize Sergei Eisenstein's (1988) intuitions that films aim at '*influencing [the] audience in a desired direction* through a series of calculated pressures on its psyche' (39). Hasson's experiment, however, limits itself to the gathering of quantitative data or to the mere topological identification of the brain areas of different spectators that activate during collective film viewing, and has no interest in the stylistic and aesthetic aspects of film, with the exception the narrative/non-narrative organization of the audio-visual content, which is quite a generic and rough distinction.

Despite these limits, neuroscience seems to have officially become part of the cognitivist studies programme. In fact, some distinguished cognitivist scholars are gradually developing a position open to neuroscience, as in the cases of Murray Smith and Torben Grodal. Smith (2017) has recently proposed to 'triangulate' between phenomenological, psychological, and neural levels and to integrate 'methods and knowledge drawn from across the humanities, the social and the natural science' (4). Grodal (1997; 2009), who has always been close to an evolutionary bio-cultural account of film viewing, reinforced his idea that the film experience is a stream that follows the brain's architecture; from perception, through emotional activation and cognitive processing, to motor action (the so-called PECMA model). Given that the human species is part of the natural word, and that the resources and dynamics involved in the perception and comprehension of a film are the same as those relied upon in everyday interaction with the real world, both Smith and Grodal stress the importance of including the methods and knowledge of neurosciences and the embodied simulation hypothesis in an effort to explain our engagement with the moving image.

However, with these exceptions, which I will discuss extensively in the next chapter in regard to the notion of empathy, the general position of cognitivists is quite clear: neuroscience provides no real explanation for how the mind works. Since film studies should remain in the area of humanities and should adopt a philosophical approach, it is instead psychocinematics that offers explanations for the functioning of the brain. As Nannicelli and Taberham (2014) significantly underline, naturalism is not at all a pacific option in film studies and risks putting its methods and agenda in danger:

> Cognitive theory's increasingly cross-disciplinary nature raises questions not only about what its boundaries are, but what they should be.

> In particular, we ought to acknowledge that while greater collaboration with the sciences presents enormous opportunities, it also requires us to engage in a kind of meta-theoretical reflection. That is, we need to carefully consider what sorts of questions about film and film viewing might be answered by appealing to scientific models and explanations and what sorts might not be. [...] Nevertheless, the question of what precisely science's role in film and media theorizing should be is an open one, and cognitivists diverge in their answers to it (3).

Malcom Turvey has recently expressed his serious scepticism on mirror neurons due to a series of reasons, including the deductive extension of the presence of these brain cells neurons detected in monkeys to humans, the generalization of assumptions based on single experiment, and the careless mixture of natural sciences and humanistic methods. As Turvey (2020) writes in this regard: '[t]he apparent authority of a scientific paradigm, in other words, can lead scholars to cherry-pick and mischaracterize our artistic practices in order to fit the science, as happened with psychoanalysis a generation ago' (25).

Among the limitations Turvey holds up, of particular relevance to my thesis is the 'egocentric' issue: the idea that in order to understand an observed movement by mirroring it neurally, this movement does not necessarily need to be part of the subject's motor repertoire. Since, as we have seen, the mirroring mechanism activates on the basis of an 'action template', the spectator can grasp the meaning of actions that he has not performed before in the same context presented in the film. Reducing understanding to a mere mental act of comprehension of the other's situation, Turvey maintains that no particular neural mirroring is required to understand an act that we have never executed. Adopting the standard simulation hypothesis (and cognitivism in general), he believes in fact that simulation is an imaginative activity, a conscious and deliberate mental act aiming at deciphering the other's situation. This is particularly valid for the complex phenomenon of empathy, which cognitivists conceive of as a conscious act of perspective-taking, that is, imagining oneself in the character's situation. In this sense, the fact that empathy relies on a neurological, pre-reflexive mechanism is simply irrelevant for the cognitivist perspective. I will discuss this argument extensively in the next chapter. Here it suffices to say that embodied simulation and its neural underpinnings as a model of action understanding will never be recognized as a reasonable hypothesis until there is agreement on the exact meaning of the word 'understanding'. While for the standard simulation hypothesis understanding is thought of as deliberate mental *comprehension*, for the embodied simulation hypothesis understanding is an implicit bodily based *prehension* of meaning: it concerns a direct, not mentally mediated experience. What is at stake is thus an epistemological turn that the cognitivist rejection of (or even fear for) *pre-rational* (or rationally inexplicable) mechanisms is ignoring or even neglecting.

The cognitivists' anxiety and mobilization against neuroscience—either in the form of Turvey's 'serious scepticism' or in David Davis' (2018) 'moderately pessimistic perspective' on Smith's 'cooperative naturalism'—is understandable and may seem a defensive strategy set up to neutralize the possible devastating effects of the rise of the precognitive realm on the domination of the cognitivist paradigm, thereby undermining its foundations. Although adopting a sceptical attitude towards neuroscience and its potential for ontological reductionism is a fitting cautionary stance; cognitivism risks falling into an alternative form of dualism based on the idea that the mind and the brain are two distinct entities.

Neurophenomenology

Beyond these meta-theoretical or epistemological concerns, embodied simulation is part of a broader ground-breaking innovation in philosophy of mind, namely the paradigm of *embodied cognition* that has permeated the humanities, social sciences and—at least in part—natural sciences in the last thirty years. This paradigm, whose fundamental theses aspire to overcome the Cartesian separation between body and mind, the metaphysical division between *res extensa* and *res cogitans*, and the distinction between the purely physiological and the purely psychological, proposes an embodied conception of human experience that offers major approaches in film studies a terrain for a productive encounter. Antonio Damasio (1994; 1999; 2003; 2010) paved the way towards a radical overcoming of the mind/body or reason/emotion dualism. For the Portuguese neurophysiologist rationality is interdependent on the biological regulation of the organism and is inevitably influenced by the latter. Conscious emotional sensations are linked to neural maps that simulate the corresponding physical state to those emotions. Consciousness itself is an emotional feeling, as it is impossible to have an emotion without having a sensation of one's body and without being physically involved in what one is observing.

Research by Mark Johnson, George Lakoff, and by Francisco Varela, inspired in turn by Merleau-Ponty's phenomenology and James Gibson's ecological approach to perception, asserts the idea that 'cognition depends upon the kinds of experience that come from having a body with various sensorimotor capacities, and [...] these individual sensorimotor capacities are themselves embedded in a more encompassing biological, psychological, and cultural context' (Varela, Thompson & Rosch 1991, 173). As Mark Johnson (2015) writes, '[e]verything we experience, understand, communicate, imagine, value, and do in our world depends critically on the nature of our bodies, the nature of the environments we inhabit, and the pattern and counters of our body-environment interaction' (9; cf. also Johnson 1987; 2017; 2018). The reciprocal dependence between cognition and lived experience forms the basis of the idea of *enaction*, according to which cognition is embodied within the entire organism and is situated in the world to the extent that it cannot be reduced to brain structures: instead, the meaning of experience is produced by continual and reciprocal interactions between the brain, the body, and the world (Noë 2004; 2009; Stewart et al. 2010; Hutto & Myin 2013; Durt, Fuchs & Tewes 2017). According to neurobiologist Varela, philosopher Thompson and psychologist Rosch—authors of a seminal book on this topic (1991)—action is constitutively embodied, that is, rooted in the nature and in the capabilities of having and being a body. Furthermore, enactivism emphasizes the fact that cognition is not pre-determined and that it *emerges* from the encounter between organism and environment: 'cognition is not the representation of a pregiven world by a pregiven mind but is rather the enactment of a world and a mind on the basis of a history of the variety of actions that a being in the world performs' (9).

Radicalizing enactivism, Varela arrived at the proposition of naturalizing phenomenology (Petitot et al. 1999). In cognitivism's classic computational approach, the 'hard problem' (Varela 1995; Chalmers 1996) of the neurosciences—the explanation of the qualitative and subjective aspects of conscious experience (or *qualia*)—is subject, on the one hand, to neuroreductionism or eliminativism, in which the pole of experience is dismissed in favour of the study of mere neural processes, and on the other, to functionalism, in which the notion of experience is forcibly assimilated to that of cognitive behaviour with the result of offering a simplistic and functionalist explanation. Varela coins the term 'neurophenomenology' to propose an interdisciplinary approach to the problem of consciousness, joining the advantages of the empirical methodology used by the neurosciences and the method of analysing first-person experience that is fundamental to phenomenology. Only by repositioning the body as the centre of inquiry and directing the transcendental philosophical approach towards the empirical study of neurological processes is it possible to truly overcome Cartesian dualism.

Naturalizing phenomenology, however, is also intrinsically problematic given phenomenology's originary vocation of programmatically opposing the methods of the natural sciences and of physiology in particular, which Edmund Husserl believed to be guilty of reducing psychic experience to a mere thing among things, and unable to bring out its constitutive dimension. Gallese (2009c) proposed instead to 'phenomenologize' the cognitive sciences, recuperating the philosophical bases of intersubjectivity and showing,

> on one hand, how important aspects of phenomenological reflection are today finding clear verification in the results of neuroscientific research, and on the other, how the results of empirical neuroscientific research can make a valid contribution to a new formulation, if not a resolution, of various problems of a philosophical nature that have for decades been and are still now at the center of phenomenological research.

These studies suggest that a relational and systemic approach based on embodiment and enaction allows, on the one hand, the overcoming of a mere disembodied conception of the film spectator—the spectator as a 'cold mind' that constantly works to interpret the narrative content of a film—and, on the other hand, the reinforcement and substantiation of the first-person and introspective (and often criticized as vague) description of the 'somatic' nature of spectatorship, that is, the spectator as a sentient body that receives multisensory stimuli without any conscious elaboration (D'Aloia & Eugeni 2014). Moving away from the reductionist presumption of localizing mental states in the brain, cognitive neuroscience can contribute to the study of the aesthetic experience by addressing numerous issues. Among them, Gallese (2018) stresses the importance of exploring the brain-body relationships 'in order to understand the constitutive elements of aesthetic experience and the genesis of aesthetic concepts' (52). The empirical attitude is also useful for the analysis of aesthetic style, as long as employed critically and with awareness of its methodological and heuristic limitations (cf. Gallese & Guerra 2019, xxi). 'The final objective', Gallese (2018) concludes, 'must be to discover how to profitably conjugate the experiential dimension through a study of the underlying subpersonal processes and mechanisms expressed by the brain-body, and promote investigations that can lead to progress in both the theoretical and philosophical stylistic fields' (53).

An enactive and embodied approach to the film experience allows for the 'systematization' of the dynamic relation between the brain, the body, and the environment. As Enrico Carocci (2018) summarizes in a recent book on narrative film and emotional involvement, '[a]ccording to this perspective, the relation between organism and environment is thought of as a *systemic* structure' (50). As Carocci states, the embodied and enactive approach promotes three main premises that are of crucial importance for the study of the film experience: that the mind emerges from the processual interaction between the organism and both the natural and cultural environment; that human cognition, even at a high level of conceptualization, is grounded in the sensorimotor experience deriving from such interactions; and that the lived body that experiences the film has a self-regulating mechanism that tends towards homeostasis (52).

A corpus of theories built up around the concept of 'enaction' offers film and media studies an array of extremely useful concepts to address the questions that I mention at the beginning of this chapter. Adopting such an approach allows to better understand how the hypothesis of embodied simulation could represent a productive pathway for the investigation of the complex dynamics of the film experience, rather than a reductionist explanation of already known phenomena. At the same time, enaction allows us to adequately weigh the role of neuroscience in explaining some of the fundamental dynamics of film participation, at a safe distance from both excessive enthusiasm and rigid scepticism (in particular, regarding the discovery of mirror neurons and their role in supporting empathy also in the aesthetic experience—an argument that has been largely but often superficially discussed).

Embodying spectatorship

The neurophysiological propensity of human beings to internally mirror gestures executed by other subjects, and even to understand their emotions in an immediate and prelinguistic form, seems to constitute the biological premise of a new phenomenology of the film experience. On the basis of Gilles Deleuze's (1989; 2000) forward-looking proposal for a 'neurobiology of cinema', Patricia Pisters (2009; 2012) has suggested the usefulness of drawing on the neurosciences to explain the film experience. Relying on Lakoff and Johnson's (1999) cognitive linguistics, Maarten Coëgnarts and Peter Kravanja (2015) combined Conceptual Metaphor Theory and embodied cognition with the aim to 'show how film is an exemplary case of embodied, immanent meaning' (63). Film scholars and philosophers are collaborating with neuroscientists for the design, conduction, and interpretation of lab experiments aimed at exploring the validity of the embodied simulation hypothesis in the filmic experience (Gallese & Guerra 2012; Fingerhut & Heimann 2017; Gallese & Guerra 2019). As Michele Guerra (2015) states, although often limited to a quantitative confirmation of the same processes already studied with qualitative methods, 'experimental aesthetics can help us in better understanding the complexity of our experience, making clear that meaning-making processes are not confined to the domain of the (disembodied) mind, but grow out of the bodily and precognitive contact between us and the work of art' (144). The most interesting idea that the cognitive neurosciences offer to film theory is, in fact, that the activity of visuomotor neurons constitutes the anatomical-functional substrate of empathy, insofar as they lead the subject observing the actions and emotions of others to internally generate the representation of the corporeal states associated with those actions and emotions, as though the subject were carrying out those actions or experiencing those emotions. As Gallese and Guerra (2019) explain,

> Embodied simulation is a basic functional mechanism of the brain by means of which part of the neural resources that are normally employed to interact with the world around us, shaping our relationships and relations, are reused for perception and imagination. Our understanding of the meaning of much of the behavior and the experiences of other beings relies on this reuse of the neuronal circuits on which our personal agentive, emotional, and sensory experiences are based. We reuse our mental states and processes, represented in corporeal form, to attribute them functionally to others. Embodied simulation provides an integrated and neurobiologically credible framework for this type of intersubjective phenomena (1-2).

Through embodied simulation the subject is able to 'grasp' the intentions implicit in the gestures and expressions of the other without any inference. As Guerra (2015) summarizes, 'the ways through which the viewer is involved in the story are not just off-line mental processes, but ordinary on-line bodily forms of intersubjectivity' (151). This is true not only in respect to the film characters but also to specific formal low-level features of filmmaking style (e.g. editing and camera movements), or what Sobchack would call the 'film's body'. Recent experiments showed that embodied simulation is particularly effective for certain types of camera movements and in particular for those realized with the steadycam. The steadycam, in fact, evoke a stronger activation of the motor simulation mechanism expressed by the mirror neurons than still camera, zoom, or dolly (cf. Heimann et al. 2014; Heimann et al. 2019), and this happens for an obvious reason: the '[s]teadicam most closely reproduced the effect of someone really walking towards the scene' and its movement is perceived 'as being the most natural and therefore having the highest potential of evoking the sensation of walking towards the scene' (Gallese & Guerra 2019, 111-112). If, on the one hand, this conclusion may appear obvious, on the other it indirectly gives consistency to one of the most original (and controversial) innovations offered by Sobchack's theory, namely the attribution of intentionality to the film as a pseudo-human-subject equipped with its own consciousness. As Sobchack (1982) argues,

> Intentionality can also be seen to characterize camera movement. It is our recognition of camera movement as intentionally structured that allows us to understand it as always meaningful and directed, and to identify it with consciousness, with an animate—if anonymous—'other' rather than with the inanimate existence and motor locomotion of a machine (321).

I will return to the issue of the film's body as capable of expressing intentionality in the final chapter in order to demonstrate how each of the five tensive motifs is capable of positioning and moving their relative *intentional* object by putting it *in tension* with the spectator's relational experience.

It bears noting that, paradoxically, it is exactly the seemingly passivity of the film spectator that facilitates embodied simulation. Since it is the spectator's physiological body yet not his lived body that remains essentially immobile in front of the screen, one can hypothesize that the internal simulation of the represented actions, emotions, and intentions is the fundamental principle that allows filmic participation to take place. As Gallese and Guerra (2019) remark, this experience 'has *its roots in transcending the body while remaining within its bounds*' (39). Accordingly, despite the fact that the spectator does not have real contact with any of the objects on the screen, nor a real relationship with the characters, he experiences a meaningful relationship with filmic objects and subjects in an empathetic form. As a sort of compensation for the lack of actual interactivity in film spectatorship, embodied simulation of the characters' and film's movements provides directness and immediacy. The spectator's physical stillness can even be considered as a facilitator of this form of enaction since it offers a fundamental condition and the necessary experiential gap-to-be-filled for *em*-bodiment and immersion in the filmic environment. Rather than stillness as a basic condition of the 'filmic situation' (as classic Filmology would call it), the tensive motifs show that an *un*-acted and *un*-body condition—that is, a temporary and voluntarily subtraction of constitutive experiential elements—is required for responding to the need for action to be *en*-acted, or for body to be *em*-bodied. As Gallese (2018) explains, immobility

> allows us to allocate more neural resources to the task at hand, intensifying the activation of embodied simulation and, in so doing, making us adhere more intensely to what we are simulating. [...] Perhaps it is no coincidence that some of the most vivid fictional experiences we entertain, as those occurring during dreams, are paralleled by the massive inhibition of the muscle tone in our body (56).

Based on these premises, enaction offers film studies the opportunity to expand (epistemologically) and reinforce (methodologically) its traditional theoretical and analytical tools. In turn, neuro-informed film studies offer other humanistic disciplines a renewed conceptual platform upon which to build an expansion of knowledge that derives from an up-to-date study of that peculiar form of life that is the film experience.

Neurofilmology

The *neural turn* that characterized the 2000s affected film studies with particular regard to models of spectatorship. Interestingly enough, both the cognitivist and the phenomenological approaches to film spectatorship are sceptical about the general use of neuroscience or empirical sciences in film studies, believing that they cannot not really add much to their consolidated analytical or speculative methods. As I have briefly discussed, there are many understandable reasons for such scepticism but just as many for trying to take a more open attitude instead. An enactive approach not only provides the theoretical basis for the elaboration of a sound and up-to-date account of film spectatorship; it also makes room for the relaunching of the original endeavour of a systematic and scientifically based study of the film experience.

The 'Neurofilmology' I advocate here is, in fact, inspired by the interdisciplinary spirit of classic Filmology, launched by Gilbert Cohen-Séat through the *Revue internationale de filmologie* in 1947. This goal was to have been achieved through the construction of an interdisciplinary theoretical platform that involves aesthetics, psychology, philosophy, art history, sociology, and anthropology, as well as the adoption of the empiric methods of hard sciences. The epistemological challenge for Filmology as a *nouvelle science* was that of overcoming an impressionistic explanation of the effects of the film on the spectator through the adoption of the experimental method (hypothesis, experiment, theorization). As can be read in the first issue of the *Revue*:

> At the scientific level, filmology is the study or research of the effects [of the film] that can be analyzed at the psychological and psycho-physiological levels: effects on perception, judgment, habit, memory, association of ideas, attention [...] the film is undoubtedly the most powerful generator of movements and haltings of movement in the nascent state, which has ever attacked itself in such a corrosive way, in the normal state of the human mind and behind him, perhaps, to the organism (95, my trans.).[1]

In accordance with this manifesto, several innovative laboratory experiments were carried out to empirically analyse the spectator's responses to cinematic projection. In 1954, an issue of *Revue* was devoted entirely to the 'Études expèrimentales de l'activité nerveuse pendant la projection du film'. The electroencephalogram (EEG) in particular was used to objectively measure such responses (Cohen-Séat, Gastaut & Bert 1954; Cohen-Séat & Faure 1954; Heuyer et al. 1954; Heuyer & Bert 1954). The main discovery of these experiments was that the desynchronization of the mu rhythm occurs not only during active movements of the subject, but also during observation of actions executed by someone else, even by a film character (D'Aloia & Eugeni 2014, 11). This same idea underlies the more recent experiments and theoretical speculations around the role of mirror neurons in the film experience.

This method, however, fell victim to the same scepticism that empirical methodology elicits today when applied in the humanities to aesthetic experiences. Filmologists themselves (Roques 1954) were aware of the contingent difficulties related to the use of the EEG and of the potential reductionism implied in the recreation of the 'cinematographic situation' in the laboratory. Filmology's epistemological project was also only partially achieved due to the historical factors that led to the rise and affirmation

1 'Au plan scientifique, la filmologie est l'étude ou la recherche des effets [du film] analysables aux plans psychologiques et psycho-physiologiques: effets sur la perception, le jugement, l'habitude, la mémoire, l'association d'idée, l'attention [...] le film est sans conteste le plus puissant générateur de mouvements et d'arrêts de mouvements à l'état naissant, qui se soit jamais attaqué de façon aussi corrosive, à l'état normal de l'esprit humain et derrière lui, peut-être, à l'organisme.'

of Christian Metz's psychoanalytical semiology as of the mid-1960s (Albera & Lefebvre 2009, 13-56).

In a similar vein—yet with significant updating of the disciplines that contribute to its programme—Neurofilmology aims at combining traditional methodologies, such as semiotics, aesthetics, psychology of perception, and philosophy of mind, with a critical use of the findings of cognitive, social, and aesthetic neurophysiological research. Although no neuroscientific experiments have been conducted specifically for the purpose of this book, I will rely on some experimental investigations of various aspects of human perception in order to expand our knowledge of the spectator's involvement with (rather than mere response to) the film and better investigate the empathic and simulative potential of cinema.

Furthermore, rather than reducing the variety and complexity of the film's effects on the spectator in a controlled experimental setting I will, following a quasi-experimental logic, conceive the film experience itself as a sort of experiment: the cinema can be thought as a giant laboratory—a space of empirical experimentation filled with an assorted array of sensory flows. In this enhanced perceptual environment, the spectator is subject to psychophysical alteration of his systems of orientation and balance, which allows for a study of his response and parameters of toleration. The spectator here is not a guinea pig, compelled to keep his eyes open before horrifying images in an attempt—as in a Kubrickian 'Ludovico Technique'—to re-educate him to behave civilly, but a subject that has knowingly and willingly put himself to the test in order to ascertain his own limits, or at least to feel in his own body the sensation of a dizziness that dazes the senses, disturbs perception, and leads to the loss of control.

As in the method used by the natural sciences, it is pathological states that allow for the acquisition of general knowledge about the structure and functioning of the brain and the organism. To this deliberate pathological state, however, the film systematically proposes a remedy or rapidly brings the level of stimulation to an acceptable threshold. The five tensive motifs that the chapters of this book deal with can thus be considered cases of the induction of temporary pathology, moments of interference, interruptions, or malfunctions of the spectator's normal biological functioning, which are then followed by the restoration of normality. This twofold dynamic reflects the tension between the search for a sensational experience and the need for intelligibility that is characteristic of contemporary times.

Neurofilmology is thus a sort of 'neofilmology', an interdisciplinary research programme that observes the film experience by adopting an epistemological and methodological approach based on dialogue with both the experimental findings and the speculative tools of cognitive psychology and neurocognitive sciences. Neurofilmology embraces an approach that combines the first-person observation typical of phenomenological philosophy and the attention to third-person inquiry typical of experimental psychology and behavioural neuroscience for film and media studies. Advancing the proposition of a neurofilmology means giving room to an integration of analytic and continental approaches, joining the focus on the mind and the focus on the body within an epistemological field with the more comprehensive concept of the *organism-environment* at its core.

The hypothesis that a process of pre-reflexive and empathetic engagement that mirrors the modalities through which we tend to understand other human beings in real life (cf. Hoffner & Cantor 1991) takes place during the film experience thus appears highly reasonable, and empathy, understood in this way, represents one of the essential keys for understanding spectatorial experience. The argument of this book, however, emerges from the necessity of reacting to the dangers of both a reductionist 'neuralistic' definition of empathy and an overly broad and vague approach at that. In the film experience, the correlation between action and cognition is, at least in part, already structured according to criteria that resemble a laboratory experiment. Stimuli (the film) are administered to a subject (the spectator) within a space characterized by specific environmental conditions (the cinema) by way of an experimental apparatus capable of regulating, intensifying, tracking, controlling, repeating, and varying the experiment. So long as they recognize and are aware of the phenomenological aspects involved in the functioning of the brain—that is, as long as they do not fall into reductionism—the neurosciences may be able to make new contributions to the study of spectatorial participation.

On Icarus' wings

Each of the following chapters discusses a different tensive motif. Chapter II is dedicated to the motif of *acrobatics* and takes as a starting point the debate between the psychologist Theodor Lipps and the philosopher Edith Stein on the nature of empathy—a crucial question in aesthetic and philosophical discussion in the late 19th and early 20th centuries. Significantly, this debate proceeds from the example of an acrobat walking on a tightrope during a circus performance and the ways by which spectator experiences his movements. Retracing the complex debate on empathy, I counterpropose to recover the filmological account of the terms developed in the 1950s by Michotte and to rework this account through the application of Stein's phenomenological model. The analyses of acrobatic actions of characters in contemporary cinema will illuminate the importance of the unbalancing/rebalancing dynamic in creating the spectator's sensation of disequilibrium. Empathy seems to be inextricably linked to the moving image's capacity to express a tension, an oscillation, and a loading of energy experienced in the first person by the observer. Such a tension, however, must be intrinsic to the action of the film. In this sense, acrobatics not only provides sensory stimuli, but also offers clues for a full and *balanced* narrative understanding of the situation. Robert Zemeckis' *The Walk* (2015) will be analysed as a paradigmatic example of this dynamic.

Abandonment to vertigo implies something irremediably destructive and self-destructive. A common outcome of acrobatics, and a motif often combined with it, is the *fall*, which is dealt with in Chapter III. Instability is insufficient; the spectator must also feel the thrill of speed and confront death even more closely, or even directly meet it in the absence of wings, parachute, or safety net. A headlong descent—voluntary or involuntary, fatal or non-fatal—allows us to experience a sense of liberty or to search for liberation. Starting with the found footage film *Maybe Not* (Pietsch 2005), which deals with the significant recurrence of the motif of the falling human body in contemporary cinema, this chapter describes characters' unstoppable descending movements as intentional acts that the spectator experiences in a simulative modality. The uncontrolled speed with which the fall takes place leads to a sudden and dramatic nearing of the body to its *end*: to its object. Drawing on Torben Grodal's terminology, referring to the use of cinema as metaphor for the mind as proposed by Antonio Damasio, and interpreting several experiments on the perception of movement in sequences in which temporality has been manipulated, I will describe the modality through which cinema 'regulates' the fall by adopting a homeostatic process that reduces its 'traumaticness' and, at the same time, enhances its expressive effectiveness.

The fall tends inalterably to its completion: its inevitable end is the *impact*, a literally traumatic moment that is programmatically 'censored' precisely due to both the visceral and the psychological violence that its explicit display would cause. Inspired by Alejandro G. Iñárritu's short film *11'9"01* (2002), Chapter IV describes the ways in which the spectator experiences the *non-representation* of the human body hitting the ground, beginning with a reflection on the traumatic events of September 11, 2001. The analysis will show that contemporary cinema adopts a series of formal strategies in order to represent the 'unrepresentable'. To explain the modalities in which these strategies concretely operate, I will draw upon several recent experiments on visual occlusion carried out in the neuroscientific field, as well as several classic demonstrations from experimental psychology that explain how we tend to internally complete the movement of a body whose final stage is 'screened' from view.

Chapter V deals with the motif of *overturning*. The film experience is usually oriented in the same way as ordinary experience, with the head up. What happens to the spectator, whose corporeal position is invariable, when the body (and the face in particular) of the character is represented upside down? The argument builds off of Merleau-Ponty's reflections on the phenomenology of the perception of space, carried out on the basis of several classic experiments on retinal inversion and oblique vision. These insights are applied to the specificity of the film experience through a juxtaposition with Rudolf Arnheim's reflections on the artistic potential a film can derive from the relativity of point of view and movement. The analysis leads to the identification of a dynamic that moves from the disorientation produced by the representation of overturned faces to an 'un-overturning', a move that restores vision to its usual axes of orientation, while still continuing to convey its internally 'inverted' aspect to the spectator. A subtle and deceptive move depicting the Joker in Christopher Nolan's *The Dark Knight* (2008) will fuel my argument.

The directionality and intentionality inherent in the previous tensive motifs is broken down in the case of the *drift*, a term by which I designate the movement of characters in environments without gravity. Chapter VI adopts an ecological approach to visual perception, one fundamentally based on James Gibson's concept of affordance as a property that emerges from the organism-environment interaction. The analysis of scenes depicting astronauts' spacewalks highlights how they convey the weakening of the human capacity to intentionally grasp objects and how they can have a stable sense of one's own body in space. Feelings of ungraspability and deanchoring depend on the interference between the visual data furnished by the screen and the 'tactile' and proprioceptive data provided to the spectator by his own body. The 'sense of void' experienced on a psychophysical level also affects the spectator in symbolic terms. Alfonso Cuarón's *Gravity* (2013) will offer several insights for this reflection.

The final chapter offers, as a conclusion, an examination of the characteristics of the five tensive motifs dealt with in the preceding chapters, carrying out a kind of general anatomy of those strategies used to generate cinematic tension. In line with the phenomenological approach adopted throughout the analysis, the concept of *intentionality* will be linked with *tension* and *intensification*: each of the tensive motifs deploys its own intentional object in a way specific to the conditions of the aerial space in which it takes place.

As in *Inception*, the tensive motifs are often found in combination and some are inextricably linked. Although discussed separately, these emblematic *momenta* of perceptual bodily intensification should be conceived as the progressive development or variants of a sole aerial motif. The fall, for example, is often the outcome of a feat of acrobatics or an overturning, and inevitably leads to an impact. Furthermore, the tension that a spectator perceives before an acrobatic action is determined by the risk of falling, almost as though it accumulated in anticipation of the trauma of the impact. Similarly, overturning is often a 'symptom' of drifting, which is in turn what causes the sense of a void. In a nutshell, this book carries out an exploration of the recurrent *vertiginous* forms through which cinema, today in a radical way, offers the spectator an intense experience; a concentration of motor and emotional stimuli that aims to generate the same alteration in balance to which the character is subject, but then (and often simultaneously) to offer a remedy and a compensation for the breakdown of equilibrium in order to make an excessive experience experienceable. In this way, the book also offers a reflection on the presence of cinema in everyday life as a sort of laboratory of experimentation on human fears and desires. The aesthetic-homeostatic dynamic involved in the functioning of all of the motifs can be understood as a means of negotiation between the desire for vertigo and excess and the necessity of bringing overstimulation back beneath the threshold that assures the legibility of and receptivity to the film, in perceptual as well as moral, social, and commercial terms. Let me anticipate how exactly this homeostatic dynamic works.

Disembodying-Reembodying

The tensive motifs do not seem to correspond with what Marcel Mauss (1973) called 'techniques of the body'; for example, marching, running, dancing, jumping, climbing up or down, swimming, and so forth. These *techniques* are all the result of acquisition and education, they are the manifestations of the cultural nature of the individual, whether in positive terms, as social education, or in negative (and Foucauldian) tems of being subjected to discipline. The tensive motifs are instead *authentic* actions, considering their distance from the harmony and coordination of athletic movement. They are far from being predetermined and from being socially learnable due to the simple fact that they are actions that are foreign to routine, daily life, and educational and disciplinary protocols; they are extreme, uncontrollable, dangerous, and sometimes fatal, so both society and the individual by his very nature tend to avoid them. In this sense, the tensive motifs, rather than being disciplinary or punitive, are destabilizing and liberating. They somewhat resemble the activities of voluntary risk (from extreme sports to gambling) described by the sociology of risk as actions in which a subject voluntarily puts his own life in danger for the sole purpose of obtaining pleasure (Goffman 1967; Lyng 2005). The film spectator, in effect, voluntarily chooses to submit himself to an intensification of stimuli, thereby intentionally looking for the thrill of vertigo, pushing himself as close as possible to the limits and defying death.

Rather than techniques embodied in society, the tensive motifs can be thought of as a play activity of the kind that Roger Caillois (2001) would categorize as *Ilinx* (the Greek term for whirlpool, from which is also derived the word *ilingos*, meaning vertigo), that is, games that cause 'a disorder that may take organic or psychological form' (24). As he writes,

> Various physical activities also provoke these sensations, such as the tightrope, falling or being projected into space, rapid rotation, sliding, speeding, and acceleration of vertilinear movement, separately or in combination with gyrating movement. In parallel fashion, there is a vertigo of a moral order, a transport that suddenly seizes the individual. This vertigo is readily linked to the desire for disorder and destruction, a drive which is normally repressed (24).

Of course, cinema is a playful activity that offers such a vertiginous disorder and destruction experience in a 'safe mode', since in the cinema one only finds innocuous dangers, thrills, and sensations of vertigo that are sources of pleasure and entertainment rather than actual threats to one's safety. The experiences offered by cinema, however, do not differ from those of daily life in simply quantitative terms. The motor and emotional engagement provided by a mediated event in fact depends on the *forces* released by the represented objects and subjects, as well as on the tensions emerging from the fictional environment and on the movements issuing from the film itself (camera movement, editing, framings, points of view, etc.). This specifically cinematic corporeality offers the spectator an opportunity to bond with a character and an immersion into an environment that is qualitatively different from what would be experienced if one were physically present on the scene. For this reason, film's corporeal mediation takes on an essential role. It is only through the film's expressivity that we can corporeally experience actions that would be impossible, dangerous, or self-destructive in real life: we can fly, fall, remain suspended in the air, or float through the void. We can risk our lives and even die since, as in *Inception*, this would only mean waking up from a dream.

Now, the forces characteristic of the motifs of air are intensified through a modulation of energetic tension, which films manage through both the narrative construction of the characters and the use of formal techniques. Often, such an intensification pushes energetic tension up to the maximum threshold. What is important here is that intensification carries with it the possibility of disturbing perception or disrupting the spectator's state of equilibrium. Quoting Caillois (2001) once more, play activities of the category of *Ilinx*

> include those which are based on the pursuit of vertigo and which consist of an attempt to momentarily destroy the stability of perception and inflict a kind of voluptuous panic upon an otherwise lucid mind. In all cases, it is a question of surrendering to a kind of spasm, seizure, or shock which destroys reality with sovereign brusqueness (23).

Similarly, the tensive motifs have the function of temporarily modifying perception up to the point of distorting, suspending, or invalidating the dynamic forces that are experienced on a corporeal level and thus call for, in a more or less automatic and systematic way, a restoration of conditions more amendable to perception and comprehension. I call this first moment the *disembodying* phase and the second the *reembodying* phase.

The first term designates the spectator's deliberate search for imbalance, excess, disequilibrium, disturbance, and danger through a 'corporeal estrangement' based on the intensification, or even the breaking of the 'energetic circuit' of sensory stimulation. Acrobatics, fall, impact, overturning, and drift are motifs that offer first and foremost a sudden interruption of the 'continuous current' that allows for the spectator's engagement. In narrative cinema, the phenomenon of the impression of reality, the state of suspended disbelief, and the immersivity of the environmental and cognitive situation are all factors that work to obscure not only the presence of a textual enunciative instance, but also that of the spectator's body. The spectator loses the sense of his own body and accesses the represented actions and events in a modality that might be called *en abyme* in respect to the corporeal materiality of his subjectivity. Even when stimulated on a physical level, the spectator continues to be 'taken' by the energy that the film generates, provided that this energy does not pass a given threshold.

Through the tensive motifs, the film brings the energy level up to this threshold, sometimes crossing over it and making the spectator distinctly sense his own body, thus breaking the enchantment of self-forgetting. Disembodiment arises when hyperstimulation becomes overstimulation and the spectator's body re-emerges from its obscured position. The 'transparency' of continuity thus turns into self-reflexive moments that pull the spectators out of their narrative immersion, making them aware of their own body as the real point of orientational reference in the experiential environment. This mismatch between embodied experience and the embodiment of experience is at the basis of contemporary cinema's expressive potential: the spectator's ability to immediately grasp the intentionality of a movement can be frustrated, slowed down, disrupted, disturbed, distanced, slackened, and so forth.

Let me clarify an important terminological issue: by saying that a characteristic of the tensive motifs is the 'disembodying' phase, I am not by any means arguing that the film experience, in general, *is* disembodied. On the contrary, relying on an enactive approach, I adopt a neurofilmological account based on the embodied cognition paradigm. In opposition to disembodied 'classic' cognitive film theory, I assume that the spectator participates in the film with his *organism*, a lived body that perceives and elaborates multisensory stimuli and that, in a simulative form grounded in the neural substratum and both embedded and extended in an experiential (natural *and* cultural) environment, enacts a series of internal movements that accompanies both the character's and the film's body movements. In this sense, the disembodying phase is precisely a specific moment in the course of a film experience in which a tensive motif emerges and 'puts in tension' the embodied and intentional nature of the perceptual experience while avoiding its complete and definitive destruction.

At the beginning of the 1930s, Rudolf Arnheim (1957) observed cinema's capacity to induce *vertigo*, underscoring that this effect arose from the insurmountable discrepancy between the spectator's physical state and the specific optical-acoustic state in which the film experience takes place, an interference between two frames of reference:

> Our eyes are not a mechanism functioning independently of the rest of the body. They work in constant cooperation with the other sense organs. Hence surprising phenomena result if the eyes are asked to convey ideas unaided by the other senses. Thus, for example, it is well known that a feeling of giddiness is produced by watching a film that has been taken with the camera traveling very rapidly. This giddiness is caused by the eyes participating in a different world from that indicated by the

> kinesthetic reactions of the body, which is at rest. The eyes act as if the body as a whole were moving; whereas the other senses, including that of equilibrium, report that it is at rest. Our sense of equilibrium when we are watching a film is dependent on what the eyes report and does not as in real life receive kinesthetic stimulation (30).

Arnheim considered the potential interference between the movement of the camera and the immobility of the spectators' bodies—termed 'motion sickness' by contemporaneous psychophysiological studies—as a 'differential factor', that is, an expressive tool for the art of cinema deriving from the inability of the cinema to render an exact copy of the real world. Although he intuited that movement in cinema was not 'simple locomotion' perceived as the mere displacement of the elements of the visual field, he nevertheless did not yet grasp the spectator's propensity to simulate the movements of the film and the emotions of the characters within his own body. His approach aimed not so much to understand the spectator's physical propensity to empathize with movement, as to show the expressive nature of the dynamics of movement, understood in terms of visuals and content. As he would write later, '[o]f course, physically all motion is caused by some kind of force. But what counts for artistic performance is the dynamics conveyed to the audience visually; for dynamics alone is responsible for expression and meaning' (Arnheim 1954, 408).

Implied in Arnheim's perspective, however, is the idea that, while film as a medium is visual, the modalities of film perception are not merely such, since they involve proprioception, equilibrioception, and others kinds of perceptions that are obtained visually but that are different in quality. As a sort of Arnheimian 'differentiating factor', a tensive motif creates a conflict of visual, sensorimotor, and vestibular information and uses the *tension* between visual and kinaesthetic perception to create a gap in the embodied structure of the film experience. In other words, it is exactly because the film experience is constitutively 'bodied' that it can be subject to a disembodying process. In sum, I do not posit disembodiment as a precondition or a result of the film experience, but rather something that occurs at moments in which the spectator is subject to a sort of an attack on the embodied nature of the perceptual experience.

Another dynamic is, in fact, counterposed against this one: just before the passing of the threshold, or in any case not long after, the disembodying phase is balanced out and compensated for by an inverse dynamic that tends to 'reembody' the lost, diffused, distorted, or disjointed intentionality. Confronted with the 'displacement' of the body, the cinema can then offer a compensation, a rebalancing, a move that brings the imbalance back under an acceptable threshold and makes the tensive motif intense but possible as well as fully experienceable. On the one hand it is the spectator himself, in his biological corporeality, who naturally reacts to the attack and attempts to restore balance. The physiological responses of the organism are aimed precisely at re-establishing equilibrium, slowing down excessive speed, censoring the unrepresentable, completing the fragmentary, uprighting the overturned, and providing a foothold for movements performed in zero-gravity. However, this compensation is also systematically carried out directly by the film soon after the imbalancing, through stylistic forms that *embody* the biological functions of homeostasis and the cognitive regulation processes instinctively activated by the spectator. Before these are used, or when they are still in their early stages, the film's body takes on aspects of the spectator's body and remedies an imbalance that would be fatal to the smooth functioning of affective engagement, narrative continuity, the interpretation of the meanings being conveyed, and so forth; in short, to the pleasure of the experience. As though trying to facilitate the spectator's task, the film in fact takes his place, anticipating her physical, perceptual, or mental effort to attenuate a trauma, his reorganization of the visual field, her narrative comprehension, and his interiorization of the values in play. The *reembodying* phase thus consists of a mitigation of excess, a reestablishment of equilibrium, a filling of the gap between visual and kinaesthetic perception, and a reconstitution of 'experiential continuity', carried out by the film on the spectator's behalf, through stylistic and formal techniques: reequilibrium, slowing down, hiding, uprighting, or gravitational aesthetics. In this sense, the cinema does not 'replace' human physiology or mental activity—as in the film/mind analogy (or the cinema as the objectification of perception, memory, attention, imagination, emotion) postulated by Hugo Münsterberg (2002) at the dawn of film theory—but incorporates and acts itself as a lived body, creating a sort of 'embodied isomorphism'.

As Francesco Casetti (2008) has argued, one of the functions of cinema, as the elective medium of Modernity, is precisely the *negotiation* between the thrills of movement, change, and the sensorial excitement of mass and urban society that it has reflected since its beginnings and the many dangers associated with these euphorias. According to its etymology, each medium has a double function: connection and separation, exposure and protection, freedom and impediment, power and limitation. Cinema negotiates between thrill and risk by putting into play 'an excited gaze that gathers stimuli and boosts them, yet it also gives this gaze adequate defenses, which protect it from possible dangers' (135). Cinema mediates between sensations and sense, between sensoriality and meanings, conveying and organizing stimuli into a story, regulating, disciplining, and balancing the spectator's excitement.

> The cinema is exactly this: an experience that vacillates between the possibility of an excitement beyond measure, and an adherence to measures that avoid all risk. It is the space between, in which the comings and goings serve to recover a balanced turmoil in order to arrive at what modern man needs: good emotion (140).

This 'homeostatic' dynamic—the transformation of 'strong emotions' into 'good emotions'—has gained an even more crucial relevance in intensified contemporary cinema, where the system of bodies involved acquires a crucial role in modulating the relationship between continuity and discontinuity, proximity and distance, immersion and self-reflection. As I will show in the analysis of the tensive motifs, they not only offer the multistable perception typical of visual illusions but also the entire dynamic of rupture of stability and its restoring on a bodily and multisensorial scale rather than merely visually. Rather than an oscillation between the continuity of narrative content comprehension and the emerging of the medium that communicates that content as a self-reflexive 'break', the experience of the tensive motifs turns the diachronic rupture into a synchronic suture. The awareness of one own's body that results from the disembodying phase should not be considered as a temporarily disembodiment, but rather as a precondition for reinforcing the embodiment, which is the taken-for-granted condition of the film (and in general the human) experience.

Post-postmodernity

The general tendency for intensification of contemporary cinema can be ascribed to the fact that the latter has had to react to radical changes that have affected technological, economic, and cultural spheres in the last decades. The advent of digital technology and media convergence has led to the establishment of new occasions for and practices of the consumption of audio-visual products. Forms of viewing have multiplied and been detached from specific places and times: one thinks of the spread of screens within urban public spaces, or the increasingly widespread diffusion of devices that allow for the use of audio-visual products while on the go. The film experience seems to have dissolved into a wider and more composite media experience. Cinema has 'relocated' itself from theatre big screens to smart phones and laptop displays, computers monitors, and the screens spread throughout cities, meeting places, spaces of transit, and means of transport. This relocation has brought about a weakening of the spectacular and immersive character of the film experience in respect to its 'traditional' form. The cinema, and with it the 'canonical' film experience, has certainly not disappeared, but has become just one of the ways in which individuals access the experience of film today. The tensive motifs described in this book are perhaps cinema's 'reaction' to this double weakening, the way that this form of experience attempts to protect its unstable borders (Casetti 2015). One among many possible locations for the viewing of a film, and one among many possible audio-visual narrative products, the theatre and the film have reshaped themselves to respond to new demands but they have also conserved—and indeed strengthened—the originary seed of their own existence, their *raison d'être*: to offer a spectacle; to provide a concentration of 'strong sensations'. As I will show, this 'revolutionary conservation' consists in the implementation of intensified styles and models of engagement.

The tensive motifs are certainly indicators of the socio-economic and cultural context in which they have arisen. Michel Lacroix (2001) has written that contemporary society seems to be devoted to the 'cult of emotion'. For Lacroix, a paradox emerges: now that the emotion can mitigate the excesses of rationalization, the *homo sentiens* risks not being able to feel anymore, and the overconsumption of strong sensations anesthetizes human sensitivity. At the turn of the Millennium, the re-emergence and the exacerbation of the tension between the rational and the irrational, or between reflection and emotion, was at the heart of the debate on postmodern cinema. The progressive intensification and polarization of film style, developed over the previous fifty years, reached its peak, and the use of special effects enhanced the spectacularity of popular media in general and blockbuster films in particular.

As Vincent Amiel and Pascal Couté (2003) argue, the American contemporary blockbuster bases its aesthetic on stimulus and on perceptual intensification, one that places emphasis on form rather than content and in which rhythm, speed, and action impose themselves as elements with an intrinsic value, no longer necessarily functional to the story. In respect to action and sci-fi films, for Geoff King (2000) Hollywood's blockbusters adopted an *impact aesthetic* by which 'viewers are not seeking to be awoken to some new understanding of the world [...] but to be stimulated physically for its own sensuous pleasure. They want [...] 'to participate in the film,' to be directly acted upon by the film' (99). For Linda Williams (2000) the film spectator goes the movie to feel excitation and visceral fright, without paying too much attention to narrative coherence (at least beginning with *Psycho*). Inspired by Jean Baudrillard's notion of simulacrum (1983) and Fredric Jameson's discourse on the 'absence of depth' and on the 'waning of affect' as typical traits of postmodern society (1991), Laurent Jullier (1997) argues that postmodern cinema reflects an era of surface, of superficial discourses, and of a lack of critical distance, replaced by the immersion in a world of completely autonomous and images—a 'bath of sensations'. In this 'passage from *communication* [...] to *fusion*', the postmodern spectator finds himself implicated in a discontinuum of stimulations that he is hardly able to rationalize. The conflict between sensation and narration, or between the need to experience the thrill of vertigo and the need to order and understand the content of storytelling, is heightened.

The obsession of postmodern cinema with the body and perceptual shock can be traced back to the experiments that preceded and contributed to the birth of the moving image. From the very beginning, cinema has proposed an intensified sensorial experience, placing itself in the history of popular spectacles that aimed to amaze the audience with tricks, wonders, and phantasmagorias. In the wake of Marey and Muybridge's 'scientific' attention to the body in motion, the first cinematographic cameras set their eye on muscular bodies, acrobatics and circus acts, sporting feats, and scenes of dance or combat between men and animals, often with a comic or burlesque vein. For Scott Bukatman (2003), since the very beginning, the 'panoramic perception' characteristic of the first cinematographic *views* was accompanied by 'kaleidoscopic perception', more frenetic and corporeal, 'which operated through a combination of delirium, kinesis, and immersion' (3), similar to the experience offered by phantasmagorias, amusement parks, halls of mirrors, and other spectacular shows. Contrary to panoramic perception, in which '[a] continuum of views replaced 'the' view, as our bodies no longer belonged to the world we saw', in kaleidoscopic perception 'The spectator was no longer at a safe remove but was plunged into a jagged discontinuum of views' (3). The same experience is thus characterized by continuity (cinema as a new medium for the rationalization of a world with expanded boundaries yet reduced distances) and discontinuity (cinema as part of the sensory bombardment and intensification of nervous life in modern metropolis). As Bukatman argues, '[k]aleidoscopic perception served to turn the fear of instability into the thrill of topsy-turveydom' (3). The coexistence of opposite poles thus results in a paradoxical synthesis in which *fear* turns into *thrill*, that is, in which 'ludification' replaces rationalization as the main form employed to face the complexity of reality.

As the result of this tendency, postmodern cinema seems to offer a new and intensified version of the 'attractions' that characterized the exhibitionistic origins of cinema, a sort of automatic distributor of adrenaline and violent impulses, visceral feelings and instantaneous emotions that have to be consumed immediately by compulsive seekers of superficial excitement. I will return extensively to this topic in the final chapter, where I will relate the narrative function of the tensive motifs to contemporary spectatorship in the light of the whole analysis and in the theoretical framework of embodied cognition. I should clarify here that I believe that the postmodern cinema debate produced a radical position that overemphasizes the sensory and physical (as well as ludic) dimension of both everyday life and the media experience as a reaction to the domination of the mind and of the eye that, although in different forms, was implied in both classic and modern cinemas. Two conflicts (or two variants of the same dichotomy) seem to lie in the postmodern cinema debate: between the mind and the body, and between narration and sensation. As the analysis of the tensive motifs will show, they both are manifestations of an unproductive dualism that should be overcome. Differently from postmodern cinema (or from postmodern theorization), contemporary cinema adopts an intensified aesthetic that plays at interfering yet does not destroy the body-mind unity nor narrative continuity.

Learn to fly

Steven Shaviro (2015) affirms that today the shocking effect of cinema as the emblem of Modernity has been replaced by an 'accelerationist aesthetic', a strategy that reflects the trend of capitalism to radicalize and exacerbate the dissolutive forces that animate it in order to feed itself. Rather than the pure expression of neoliberal society, however, the five motifs of air embody a more visceral concern. The strategy of disarticulation and rearticulation of intentionality that underlies the motifs reflects the clash of desires and fears, attitudes and concerns, and aspirations and preoccupations. Cinematic acrobatics, falls, impacts, overturnings, and drifts are expressive experiences that communicate in an 'immediate', sensible, and only seemingly superficial manner, the deep meaning of human existence—the innate propensity of the individual and of society to transcend the limits of their own condition, to know the thrill of speed, to liberate themselves on the wings of liberty and defy death. At the same time, they provide a compensation for the perturbation of perception by adopting embodied forms of regulation of stimuli and a dynamic restoration of equilibrium. The spectator is invited to stand empathically in the shoes of the film character—whether a tightrope walker, an angel, a superhero, an astronaut, or an 'ordinary' person—and thus to carry out acts of tensive aerial experience in order to test in a safe way and reflect upon the limits of our human condition.

In this sense, the undecidability that characterizes the motif of *acrobatics* is in a way a reflection of the indecision and doubt that eats at the contemporary individual. The precipitousness of the *fall* gives form to the relationship between individual and environment not only in a spatial sense, but also a social, cultural, and historical one, that is, perhaps, most relevant after September 11, 2001. In cinema, the fall reminds us of the decline of a civilization that has built itself up to great heights, believing itself to be in a utopian state of invincibility. The fall is perhaps an extreme way of emancipating oneself from the constraints of the body and from everyday life, a 'liberation' from gravity, but the conclusion of this act is almost always violent, dramatic, and traumatic. If the fall expresses physical and moral collapse, decline, transience, and decadence, the *impact* expresses failure, and for this reason is always subject to self-censorship. While the fall preserves as much of a principle of orientation as possible thanks to the force of gravity, *overturning* calls into question the fundamentals of the physics of daily life, upsets them, and makes them ambiguous, impenetrable, and indecipherable. Then there is the extreme case of the *drift*, in which the individual definitively loses attachment to the ground and the ability to grasp the meaning of life. In the abyss of outer space, the indeterminate and the unknown prevail in a void that negates the very existence of a ground into which we could deposit our mortal remains.

Undecidability, liberation, trauma, indecipherability, and the unknown: cinema increasingly tends to offer us the sensation of vertigo and to push us onto the wings of the air, allowing us to explore unknown worlds. At the same time, it takes our breath away, knocks us over, flings us against a wall, overturns us, and abandons us in the void, placing us before our insecurities, vulnerabilities, and obsessions. Human beings, irremediably chained to the weight of their own body, their own immanence, and to gravity, seek in cinema a lightness that would otherwise be impossible, and to receive the opportunity for a transcendent experience; one that loosens the chains of human nature and condition and, at the same time, reaffirms these limitations, offering an unprecedented modality of exploration and reflexive consciousness. More radically, then, the tensive motifs reveal the flowering, on the terrain of cinema, of a Heideggerian rediscovery of our *being-towards-death*.

Bibliography

Albera, François, & Martin Lefebvre, eds. 2009. *La filmologie, de nouveau. Cinémas: revue d'études cinématographiques / Cinémas: Journal of Film Studies*. 19 (2-3). DOI:10.7202/037546ar.

Allen, Richard, & Murray Smith, eds. 1997. *Film Theory and Philosophy*. Oxford: Clarendon Press.

Amiel, Vincent, & Pascal Couté. 2003. *Formes et obsessions du cinéma américain contemporain*. Paris: Klincksieck.

Arnheim, Rudolf. 1954. *Art and Visual Perception: A Psychology of the Creative Eye*. Berkeley: University of California Press.

Arnheim, Rudolf. 1957. *Film as Art*. Berkeley: University of California Press.

Bachelard, Gaston. 1988. *Air and Dreams: An Essay on the Imagination of Movement*. Translated by Edith Farrell & Frederick Farrell. Dallas: Dallas Institute of Humanities and Culture.

Baudrillard, Jean. 1983. *Simulations*. Translated by Paul Foss, Paul Batton & Philip Beitchman. New York: Semiotext(e).

Bordwell, David, & Noël Carroll, eds. 1996. *Post-Theory: Reconstructing Film Studies*. Madison: University of Wisconsin Press.

Bordwell, David. 1985. *Narration in the Fiction Film*. Madison: University of Wisconsin Press.

Bordwell, David. 1989. *Making Meaning: Inference and Rhetoric in the Interpretation of Cinema*. Cambridge, MA: Harvard University Press.

Branigan, Edward. 1992. *Narrative Comprehension and Film*. London/New York: Routledge.

Buckland, Warren. 2009a. *Film Theory and Contemporary Hollywood Movies*. New York and Abingdon: Routledge.

Bukatman, Scott. 2003. *Matters of Gravity: Special Effects and Supermen in the 20th Century*. Durham: Duke University.

Caggiano, Vittorio, Leonardo Fogassi, Giacomo Rizzolatti, Joern K. Pomper, Peter Thier, Martin A. Giese, & Antonino Casile. 2011. 'View-Based Encoding of Actions in Mirror Neurons of Area F5 in Macaque Premotor Cortex'. *Current Biology*. 21 (2): 144-148. DOI:10.1016/j.cub.2010.12.022.

Caillois, Roger. 2001. *Man, Play and Games*. Translated by Meyer. Barash. Urbana/ Chicago: University of Illinois Press.

Carocci, Enrico. 2018. *Il sistema schermo-mente. Cinema narrativo e coinvolgimento emozionale*. Roma: Bulzoni.

Carroll, Noël. 1988. *Mystifying Movies: Fads and Fallacies in Contemporary Film Theory*. New York: Columbia University Press.

Carroll, Noël. 1990. *The Philosophy of Horror, or Paradoxes of the Heart.* New York: Routledge.

Casetti, Francesco. 2008. *Eye of the Century: Film, Experience, Modernity.* New York: Columbia University Press.

Casetti, Francesco. 2015. *The Lumière Galaxy: Seven Key World for the Cinema to Come.* New York: Columbia University Press.

Chalmers, David J. 1996. *The Conscious Mind: In Search of a Fundamental Theory.* New York: Oxford University Press.

Coëgnarts, Maarten, & Peter Kravanja. 2015. *Embodied Cognition and Cinema.* Leuven: Leuven University Press.

Cohen-Séat, Gilbert, & Jacques Faure. 1954. 'Retentissement du 'fait filmique' sur les rythmes bioélectriques du cerveau'. *Revue internationale de filmologie.* 16: 27-50.

Cohen-Séat, Gilbert, Henry Gastaut, & Jacque Bert. 1954. 'Modification de l'E.E.G. pendant la projection cinématographique'. *Revue internationale de filmologie.* 16: 7-26.

Cutting, James E., & Ayse Candan. 2015. 'Shot Durations, Shot Classes, and the Increased Pace of Popular Movies'. *Projections.* 9 (2): 40-62. DOI:10:3167/proj.2015.090204

D'Aloia, Adriano, & Ruggero Eugeni, eds. 2014. 'Neurofilmology: An Introduction'. *Cinéma&Cie. International Film Studies Journal.* 14 (22-23): 9-25.

Damasio, Antonio R. 1994. *Descartes' Error: Emotion, Reason, and the Human Brain.* New York: Grosset/Putnam.

Damasio, Antonio R. 1999. *The Feeling of What Happens: Body and Emotion in the Making of Consciousness.* New York: Harcourt.

Damasio, Antonio R. 2003. *Looking for Spinoza: Joy, Sorrow and the Feeling Brain.* New York: Houghton Mifflin Harcourt.

Damasio, Antonio R. 2010. *Self Comes to Mind: Constructing the Conscious Brain.* New York: Pantheon.

Davis, David. 2018. 'A Moderately Pessimistic Perspective on "Cooperative Naturalism"'. *Projections.* 12 (2): 9-18. DOI:10:3167/proj.2018.120203.

Deleuze, Gilles. 1989. *Cinema 2: The Time Image.* Translated by H. Tomlinson and R. Galeta. Minneapolis: University of Minnesota Press.

Deleuze, Gilles. 2000. 'The Brain Is the Screen', in *The Brain Is the Screen: Deleuze and the Philosophy of Cinema.* Edited by Gregory Flaxman, 365-373. Minneapolis: University of Minnesota Press.

di Pellegrino, Giuseppe, Luciano Fadiga, Leonardo Fogassi, Vittorio Gallese, & Giacomo Rizzolatti. 1992. 'Understanding Motor Events: a Neurophysiological Study'. *Experimental Brain Research.* 91: 176-180.

Durt, Christoph, Thomas Fuchs, & Christian Tewes, eds. 2017. *Embodiment, Enaction, and Culture. Investigating the Constitution of the Shared World.* Cambridge, MA/London: The MIT Press.

Eisenstein, Sergei M. 1988, *Selected Works*. Volume I: *Writings, 1922-34*. Edited and translated by Richard Taylor. London: British Film Institute.

Elliott, Paul. 2010. 'The Eye, the Brain, the Screen: What Neuroscience Can Teach Film Theory'. *Excursions*. 1: 1-16. DOI:10.20919/exs.1.2010.123.

Ferrari, Pier Francesco, & Giacomo Rizzolatti, eds. 2015. *New Frontiers in Mirror Neurons Research*. New York: Oxford University Press.

Fingerhut Joerg, & Katrin Heimann. 2017. 'Movies and the Mind: On Our Filmic Body'. In Durt, Fuchs & Tewes, eds., 353-377.

Freedberg, David, & Vittorio Gallese. 2007. 'Motion, Emotion and Empathy in Aesthetic Experience'. *Trends in Cognitive Sciences*. 11 (5): 197-203. DOI:10.1016/j.tics.2007.02.003.

Gallagher, Shaun. 1986. 'Lived Body and Environment'. *Research in Phenomenology*. 16: 139-170.

Gallese, Vittorio, & Alvin I. Goldman. 1998. 'Mirror Neurons and the Simulation Theory of Mind-Reading'. Trends in Cognitive Sciences. 2 (12): 493-501. DOI:10.1016/s1364-6613(98)01262-5.

Gallese, Vittorio, & Michele Guerra. 2012. 'Embodying Movies: Embodied Simulation and Film Studies'. *Cinema: Journal of Philosophy and the Moving Image* 3: 183-210. http://cjpmi.ifilnova.pt/storage/3/3_Gallese_Guerra.pdf.

Gallese, Vittorio, & Michele Guerra. 2019. *The Empathic Screen: Cinema and Neuroscience*. Translated by Frances Anderson. New York: Oxford University Press.

Gallese, Vittorio, Christian Keysers, & Giacomo Rizzolatti. 2004. 'A Unifying View of the Basis of Social Cognition'. *Trends in Cognitive Sciences*. 8 (9): 396-403. DOI:10.1016/j.tics.2004.07.002.

Gallese, Vittorio, Luciano Fadiga, Leonardo Fogassi, & Giacomo Rizzolatti. 1996. 'Action Recognition in the Premotor Cortex'. *Brain*. 119: 593-609. DOI:10.1093/brain/119.2.593.

Gallese, Vittorio. 2001. 'The "Shared Manifold" Hypothesis: From Mirror Neurons to Empathy'. *Journal of Consciousness Studies*. 8 (5-7): 33-50.

Gallese, Vittorio. 2003. 'The Roots of Empathy: The Shared Manifold Hypothesis and the Neural Basis of Intersubjectivity'. *Psychopatology*. 36 (4): 171-180. DOI:10.1159/000072786.

Gallese, Vittorio. 2005a. '"Being Like Me": Self-Other Identity, Mirror Neurons and Empathy'. In *Perspectives on Imitation: From Cognitive Neuroscience to Social Science Volume 1*. Edited by Susan Hurley & Nick Chater, 101-118. Cambridge, MA: The MIT Press.

Gallese, Vittorio. 2005b. 'Embodied Simulation: From Neurons to Phenomenal Experience'. *Phenomenology and the Cognitive Sciences*. 4 (1): 23-48. DOI:10.1007/s11097-005-4737-z.

Gallese, Vittorio. 2007. 'Before and Below 'Theory of Mind': Embodied Simulation and the Neural Correlates of Social Cognition'. *Philosophical Transactions of the Royal Society B-Biological Sciences*. 362: 659-669. DOI:10.1098/rstb.2006.2002.

Gallese, Vittorio. 2009a. 'Mirror Neurons, Embodied Simulation, and the Neural Basis of Social Identification'. *Psychoanalytic Dialogues*. 19 (5): 519-536. DOI:10.1080/10481880903231910.

Gallese, Vittorio. 2009b. 'Motor Abstraction: A Neuroscientific Account of How Action Goals and Intentions are Mapped and Understood'. *Psychological Research*. 73 (4): 486-498. DOI:10.1007/s00426-009-0232-4.

Gallese, Vittorio. 2009c. 'Neuroscienze e fenomenologia'. In *Treccani XXI secolo*. http://www.treccani.it/enciclopedia/neuroscienze-e-fenomenologia_%28XXI-Secolo%29.

Gallese, Vittorio. 2010. 'Mirror Neurons and Art', in *Art and the Senses*. Edited by Francesca Bacci & David Melcher, 441-449. Oxford: Oxford University Press.

Gallese, Vittorio. 2018. 'Naturalizing Aesthetic Experience. The Role of (Liberated) Embodied Simulation'. *Projections*. 12 (2): 50-59. DOI:10.3167/proj.2018.120207.

Goffman, Erving. 1967. *Interaction Ritual: Essays on Face to Face Behavior*. Garden City, NY: Doubleday.

Goldman, Alvin I. 2006a. 'Imagination and Simulation in Audience Responses to Fiction'. In *The Architecture of the Imagination: New Essays on Pretence, Possibility, and Fiction*. Edited by Shaun Nichols, 41-56. Oxford: Clarendon Press.

Grèzes, Julie, Jorge L. Armony, James Rowe, & Rrichard E. Passingham. 2003. 'Activations Related to "Mirror" and "Canonical" Neurones in the Human Brain: an fMRI Study'. *Neuroimage*. 18 (4): 928-937. DOI:10.1016/S1053-8119(03)00042-9.

Grodal, Torben. 1997. *Moving Pictures: A New Theory of Film Genres, Feelings, and Cognition*. Oxford: Clarendon Press.

Grodal, Torben. 2009. *Embodied Visions: Evolution, Emotion, Culture, and Film*. New York: Oxford University Press.

Guerra, Michele. 2015. 'Modes of Action at the Movie, or Re-Thinking Film Style from the Embodied Perspective'. In Coëgnarts & Kravanja, eds., 139-154.

Hari, Riitta, Nina Forss, Sari Avikainen, Erika Kirveskari, Stephan Salenius, & Giacomo Rizzolatti. 1998. 'Activation of Human Primary Motor Cortex during Action Observation: A Neuromagnetic Study'. *Proceedings of the National Academy of Sciences*. USA 95: 15061-15065.

Hasson, Uri, Ohad. Landesman, Barbara Knappmeyer, Ignacio Vallines, Nava Rubin, & David J. Heeger. 2008b. 'Neurocinematics: The Neuroscience of Film'. *Projections*. 2 (1): 1-16. DOI:10:3167/proj.2008.020102

Hasson, Uri, Ori Furman, David Clark, Yadin Dudai, & Lila Davachi. 2008a. 'Enhanced Intersubject Correlations During Movie Viewing Correlate with Successful Episodic Encoding'. *Neuron*. 57 (3): 452-462. DOI:10.1016/j.neuron.2007.12.009.

Heimann, Katrin, Maria Alessandra Umiltà, Michele Guerra, & Vittorio Gallese. 2014. 'Moving Mirrors: A High-Density EEG Study Investigating the Effect of Camera Movements on Motor Cortex Activation During Action Observation'. *Journal of Cognitive Neuroscience*. 26 (9): 2087-2101. DOI:10.1162/jocn_a_00602.

Heimann, Katrin, Sebo Uithol, Marta Calbi, Maria Alessandra Umiltà, Michele Guerra, Joerg Fingerhut, &Vittorio Gallese. 2019. 'Embodying the Camera: An EEG Study on the Effect of Camera Movements on Film Spectators' Sensorimotor Cortex Activation'. *PlusOne*. DOI:10.1371/journal.pone.0211026.

Heuyer, Georges, & Jacque Bert. 1954. 'EEG Changes During Cinematographic Presentation; Moving Picture Activation of the EEG'. *Electroencephalogr Clin Neurophysiol*. 6 (3): 433-444. DOI:10.1016/0013-4694(54)90058-9.

Heuyer, Georges, Gilbert Cohen-Séat, Serge Lebovici, Monique Rebeillard, & M.lle Daveau. 1954. 'Note sur l'électroencéphalographie pendant la projection cinématographique chez des adolescents inadaptés'. *Revue internationale de filmologie*. 16: 51-64.

Hoffner, Cynthia, & Joanne Cantor. 'Perceiving and Responding to Mass Media Characters'. In Bryant & Zillmann, eds., 63-101.

Hurley, Susan. 2002. *Consciousness in Action*. Cambridge, MA: Harvard University Press.

Hutto, Daniel D., & Erik Myin. 2013. *Radicalizing Enactivism: Basic Minds Without Content*. Cambridge, MA: The MIT Press.

Iacoboni, Marco. 2009. *Mirroring People: The New Science of How We Connect with Others*. New York: Picador.

Jameson, Fredric. 1991. *Postmodernism, or, the Cultural Logic of Late Capitalism*. Durham: Duke University Press.

Johnson, Mark. 1987. *The Body in the Mind: The Bodily Basis of Meaning, Imagination, and Reason*. Chicago: University of Chicago Press.

Johnson, Mark. 2015. 'Foreword'. In Coëgnarts & Kravanja, eds., 9-13.

Johnson, Mark. 2017. *Embodied Mind, Meaning, and Reason: How Our Bodies Give Rise to Understanding*. Chicago: University of Chicago Press.

Johnson, Mark. 2018. *The Aesthetics of Meaning and Thought: The Bodily Roots of Philosophy, Science, Morality, and Art*. Chicago: University of Chicago Press.

Jullier, Laurent. 1997. *L'écran post-moderne: Un cinéma du recyclage et du feu d'artifice*. Paris: L'Harmattan.

Keysers, Christian. 2011. *The Empathic Brain. How the Discovery of Mirror Neurons Changes Our Understanding of Human Nature*. Sydney: Social Brain Press, Kindle Edition.

King, Geoff. 2000. *Spectacular Narratives: Hollywood in the Age of the Blockbuster*. London: I.B. Tauris.

Lacroix, Michel. 2001. *Le culte de l'émotion*. Paris: Flammarion.

Lakoff, George, & Mark Johnson. 1999. *Philosophy in the Flesh: The Embodied Mind and Its Challenge to Western Thought*. New York: Basic Books.

Lyng, Stephen, ed. 2005. *Edgework: The Sociology of Risk-Taking*. New York: Routledge.

Mauss, Marcel. 1973. 'Techniques of the Body'. *Economy and Society*. 2 (1): 70-88.

Merleau-Ponty, Maurice. 1964. 'Eye and Mind'. In *The Primacy of Perception*. Edited by James E. Edie. Translated by Carleton Dallery, 159-190. Evanston, IL: Northwestern University Press.

Merleau-Ponty, Maurice. 1967. *The Structure of Behavior*. Translated by Alden Fisher. Boston: Beacon Press.

Merleau-Ponty, Maurice. 1968. 'The Film and the New Psychology'. In *Sense and Non-Sense*. Translated by Hubert L. Dreyfus & Patricia Dreyfus, 48-59. Evanston, Ill.: Northwestern University Press.

Merleau-Ponty, Maurice. 2002. *Phenomenology of Perception*. New York: Humanities Press/London: Routledge & Kegan Paul.

Mukamel, Roy, Arne D. Ekstrom, Jonas Kaplan, Marco Iacoboni, & Itzhak Fried. 2010. 'Single-neuron Responses in Humans during Execution and Observation of Actions'. *Current Biology*. 20 (8): 750-756. DOI:10.1016/j.cub.2010.02.045.

Mullarkey, John. 2009. *Refractions of Reality: Philosophy and the Moving Image*. Houndmills: Palgrave-Macmillan.

Münsterberg, Hugo. 2002. *Hugo Münsterberg on Film:* The Photoplay: A Psychological Study *and Other Writings*. Edited by Allan Langdale. New York/London: Routledge.

Nannicelli, Ted, & Paul Taberham. 2014. *Cognitive Media Theory*. New York/London: Routledge.

Noë, Alva. 2004. *Action in Perception*. Cambridge, MA: The MIT Press.

Petitot, Jean, Francisco J. Varela, Bernard Pachoud, & Jean-Michel Roy, eds. 1999. *Naturalizing Phenomenology: Issues in Contemporary Phenomenology and Cognitive Science*. Stanford: Stanford University Press.

Pisters, Patricia. 2009. 'Illusionary Perception and Cinema: Experimental Thoughts on Film Theory and Neuroscience'. In *Deleuze and New Technology*. Edited by Mark Poster & David Savat, 224-240. Edinburgh: Edinburgh University Press.

Pisters, Patricia. 2012. *The Neuro-Image: A Deleuzian Film-Philosophy of Digital Screen Culture*. Stanford: Stanford University Press.

Plantinga, Carl, & Greg M. Smith, eds. 1999. *Passionate Views: Film, Cognition and Emotion*. Baltimore: Johns Hopkins University Press.

Rizzolatti, Giacomo, & Corrado Sinigaglia. 2007a. *Mirrors in the Brain: How our Minds Share Actions, Emotions, and Experience*. Translated by Frances Anderson. New York: Oxford University Press.

Rizzolatti, Giacomo, & Corrado Sinigaglia. 2007b. 'Mirror Neurons and Motor Intentionality'. *Functional neurology*. 22 (4): 205-210.

Rizzolatti, Giacomo, & Laila Craighero. 2004. 'The Mirror-Neuron System'. *Annual Review of Neurosciences*. 27: 169-192. DOI:10.1146/annurev.neuro.27.070203.144230.

Rizzolatti, Giacomo, Leonardo Fogassi, & Vittorio Gallese. 2001. 'Neurophysiological Mechanisms Underlying the Understanding and Imitation of Action'. *Nature Reviews: Neuroscience*. 2: 661-670. DOI:10.1038/35090060.

Rizzolatti, Giacomo, Luciano Fadiga, Vittorio Gallese, & Leonardo Fogassi. 1996. 'Premotor Cortex and the Recognition of Motor Actions'. *Brain Research: Cognitive Brain Research*. 3: 131-141. DOI:10.1016/0926-6410(95)00038-0.

Rizzolatti, Giacomo. 2005. 'The Mirror Neuron System and its Function in Humans'. *Anat. Embryol.* 210 (5-6): 419-421. DOI:10.1007/s00429-005-0039-z.

Rodowick, David N. 2007. 'An Elegy for Theory'. *October.* 122: 91-109.

Rodowick, David N. 2014. *Elegy for Theory*. Cambridge, MA: Harvard University Press.

Roques, Mario. 1954. 'Introduction'. *Revue internationale de filmologie*. 16: 3-6.

Shaviro, Steven. 2015. *No Speed Limit*. Minneapolis: University of Minnesota Press.

Shimamura, Arthur P., ed. 2013. *Psychocinematics: Exploring Cognition at the Movies*. New York: Oxford University Press.

Sinnerbrink, Robert. 2011. *New Philosophies of Film: Thinking Images*. London/New York: Continuum.

Sinnerbrink, Robert. 2019. 'Phenomenology Encounters Cognitivism'. *Projections*. 13 (2): 1-19. DOI:10:3167/proj.2019.130201.

Slugan, Mario. 2020. 'Film Studies and the Experimental Method'. *NECSUS*. European Journal of Media Studies. Autumn. https://necsus-ejms.org/film-studies-and-the-experimental-method.

Smith, Murray. 1995. *Engaging Characters: Fiction, Emotion, and the Cinema*. Oxford: Clarendon Press.

Smith, Murray. 2017. *Film, Art, and the Third Culture: A Naturalized Aesthetics of Film*. New York: Oxford University Press.

Smith, Tim. 2012. 'The Attentional Theory of Cinematic Continuity'. *Projections*. 6 (1): 1-27. DOI:10.3167/proj.2012.060102.

Sobchack, Vivian. 1982. 'Toward Inhabited Space: The Semiotic Structure of Camera Movement in the Cinema'. *Semiotica*. 41 (1-4): 317-335.

Sobchack, Vivian. 1992. *The Address of the Eye: A Phenomenology of Film Experience*. Princeton: Princeton University Press.

Sobchack, Vivian. 2004. *Carnal Thoughts: Embodiment and Moving Image Culture*. Berkeley: University of California Press.

Stewart, John, Olivier Gapenne, & Ezequiel A. Di Paolo, eds. 2010. *Enaction: Toward a New Paradigm for Cognitive Science*. Cambridge, MA: The MIT Press.

Tan, Ed. 2013. 'The Empathic Animal Meets the Inquisitive Animal in the Cinema: Notes on a Psychocinematics of Mind Reading'. In Shimamura, ed., 337-367.

Turvey, Malcom. 2020. 'Mirror Neurons and Film Studies. A Cautionary Tale from a Serious Pessimist'. *Projections*. 14 (3): 21-46. DOI:10.3167/proj.2020.140303.

Varela, Francisco J. 1995. 'Neurophenomenology: A Methodological Remedy for the Hard Problem'. *Journal of Consciousness Studies*. 4 (3): 330-349.

Varela, Francisco J., Evan Thompson, & Eleanor Rosch. 1991. *The Embodied Mind: Cognitive Science and Human Experience*. Cambridge, MA: The MIT Press.

Williams, Linda. 2000. 'Discipline and Fun: Psycho and Postmodern Cinema'. In *Reinventing film studies*. Edited by Linda Williams & Christine Gledhill, 351-378. London: Arnold.

II Acrobatics

On the wires of empathy

Abstract
The chapter 'Acrobatics. On the wires of empathy' takes as a starting point Edith Stein's critique of psychologist Theodor Lipps' notion of empathy (*Einfühlung*) and her original proposal for a phenomenology of intersubjectivity. Since this debate revolves around the example of an observer watching an acrobat walking on a wire in mid air, the chapter offers an analysis of acrobatic actions in contemporary cinema (such as in Zemeckis' *The Walk*) and reflects on both disembodied and embodied accounts of empathy in film studies. Recovering the filmological meaning of this term (introduced into film studies by psychologist Albert Michotte) and developing a model of cinematic empathy along the lines of Stein's theory, the chapter illuminates the importance of the unbalancing/rebalancing dynamic in creating the spectator's proprioceptive experience of disequilibrium.

Keywords: Cinematic empathy, *Einfuhlung*, Edith Stein, Albert Michotte, Mirror Neurons, *The Walk*

> Thus all of us may get vicariously the experience which we could not get or would not want in actual life.
>
> —Victor O. Freeburg, *The Art of Photoplay Making* 1918 (16)

The green abyss

In September 2015, at the press conference that followed the world premiere of Robert Zemeckis' *The Walk* at the New York Film Festival, both film critics and audience members reported that they experienced unpleasant sensations while watching the film or got physically sick shortly after. Indeed, the 20-minute-long finale showing Philippe Petit (Joseph Gordon-Levitt)'s

D'Aloia, A., *Neurofilmology of the Moving Image. Gravity and Vertigo in Contemporary Cinema*. Taylor & Francis Group 2021
DOI: 10.5117/9789463725255_CH02

tightrope walk between the digitally restored Twin Towers offers a vertiginous view that caused nausea, anxiety, dizziness, tingling, and drowsiness.[1] Newspapers reported excited testimonies: 'It felt very real. I felt a knot in my stomach. It's like my head was reeling but I was not dizzy. The audience got a fear of him falling. It's like actually picturing in your mind him falling. You really get a sense of depth'; 'The last 20 minutes of the film I had to look away a couple of times because of the sensation of the height. I felt a little bit queasy. I felt nervous. It was a tingling sensation and some anxiety' (Child 2015) The director intentionally used computer-generated imagery and special 3D-effects to evoke such visceral responses from the audience: '[the goal] was to evoke the feeling of vertigo. We worked really hard to put those audiences up on those towers and on the wire' (Lee 2015), Zemeckis said.

The idea of 'putting the audience up', i.e. giving the spectator the vivid feeling of being precariously balanced in the fictional space, is the fundamental concern of this chapter. More precisely, the aim is to bring to light the central role of *kinaesthetic empathy*, i.e. the human ability to intuit what others are experiencing based upon their bodily behaviour, in the spectator's experience of narrative fiction film. In the particular spatial and psychological situation of the cinema auditorium, and especially in respect to the main characters, involvement with the characters entails both motor and emotional participation, despite the consciousness of the fictional nature of filmic events. This participation is mostly realized via the activation of empathy, a factor that reduces the psychological separation between the spectator and the characters. In cinema practice, a series of film techniques (including 3D) are used in order to artificially construct empathy and to enhance the feeling of 'being there'. The case of *The Walk* is clearly one of overstimulation, one that questions the nature, range, and function of kinaesthetic empathy. The strong audience responses, in fact, suggest that although the film is successful in 'putting the audience up', it does not succeed in keeping the audience *there*: the need to look away or even the urge to leave the seat to go to the bathroom signals a clear breaking of the 'empathetic pact' between the film and its spectator.

The tree of cinematic empathies

Today, human and social sciences (e.g. psychology, philosophy, aesthetics, and even economics) and natural sciences (especially cognitive neuroscience)

1 The film is based on the real walk between the Twin Towers performed by the French high-wire artist Philippe Petit on August 7, 1974.

have revived and reanimated an interdisciplinary debate around empathy and film (Agosta 2004; Coplan 2004; Stueber 2006; Anderson & Fisher Anderson 2007; Curtis & Koch 2008; Coplan & Goldie 2011; Reynolds & Reason 2012; Lux & Weigel 2017). Empathy in fact is an extremely complex and articulated notion to which different disciplines in different epochs give distinct values, meanings, and characterizations (cf. Batson 2009; Pinotti 2016; Pinotti & Salgaro 2019). Like a sort of a conceptual 'tree', its roots are grounded in ancient thought and its foliage is extensively ramified. The concept of empathy was developed by Anglo-Saxon empiricism in the 18th and 19th centuries, although under the label of sympathy (Locke 1690; Hume 1739; Darwin 1871; Mill 1867). Interestingly enough, in 1759 Adam Smith (2002) used the example of a tightrope walker to describe the phenomenon of 'fellow feeling': 'The mob, when they are gazing at a dancer on the slack rope, naturally writhe and twist and balance their own bodies as they see him do, and as they feel that they themselves must do if in his situation' (12). This natural tendency to imaginatively change one's own place with that of the acrobat was the first precise formulation of empathy in modern thought. For Smith,

> As we have no immediate experience of what other men feel, we can form no idea of the manner in which they are affected, but by conceiving what we ourselves should feel in the like situation. [...] By the imagination we place ourselves in his situation, we conceive ourselves enduring all the same torments, we enter as it were into his body, and become in some measure the same person with him, and thence form some idea of his sensations, and even feel something which, though weaker in degree, is not altogether unlike them (11-12).

In the neo-Romantic aesthetics of the 19th and 20th centuries, *Einfühlung* become a keyword for understanding the process of viewing works of art as a *projection* of the observer, who 'transfers' her own emotions into the work of art, attributing to the latter the emotional content and affective qualities that she feels subjectively (Vischer 1873; 1927; Wölfflin 1886; von Hildebrand 1893; Warburg 1893; Mallgrave, Ikonomou & Vischer 1994). German philosopher Theodor Lipps had a crucial role in the elaboration of this concept. According to Lipps (1965), *Einfühlung* is a form of 'inner imitation' (involuntary, physiological, kinaesthetic) by which 'I enjoy myself in a sensuous object distinct from myself' (493) 'not a sensation in one's body, but feeling something, namely, oneself into the esthetic object' (Lipps 1979, 381). 'Esthetic object' here means either other people and animals, or even inanimate objects and structures, such as works of art and human creations whose formal qualities evoke in the observer a vicarious action that projects her into the artwork. At the centre of the empathetic experience is the ego because the cause of aesthetic enjoinment is the observer's self and empathy is not a feeling related to an object (which in this case is instead the ego). As Lipps (1979) concludes, in aesthetic empathy there is identity between the self and the object:

> In a word, I am now with my feeling of activity entirely and wholly in the moving figure. Even spatially, if we can speak of the spatial extent of the ego, I am in its place. I am transported into it. I am, so far as my consciousness is concerned, entirely and wholly identical with it. Thus feeling myself active in the observed human figure, I feel also in it free, facile, proud. This is esthetic imitation and this imitation is at the same time esthetic empathy (379).

The relational intersubjective meaning of empathy led to a convergence between the two genealogies—empiricism and aesthetics—starting when Edward B. Titchener (1909) coined the term 'empathy' (cf. Lanzoni 2012) as the English translation of Wilhelm Wundt's *Einfühlung* ('feeling-into'). Following this theoretical framework, empathy has been defined as a human form of understanding the other's mind through a 'substitution', or the act of 'putting oneself in the other's shoes', and as a form of deep enjoyment of works of art through a projection of one's own feelings into such work. As I will discuss in what follows, this idea of empathy as pure identification was criticized by phenomenologist philosopher Edith Stein, who offers an account of the empathetic process that I will try to apply to the film experience. First, however, I will provide a brief summary of the debate on empathy in cognitive film studies.

Disembodied empathy

The distinction between different types of emotional relationships between the spectator and the character(s) has been present in film theory since its very beginning. In 1916, in recognizing the importance of emotions in the 'photoplay' and implicitly relating the notion of *Einfühlung* to the metaphor of *projection*, Münsterberg (2002) noted that

> On the one side, we have those emotions in which the feelings of the persons in the play are transmitted to our own soul. On the other side,

> we find those feelings with which we respond to the scenes in the play, feelings which may be entirely different, perhaps exactly opposite to those which the figures in the play express (104).

Whereas those belonging to the first group, which the American psychologist considers 'by far the larger one' (104), those of the second type stem from the spectators' 'independent affective life' (105).[2] In 1918, Victor Freeburg (1918) underlined the 'twofold nature' of the spectator's emotional experience (13). On the one hand there is the 'self-emotion' similar to that experienced 'in real life face to face with real nature' (12), 'a thrill or excitement at some action or disturbance', a 'simple emotional appeals' that 'stimulates a corresponding agitation within us' (14). On the other there is the 'dramatic sympathy', or the spectator's 'social interest in the characters on the screen', that is, the film's 'tremendous power' to elicits emotions for 'people who do not exist except in imagination' and that makes that '[f]iction becomes real' (14).

These differentiations were in fact pivotal in the mid-1990s debate in cognitive film studies over the forms of the spectator's emotional participation (cf. Plantinga & Smith 1999). Empathy was the key word and concept used by 'post-theorists' to challenge the Freudian notion of identification and delineate a deliberate form of imagining being in the other's situation in order to understand his or her mental state. Relying on standard simulation theory (cf. *infra*, Ch. 1), cognitive film studies tied empathy to the notion of 'perspective taking' and kept it separate from the subjective feeling or any involvement of the spectator's body, except from autonomic reactions to audio-visual stimuli. In general terms, according to the 'disembodied' paradigm, empathy is described as a kind of imaginative act that integrates cognitive and affective processes through which a subject is 'put into the shoes' of the main character(s), assuming her perspective and 'tuning into' her emotional state (cf. Goldman 2006b; Gallese 2007). This perspective is thus based on the cognitive modelling of the character, rather than on a simulation of the latter's emotional state.

The concept of empathy in film studies, however, was far from unambiguous and took on different meanings and descriptions for different authors (for a review, see Bryant & Zillmann 1991; Zillman 2006; Neill 1996; Vaage 2010; Coplan 2012; Stadler 2017), some of whom did not consider it to be an effective or pertinent notion. Rather than empathetically 'feeling with' the character, some argued, the spectator's affective participation should

2 A detailed discussion on *Einfühlung* and *projection* in Münsterberg can be found in Brain 2012.

be described as a sympathetic 'feeling for' the character. For Noël Carroll (1999; cf. also 1996), who prefers the term 'assimilation' to both empathy and identification, the viewer's emotional state in relation to film characters is quite often characterized not by shared emotions, but rather by an asymmetry in which an understanding of their behaviour is not bound to the spectator's replication of their mental states.

For Murray Smith (1995), meanwhile, the key to understanding character engagement is the so-called 'structure of sympathy' (73-109). This includes different and progressive levels of involvement: *recognition* of the character on the basis of information provided by the film, especially his or her face and body; *alignment* with the character's perception, action, beliefs, and inner states; and *allegiance*, that is, a moral and ideological evaluation of the character.

Often in mid-1990s film studies the notion of simulation works as a metaphor for 'imagination', that is to say an offline recall and reactivation of memories and past mental states (cf. Currie 1995; Currie & Ravenscroft 2002). Smith's contribution is also important due to its distinction between *central imagining* and *acentral imagining*, elaborated in the wake of Richard Wollheim's work (1994, 407). Empathy corresponds to a kind of central imagining, that is, a form of mental substitution in which the spectator projects herself into the fictional situation, assuming the character's beliefs and desires: the spectator puts herself in the character's shoes and imagines 'from the inside'—as Kendall Walton (1990, 28-35) would say—what it is like to be in the latter's situation. Conversely, sympathy corresponds to acentral imagining, through which the spectator simply imagines the character's perceptual, emotional, cognitive, and moral point of view from the outside. Different from sympathy, empathy does not require the spectator to share the values, beliefs, or intentions of the character.

Using broader terms of categorization than those of Smith, Ed Tan (1996) distinguishes between *fictional* emotions, through which the fictional world presents itself and, ideally, engages the spectator, and *artifact* emotions, that is, cases in which the spectator's attention is focused on aesthetic elements of film (special effects, quality of photography, editing, etc.). Among fictional emotions, Tan distinguishes between *empathetic* and *non-empathetic* emotions. The latter are determined by a fictional event that is an emotional stimulus *per se*: the spectator is caught up in the spectacle, *fascinated* by the film, and immersed in the pure pleasure of watching. However, empathetic emotions are far more predominant. They are determined by the value of the event or situation represented for the characters (for example, the character's misfortune produces a negative emotion in the spectator). Tan defines empathy as 'all cognitive operations on the part of the viewer that lead to a more complete understanding of the situational meaning of the character' (173) offered by the narrative. He claims that sympathy, alongside *interest*, is 'the most important sensation evoked by the traditional feature film' and that 'a sympathetic disposition is also a precondition for empathetic enjoinment' (178). Tan identifies two further empathetic emotions. *Sympathy* is a positive emotion characterized by a state of equality and reciprocity between spectator and character. While sympathy can be described as the tendency to search for proximity and intimacy, 'a sharing of thoughts and feelings, and a sense of cherishing and being cherished' (178), two other empathetic emotions can be identified. *Compassion* is characterized by the superiority of the spectator in respect to the character: it is the tendency of the spectator to protect, help, or console the character. On the contrary, *admiration* is characterized by inferiority: the tendency of the action is that of seeking proximity, but not intimacy. The empathetic emotions are thus a source of both investment and return, costs and rewards (while the cost of sympathy is extremely low). In the end, however, Tan downplays empathy: 'the empathetic emotion experienced by the film viewer is far from an in-depth understanding of the innermost feelings of the film character. It is sufficient for the viewer to simply follow the narrative' (178) on the basis of the *appraisal* of the situation or the events eliciting emotions.[3]

For Carl Plantinga (1999), empathy is not a single emotion, but rather a variety of sorts of emotional experiences: it 'consists of a capacity or disposition to know, to feel, and to respond congruently to what another is feeling, and the process of doing so' (245). Empathy is characterized by two processes: first, the spectator undertakes a kind of mental simulation by which she imagines and dwells on the character's condition; second, the spectator's emotions must be *congruent* to those she imagines, that is, they must 'respond in a way that evinces commonality or solidarity with the person's goals or desire' (245). Plantinga's contribution helps to clarify that empathy, as the full comprehension of the character's affectivity via mental simulation, is rooted in basic, automatic, and unconscious phenomena that do not involve any understanding of the character's state of mind. These phenomena are *emotional contagion* (the 'catching' of others' emotions or affective states) induced by *affective mimicry* (the automatic tendency to mimic and synchronize with others' expressions, postures and movements) and *facial feedback* (the subject that mimics a facial expression actually catches the other's emotions). Filmmakers use the so-called 'scene of empathy', i.e.

3 Tan borrows the idea of 'situational meaning' of emotions from Frijda 1986.

the prolonged close-up of a character's face on screen, not only to represent emotion but also to elicit affective—especially empathetic—responses. This 'scene' occurs in few and strategic points of the narrative (in a way similar, yet not equal, to what I call tensive motifs). In subsequent works, Plantinga (2009) confirms his perspective but stresses his scepticism about the usefulness of distinguishing between empathy and sympathy and prefers the word sympathy as a more encompassing way to describe character engagement that depends on *affective congruence*, that is 'a state in which the viewer is concerned for the plight of a character and *may* experience emotions that have similar orientation or valences with characters yet are rarely, if ever, identical', in opposition to antipathy (101, my emphasis). In other words, for Plantinga (2018) empathy can be only the very basic, physiological layer of sympathy: 'Even the "higher" emotional responses involve automatic and bodily processes that to some extent escape conscious control' (137).

Adopting an evolutionary perspective, Torben Grodal (1997) argues that identification, empathy, and cognitive simulation are prosocial activities linked to the survival value of the human species (81-105). Mentioning the results of a neuroscientific experiment (that predate by half a decade those conducted in Italy in mid 1990s that led to the discovery of the so-called 'visuomotor neurons'), Grodal reports the existence in the monkey's brain of 'special neurons' that respond when monkeys observe human movements. These neurons fired much more strongly when the observed person walked forward than backward (because the forward movement is ordinarily more significant) and when the movement was goal-oriented, that is, directed towards a specific object (i.e. the laboratory door) rather than any other direction (cf. Perrett et al. 1990). This leads Grodal (1997) to support the idea that neural response is also an 'interpretation of significance' (86), or that 'a viewer's cognitive analysis of at least basic movements and goals, [...] is a relatively automatic process and the strong neural activity is probably 'felt'' (87), whereby 'felt' Grodal intends to indicate that 'the processing of goals and acts would activate motor-control systems'. Grodal ascribes to empathy part of the cognitive identification of the viewer with the 'agents of fiction'. While cognitive identification is a simulation by which the viewer constructs the actant's perceptions and world, empathy is 'the viewer's cued simulation of emotions in identification with an agent of fiction' (87), or 'a viewer-activation of affects and emotions in identification with the interests of a fictive being' (92), implying that cognition is intimately linked to emotions by means of *motivation* (or, evolutionarily, preferences of a given biological entity in a given situation). For Grodal, cognitive activity prevails on and regulates emotions, since although cognitive identification need not necessarily imply empathy, the latter is often the consequence of a prolonged cognitive identification. As he states,

> The cognitive activities first serve to produce emotions and affects because the relation between the preference and a given situation demands cognitive analysis. A given situation can only be evaluated as 'dangerous,' for example, by cognitive analysis. The cognitive activities then produce mental models for reducing the [negative] affects and emotions (87).

In viewing a narrative film, cognitive analysis is thus the starting and the arrival point of an evaluation structure in which cognition serves as a modulator of emotions.

Mindfeeling

More recently, the cognitivist account of empathy has been subject to an internal revision that aims at revaluating the relevance of motor mimicry, affective mimicry, emotional contagion and other low-level response to the film (cf. Coplan 2012). In the 2010s, cognitive film scholars returned to the notion of empathy in the wake of discoveries made in the field of cognitive neuroscience that suggest that the functioning of the brain allows for an immediate and pre-linguistic ability to 'catch' the *sense* of our experiences prior to any deliberate cognitive elaboration such as mind reading.

Torben Grodal (Grodal & Kramer 2010) reinforced his bio-cultural perspective and reframed the notion of empathetic response as the 'push for sharing feelings' developed by mammals and humans during evolution, which are also active during the film experience:

> These psychological mechanisms are central to the film experience since it is based on communication related to the bonds between humans in real life as well as between viewers and film characters. The film experience is embodied: the brain and the body—even viscera and the skin—constantly resonate in accordance with the film's flow, with changes in muscular tension, perspiration, stomach state, etc. (22).

Different from a mere cognitive account of empathy based on Theory of Mind, in this view '[e]mpathetic understanding is probably the default mode of human engagement building on the recruitment of the neural circuits used in our own first-hand experiences with a situation in order to understand and share the experience of another agent' (2010, 27). According to Grodal (1999, 132; 2009, 145-157), watching a film is an experience of flow that follows the architecture and general functioning of the human brain, which proceeds according to the schema perception-emotion-cognition-motor action (the so-called 'PECMA flow'). In this flow, empathy is achieved through 'first-person simulations' of the characters that 'at least to a certain degree involve emotional action tendencies' (2009, 199) and is supported by a series of brain mechanisms, namely the mirroring mechanism facilitated by a cluster of brain cells in the premotor cortex, the so-called 'mirror neurons', which discharge both when a subject (a macaque or a human being) performs or intends to perform a goal-directed action and when the subject sees another agent performing a similar action.

In his latest book, Murray Smith (2017) embraces a 'scientific-aesthetic' perspective and follows Owen Flanagan's 'natural method' to suggest a 'triangulation' of phenomenological, psychological, and neurophysiological levels of analysis of the aesthetic experience. In this framework, Smith proposes to 'fix empathy' by integrating the pure cognitive account of affective engagement into the neurological functioning of the organism, namely the mirror neuron mechanism (72-74). More precisely, Smith revisits the notion of empathy in the context of Extended mind theory (cf. Clark & Chalmers 1998; Chemero 2009; 2016), according to which the human mind exploits features of the environment to enhance its cognitive capacities, a 'coupling' between the mind and the part of the world—like a technology or a medium—through which the mind extends itself. As Smith states, empathy is a *mechanism* of such coupling, simply because '[w]hen we empathize with another person, we extend our mind to incorporate part of her mind' (Smith 2017, 188). Conceived of as a 'prosthesis' in the environment, the Other is, in fact, a way to extend the self. 'We can think, for example, of the devices of filmmaking as *cognitive prostheses*, in much the same way that we think of other devices, like the telescope or microscope, as perceptual prostheses—devices that amplify our native perceptual capacities' (188). Smith, however, limits the boundaries of such an 'environment' to 'the domain of representation, and especially to the practice of narration, that constitutes the 'environmental support' created by the mind to drive its amplified performance' (188). Recall that for Smith empathy is a kind of central imagination in the aesthetic experience, that is, the possibility of understanding human subjects 'from the inside' by imagining their thoughts and feelings. In this sense, Smith's refinement of empathy affects its '*scope* and *intensity*', because the narrative arts provide modern human beings increasingly frequent opportunities to experience different people, situations, and cultures, and because narrative has the capability to condense and enhance emotions (as in the aforementioned 'scene of empathy'), that is, to stylistically and narratively 'design' affective responses that may be more intense than those experienced in real circumstances.

In revaluating empathy in the film experience, Smith underlines its double function in respect to the spectator's informative access to the character's mind: empathy has a *mindreading* function when the spectator has a limited knowledge of the character's situation and uses it (and its neural basis) 'to probe and reveal more of what is or might be going on inside the agent'; it also, however, has a *mindfeeling* function when the spectator already has an extensive and detailed knowledge of the character situation and uses it 'to put the information that we do posses under a new description', by virtue of the 'internal' perspective acquired. 'In the case of mindreading', Smith concludes, 'empathy operates at or near the base of the narrative understanding; in the case of mindfeeling, empathy arises the apex of such understanding' (194). In this latter case, it could be added, empathy is not only a means but also the goal of spectatorial engagement. An example of the combination of these functions is provided in film scenes—e.g. the climax sequence of *127 Hours* (Boyle 2011), analysed by Smith—in which the spectator experiences so-called 'mirror thrills', that is, 'intense, bodily sensations triggered by and tracking those of the character on screen' (100), which are allowed by the activation of the mirror mechanism that constitutes the neural substratum of empathy. When the protagonist, Ralston, who has been trapped beneath a rock in a canyon for days, decides to amputate his arm to save his own life, at least three types of mirroring come into play: 'the film invites us to mirror the *sensations* of his trapped and dying arm (the constant weight of the boulder, the cutting and ripping of skin, the breaking of bone); the strenuous efforts—*motor actions*—of Ralston as he contorts his body to break his arm and cut himself free; and his *facial* and *vocal expressions* of pain' (101). Drawing on neurophysiological research on the role of mirror neurons in enabling a 'direct' and experiential form of understanding the other (cf. *infra*, Ch. I), and following geriatric medical doctor Raymond Tallis' (2011) idea of animals as 'wired into the world', Smith (2017) revaluates the relevance of spontaneous, unreflective, non-conscious, autonomic responses—the very basic layer of empathy. He claims that

> humans—like the members of many other species—are 'wired into' the minds of their fellows by virtue of somatosensory, motor, and affective mimicry, psychological capacities realized by mirror neurons. These capacities allow us to track, virtually effortlessly, the basic emotional

states of those around us, and assist us in imitating and in learning new motor skills (101).

In brief, and to return to the triangulation between phenomenology, psychology and neuroscience, Smith considers the neural mirror mechanism as 'the *neural* substrate that 'implements' our *psychological* capacities for sensory, motor, and affective mimicry, and the *experiences* that may characterize these processes' (99).

Ed Tan has also recently returned to the notion of empathy (and empathic emotion) to specify the neural underpinning of its automatically initiated forms. Tan adopts Stephanie Preston and Frans de Waal's Perception-Action Mechanism (PAM) (Preston & de Waal 2001), a mechanism comprising brain structures that combine perception of others' action with perception of one's own actions. As part of the PAM mechanism, mirror neurons play a central role in autonomic responses, such as mimicry and emotional contagion (although its implication for the identification of emotion and its contribution to empathy and sympathy are less clear). 'The PAM provides the basis for embodied representations, ones that are not only propositional or symbolic but also linked to body awareness and body movements' (Tan 2013, 345); in other words, an embodied form of simulation by which we enter the world of the other without explicit theorizing. This 'low way', however, is not sufficient to describe the multifaceted experience of empathy in the film experience. Tan, in fact, highlights that a 'high way' is also necessary: 'identifying personal, interpersonal, and narrative schemas is not an automated process; it requires voluntary effort. [...] Thus, it seems that automated resonance empathy in the cinema usually is the first building block for more complex and non-automated empathy' (351). Unconscious and conscious processes, bodily *resonance* and cognitive *enactment*—as Tan labels the two 'ways[4]—cooperate and interact.

As Grodal, Smith, and Tan's recent contributions suggest, the disembodied cognitive account of empathy is not sufficient to fully explain the nature of the empathetic spectator's involvement in the film. The neural basis of empathy provided by the mirror mechanism expands the range of empathy 'downwards'. The imaginative perspective taking, i.e. the conscious act of putting oneself into another's shoes (*mental simulation* provided by high-level

4 Tan uses the terms 'resonance' to describe an embodied representation of a feeling state experienced by the character, drawn from Goldman 2006a; and the term 're-enactement', that is the explicit simulation of an emotion using theorizing and imagination on the other's state, drawn from Stueber 2006.

cognitive activity), and the involuntary, non-conscious act of catching the other's emotions and sensations (*embodied simulation* provided by the neural substratum that implements the psychological capacities) are both active in the course of a film experience and should not be considered as mutually exclusive or competitive. The proposal of these authors is, in fact, not one that embraces embodiment uncritically or overturns the theoretical foundations of cognitivist film studies' epistemology. Rather, the idea is that empiric findings (including those coming from neuroscience) may extend the range of the consolidated heuristic tools.

Conversely, the 'implanting' of mirror neurons into cognitive film studies was met with several critiques. Malcom Turvey's (2020)—whose scepticism on neuroscience has been already discussed in the previous chapter—is drastic:

> It seems that the mirror neuron simulation theory of empathy issues in an impoverished conception of 'deep understanding' in its insistence that I have to feel the other person's emotions in order to 'really' grasp them. This is a good example of how a scientific theory can distort our understanding of artistic practice, in this case our notion of what 'comprehending a character' consists of (35).

For Turvey, mirror neurons provide evidence 'for *one form* of cinematic empathy', namely the 'unreflective' and 'immediate mimicking tendencies' (Shaw 2016, 153) that are at the basis of other and 'higher' forms of the character-spectator relationship based on cognitive appraisal and should not be confused with the latter. This stance, however, is not in contradiction with Smith's perspective, which conceives emotion as 'a dynamic somatic and cognitive apprehension of the significance of some phenomena—an object, a person, an event, a situation—by an agent' (162).

Nevertheless, the mutual opposition of 'two' empathies is counterproductive to a real understanding of the film spectator's experience. Although this opposition reflects the contrast between two obviously irreconcilable theoretical models and although the stakes are above all epistemological, I believe that rather than fighting to affirm one vision or the other, it is necessary to try to integrate the different notions of empathy in a circuit. Empathy has not been discussed exhaustively in its multifaceted and multimodal characteristics and functions and, above all, it has not been conceived of as a comprehensive and unitary process in which the body and the mind are not two poles (either allies or opponents) of a *dualistic* relation. In order to build a *holistic* rather than dualistic notion of empathy, in the following I recover a phenomenological approach to spectator engagement and integrate and expand—and partially revise—empathy's field of action. I will trace a parallel between philosopher Edith Stein's description of empathy, offered in her book *On the Problem of Empathy*, which critiques earlier accounts of *Einfühlung* (notably Theodor Lipps') from a phenomenological standpoint, and the film theory of Belgian psychologist and filmologist Albert Michotte, which explores motor and emotional empathy in the experience of watching a film. The comparison of these accounts highlights the *structural* analogy between the mediated nature of the empathic experience, as they describe it, and the mediated nature of the film experience, as well as the *processual* analogy between the two experiences in their perceptual, emotional, and cognitive stratification. I aim to demonstrate that empathy is inherent in the nature of narrative cinema itself and is pivotal to describing the variety and complexity of film spectatorship as an *intensified* experience. In order to evaluate the heuristic potential of the theoretical accounts taken into consideration, I briefly analyse the prologue of the drama film *Trapeze* (Reed 1956) and eventually return to Zemeckis' *The Walk*.

With-in the acrobat

As previously mentioned, Theodor Lipps (1903) stated that in watching the tightrope walker balancing precariously on the suspended wire, the observer *projects* and feels herself *inside* the acrobat to such an extent that her conscious self completely merges with that of the funambulist. This fusion is achieved on the basis of an 'inner imitation' through which the observer internally reproduces the movements of the observed person. Perceived movements are instinctively and simultaneously mirrored by kinaesthetic 'strivings' and the experience of corresponding feelings in the observer (cf. 121-126).

In order to discuss this neo-Romantic account of *Einfühlung*, Edmund Husserl's student Edith Stein (1964) once again invoked the case of the acrobat in *On the Problem of Empathy*. In her view, Lipps confuses the act of being drawn into the experience of the other (for instance the acrobat) with the transition from *non-primordial* to *primordial* experience (Stein 1964, 12). Primordial experience for Stein is one whose content is present and bodily given, whereas there are psychological experiences (such as memory, expectation, and fancy) in which individuals do not have their object bodily present before them (6-9). These are experiences that are primordially given, but non-primordial in their content. In the same way, the act of empathizing consists in primordially experiencing something that is non-primordially given, since the content belongs to another: 'This other subject is primordial although I do not experience its primordiality' (10). The experience of empathy, in the end, consists in the feeling of being led by the other's primordiality, which is 'not experienced by me but still there, manifesting itself in my non-primordial experience' (10); '[a]nd in these non-primordial movements I feel led, accompanied, by his movements which are only there for me in him' (17). In the empathic relation, 'I am not one with the acrobat but only "at" him. I do not actually go through his motions but only *quasi*' (17). In watching an acrobat, 'I put myself into the perceived body, as if I were his vital centre, and I perform an impulse quasi of the same type as that which could cause a movement' (Stein 1991, 200, my trans.).[5] The *quasi* describes the 'imperfect substitution' of the empathizing subject with the empathized subject, a proximity and accompaniment that does not result in a fusion or replacement and that preserves a distance, a 'unity in distinction'. The act of 'putting myself into the perceived body' is, in fact, explained with the expression 'as if I were', that is, an imaginary act that connects the internal, apperceived side of the experience to its external, perceived side. This peculiar contact does not concern the body in its natural or objective physical meaning (the *Körper* in the Husserlian sense), but rather the vital activity of the experienced, animated, sentient lived body (the *Leib*) (cf. Husserl 1960, §§ 42-62; 1989, §§ 43-47). The activation of the acrobat's lived body entails a corresponding activation of the kinaesthetic sensations of the spectator's lived body.

In brief, for Stein, rather than a projection or a fusion, empathy is an *accompaniment*, in which the spectator's subjectivity is not 'one with' the acrobat's subjectivity, but only 'with'. Differently from Scheler's (2017) conception of an undifferentiated flow of consciousness (that is, the idea that, at least initially, the two subjectivities involved are undistinguishable[6]), for Stein the empathizing subject is side-by-side with the empathized subjects,

5 'Ich versetze mich selbst in den wahrgenommenen Körper, so als habe er ein lebendiges Zentrum, und ich führe einen Impuls aus, der quasi vom selben Typ ist, wie der, der eine Bewegung verursachen könnte.'

6 For Scheler (2017), in the understanding of the other's mind, 'What occurs [...] is an immediate flow of experiences, *undifferentiated as between mine and thine*, which actually contains both our own and others' experiences intermingled and without distinction from one another. Within this flow there is a gradual formation of ever more stable vortices, which slowly attract further elements of the stream into their orbits and thereby become successively and very gradually identified with distinct individuals' (246). For a discussion of empathy in Lipps, Scheler, Husserl, and Stein, cf. Moran 2004. For a discussion on empathy in the pehenomenogical debate on intersubjectivity and social cognition, cf. Zahavi 2014.

and their adjacent position implies a clear separation and a paradoxical proximity at a distance. Moreover, do not *imagine* or *infer* the other's emotion (as the cognitivist approach to film studies, which I will discuss later, maintains), but rather I *experience* it, although that emotion is not 'originarily' mine. The form of accompaniment implies the structure of a *mediated* experience, where mediation consists both in an inevitable distance and an opportunity for contact. In this sense, the debate on *Einfühlung* seems to provide a phenomenological description that relates closely to the film spectator's experience, that is, a situation in which the other is not physically co-present in the traditional sense. As I will argue, there is an analogy between the structure and the process of empathy and the structure and process of the film experience, on the condition that we assume the *sui generis* nature of otherness implied in a film character.

Tensive movement

The case of the acrobat at the core of the *querelle* between Lipps and Stein is particularly significant for the study of empathic involvement in film because it is centred on a movement that is a powerful generator of motor and emotional imitation. Implicit in the choice of example by Lipps and Stein is the fact that the spectator is not faced with an ordinary movement (walking), but rather a movement that is characterized by tension (walking on a suspended wire). On the screen and in the cinema, a field of energy is unfolded and fills the space between the spectator and the acrobat, between two bodies that occupy different positions—the one in a situation of extreme danger, the other in a condition of full protection and security—but that seem to inhabit the same environment and to move in consonance. Lipps' and Stein's choice of example implies the fact that the empathic movement is determined by this energy field, by a force that ultimately consists in the film's ability to express a state of imminent risk and danger and the spectator's will to voluntarily run that risk and feel the thrill of that danger in her own skin. The essential element is therefore the authenticity that derives from the *impression of a real danger*.

Early film theories recognized the cinema's capacity to intensify experience, and empathy plays a pivotal role in this intensification as a form of precognitive, immediate experience. As Freeburg (1918) noted, the eyes take a 'keen pleasure' in the 'physical appeals' of the cinematic representation of bodies in movement. 'The response of our senses to human form and physical movement is primary and elemental, and takes place before our brain has time to interpret the dramatic meaning of the visual stimulus' (12). According to classic film theories, the situations with the most potential for empathy are those in which a strong kinaesthetic intensification is invited (for instance acrobatics, falling, sports performance, dance, etc.). In his *The Visible Man*, however, Béla Balázs (2010) suggested that '[i]f it is true that film is concerned exclusively with visible, that is, bodily, human actions, then it follows that sporting and acrobatic performances can constitute extremely enhanced expressions of human physical life' (64). Balázs provided the first implicit description of empathy in film spectatorship, affirming the specificity of film experience in respect to reality: 'In reality we see only a moment, a fragment of movement. In film, however, *we accompany* a *runner and drive alongside the fastest car*' (64). Cinema is capable of including the spectator in the totality of a particularly intense movement, experienced first hand and by 'accompanying' the characters. In particular, the more 'genuine', 'unpolished', and 'spontaneous' the appearance of the character's physical activity portrayed by the film, the greater the intensity and effectiveness of spectator participation. As Balázs argues, in fact,

> Movement in film is not just a sporting or 'natural' fact; it can be the highest expression of an emotional or vital rhythm. [...] Thus, the physical activities of the film hero must take care not to assume a *sporting character*, even if he has to perform the most difficult stunts. For sport means movement as a goal in itself and is useless as expressive movement (64-65).

The spectator, Balázs appears to assert, is an amateur acrobat, a tightrope walker for a day, an aerialist on her first performance, a policeman on his first chase, a criminal making his first escape:

> the character who boxes must never become 'a boxer,' a running man must never become 'a sprinter.' For the film then acquires the insidious taint of the 'professional,' arousing our doubts as to the authenticity of the performance, and robbing the action of the immediacy of life (65).

The 'immediacy' of the experience depends on the apparent genuineness of the action, on its rudimentary and provisional characterization. The expressive impact of the action is therefore undermined where the spectator's attention is focused on the prowess of the performance (as can be the case with sporting actions), rather than the intensity of movement in sensorimotor and emotional terms.

Cinematic empathy

Empathy was first discussed explicitly and extensively in film theory in 1953 in an essay by the Belgian psychologist Albert Michotte van den Berck on the 'emotional involvement of the spectator in the action represented in a film'. Michotte (1991a) states that the psycho-physiological *distance* of the spectator from the fictional events on-screen can be reduced by empathy, which acts to compensate for the 'gap' between direct and mediated experience. Empathy is defined as a process that involves an immediate form of experience, that is to say something that occurs 'when we observe what someone else is doing and we ourselves live it in some sense, rather than just understand it at an intellectual level' (209).

Given this 'unintellectual' nature of empathy, Michotte distinguishes between *motor* empathy and *emotional* empathy, connecting the sensorimotor component of movement to feelings, mental attitudes, judgments, thoughts, and all those categories of events that are intimately connected to the spectator's inner self. Motor empathy, which develops progressively, precedes and accompanies emotional empathy: a structural homology allows the spectator to identify the movement seen on the body of the actor with that which is felt and experienced from the inside of her own body. When witnessing motor performances, for instance dance, acrobatics, or sports competitions, the spectator can experience a range of a varied reactions.

Case 1: There is no empathy at all in cases where the perceived movement and the spectator's motor reaction are clearly separated, that is to say, in which there is a gap between visual impressions and their tactile-kinaesthetic correlates. At the emotional level, the spectator and the character have quite different emotions.

Case 2: At the most basic level of empathy, the movement of the spectator accords with that of the character merely in the form of synchronization, for instance following a musical or dance rhythm by tapping one's foot. The emotions of the spectator and those of the character are connected by some accidental or casual reason, such as when the criticisms made by one character about the behaviour of another also apply to the behaviour of the spectator when confronted with a similar situation in real life. The spectator is directly affected by such criticisms, albeit due to a motivation external to the film. Such a parallelism is evoked by expressions like 'sharing someone else's joy', or 'participating in their grief' (214), triggering a physiological activation in the form of *pre*-empathy. However, this form of basic activation must not be confused with empathy.

Case 3: Actual empathy occurs when the spectator reproduces the observed movement, for example assuming a facial expression similar to that of the character. This imitation takes place at the musculo-skeletal level and is less intense than the action of the body that actually performs the movement. As in the Steinian description of empathy, this mirror-effect does not result in a fusion of inner states. It is as if there is a single action presented in two different forms (visual and proprioceptive), belonging to two distinct subjectivities.

Case 4: In the extreme case, an apparent fusion of subjectivities occurs (here Michotte mentions Lipps). The spectator 'puts himself into the skin' of the character: there is not only a single motor action, but also a single 'moving I' (210-211). In this case, there may be a deep identification between the 'person' of the spectator and that of the character, in terms not only of motor imitation but also of emotional absorption (214-215).

This taxonomy requires some elucidation. Case 1 includes the possibility that not every film experience will necessarily entail involvement, whether sensorimotor or psycho-affective. In this case there is no reduction of the separation of spaces: the spectator's experience consists solely of witnessing a fictional world that remains clearly distant. Case 2 describes a physiological activation due to a form of *pre*-empathy (rhythmic synchronization). It is a basic activation that must not be confused with empathy as such, which is found in Case 3, characterized by the co-presence of visual and bodily experience belonging to two distinct subjectivities. An extreme level of fusion and identification is realized in Case 4, where the total assimilation of subjectivities results in an identification in which the viewer loses the knowledge of herself and fuses her own ego with that of the character.

It is the combination of sharing and separation that makes Case 3 akin to Stein's interpretation of the case of the acrobat. Both the spectator of the acrobatic performance described by Stein and the film spectator described by Michotte are involved in a *quasi*-intersubjective relationship, that is to say a relationship between the spectator's primordial body and the non-primordial, or *quasi*, body of the acrobat/character. The film character is a *quasi*-other, empathically experienced as the other's lived body.

In this sense, Stein's model seems to provide a philosophical account of cinematic empathy. As we have seen, in phenomenological terms, empathy consists in primordially experiencing something that is non-primordially given. It is a primordial act of a non-primordial content. Analogously, the film experience of the relationship with the character could be thought of as the primordial experience (in the spectator's lived body) of non-primordial movements and emotions (those that are performed and felt by the character's *quasi*-body). Both empathy and the film experience are intimate or 'immediate', experiences of an at-a-distance, 'mediated' experience. The nature of the film experience of narrative cinema as a *sui generis* form of intersubjective relationship between the spectator and the character is structurally empathic.

The pertinence of Stein's account of empathy for film theory lies not only in its *structural* analogy with the filmic experience, as just described, but also on the *processual* analogy between the stages of realization of the empathic act and the dynamic of the film spectator's involvement in the character. My argument is that the dynamic of empathy proposed by Stein is complete and complex enough to explain the psychological relationship between the spectator and filmic *quasi*-bodies. Here is Stein's (1964) description of the empathic process:

> When [empathy] arises before me all at once, it faces me as an object (such as the sadness I 'read in another's face'). But when I inquire into its implied tendencies (try to bring another's mood to clear givenness to myself), the content, having pulled me into it, is no longer really an object. I am now no longer turned to the content but to the object of it, am at the subject of the content in the original subject's place. And only after successfully executed clarification, does the content again face me as an object (9).

For Stein, empathy is a composite process, one that has at least three grades or modalities of accomplishment: (1) *the emergence of the experience*: suddenly, I see sadness on the character's face; (2) *the fulfilling explication*: I am involved in her inner state, I experience the sadness she does by moving 'at' her, 'with' her in front of the same object; (3) *the comprehensive objectification of the explained experience*: in the end, I am aware of the character's sadness (10). In brief, at the starting stage, I am in front of the object, and I experience it with my senses. In the middle stage, a fulfilling explication drives me towards the subject and pulls me back. At the final stage, I am again in front of the object, and I receive it into my experience, I internalize it.

In the phenomenological framework, therefore, empathy is not a purely physiological reaction, nor a purely cognitive act. Rather, it is a *feeling* composed of different levels, namely perceptual, emotional, and cognitive levels, which are grounded in the lived body. The three levels seem to be parallel to the levels of filmic experience involved in relating to a main character on screen: (1) a *perceptual* act: I perceptually face a filmic body that expresses an external and internal state and attracts my attention and my senses; (2) this act is lived as an *emotional* act: I move closer and place myself 'at' the character, 'on his side', in front of the origin of her emotion; (3) this experience is objectified by a *cognitive* act: I exit, I move back and detach myself to face the object again, to cognitively perform a new objectification. Distance, proximity, and distance again: empathy allows this psychological 'round-trip' of approaching, fulfilling, and detaching. The distanced moments correspond respectively to an optical and mental stage (emergence and interiorization of the experience), whereas the core of the process is a 'rapture' in which disbelief is temporarily suspended and the spectator is fully immersed in the fictional events and has the impression of having an intimate relational experience. The oxymoronic structure of filmic experience consists in an 'emotional' moment embedded in an optical-cognitive frame. The act of filmic empathy consists in the fulfilling of the *quasi*-intersubjective structure of the filmic relation.

The fate of the acrobat

In light of this framework, both in order to explore the structural and processual analogy of the film experience and the empathic act and to analyse them in practice, let us consider a cinematic example. In the prologue of *Trapeze* (Reed 1956), the acrobat Mike Ribble performs a triple somersault in front of two kinds of audience. The first audience is that of the spectators-*in*-the-film: extras acting as the crowd of people around the circus ring that follows the performance with bated breath. The second audience consists of the spectators-*of*-the film: real people who have gathered in a cinema auditorium to watch the acrobatic performance (and the circus audience) represented in *Trapeze*. This film excerpt allows us to focus on the different psychological situations of the two kinds of audience.

It is useful to note that every narrative text, in fact, makes a 'pact' with its spectator, whose nature depends on the interpretative route proposed (cf. Eco 1994, 75-96). This pact can be *referential* in the case where the object of the experience is reality, or *fictional*, when the spectator is invited to suspend her disbelief and accept the imaginary world represented. *Trapeze* is a narrative film that makes a fictional pact with the spectator: whereas the action of the acrobat is 'direct' for the spectators of the circus in the film, the on-screen events are taken to be far from *real* (as they would be in a documentary), but are nevertheless considered to be *realistic*, since the represented bodies appear human, the image is photographic, and actions and events obey the physical rules that the spectators use to interpret the real world (for instance the acrobat does not fly). It must be clarified that in mediated experiences, such as live television broadcasting, spectators' involvement mostly depends on the fact that the beholder knows that the events that she is watching are actually happening at that moment and cannot be manipulated (so an accident might actually occur). Cinematic images, meanwhile, can involve the spectator in a more engaging experience through the utilization of a narrative perspective (for instance the re-enactment of the performance with an actor, suspense-inducing music and fast editing).

Now, let us consider the audience reactions to Ribble's acrobatic performance and its tragic outcome. As Ribble loses his grip and falls down in the middle of the circus floor, the spectators-*in*-the-film jump to their feet in an icy silence; some of them approach his motionless body with astonishment and fear, incredulous that the show has had such a dramatic conclusion. The psychophysical suspense experienced by the spectator-*in*-the-film are strictly dependent on the actual danger of the performance, that is, on the physical presence of the acrobat's body, who is up there in the flesh—no tricks—and at risk of falling. By contrast, the spectator-*of*-the-film does not interfere with the events represented (they do not stand up or call the ambulance), since they are voluntarily disposed to view the represented events *as if* they are actually happening while still maintaining an awareness that those events are merely fictional. Given this peculiar psychological structure of the film experience, the spectator-*of*-the film (or 'spectators' for short, henceforth) can experience the character's sense of vertigo, loss of balance, and impact with the ground vicariously. Their sensorimotor and affective activations are realized by varying degrees of empathy. The degree and quality of motor activation and emotional involvement depend on the effectiveness of the forces and tensions created by the movement of on-screen bodies.

Following the framework constructed by the comparison of the Steinian account of empathy with Michotte's description of the film experience, a circuit of empathies can be recognized in the relationship between the spectator and the character. At an initial level of the involvement process, the spectator is in front of the fictional world: she is positioned 'in the middle' of the events, in a way participating in the performance, rather than only witnessing it. Through a series of techniques (for instance camera angle, shot scale, point-of-view), the spectator is brought closer to the action. In *Trapeze*, thanks to the alternation of long shots and close-ups, only spectators in front of the screen can see the fatigue on Ribble's face and the sweat on his forehead, or watch the action from above or just under the safety net, from behind the trapeze, or even clinging to the trapeze artist's belt.

In addition to camera shots, camera movements also have to be considered. Camera movements do not simply produce a motor activation, but rather are capable of generating or implicitly suggesting a relation between the movement perceived on the screen and the movement that is internally experienced by the spectator. In the prologue of *Trapeze*, Ribble's pendulum movement in mid-air is shown not only by the overall view provided by the extreme long shot; rather, the camera follows the acrobat and sways, on both the horizontal and vertical axes alternately, in order to keep him in the centre of the visual frame. This movement *simulates* the character's movement, but it is also different and autonomous. As a result of this technique, the spectator can perceive the loss of balance elicited by the movements of the camera as it follows the acrobat. In this sense, he has an experience that is available only through film.

Emotional participation is connected to cognitive and narrative factors (for instance, if the character is shown in close-ups and his action dominates that of the other characters, then he must be the main character—and if he is, he cannot die in the first scene—but if the stunt is shown in the prologue, something bad is going to happen). Here the series of close-ups that precede Ribble's fall and the related camera movements enrich the involvement strategy. This group of shots places the spectator in the midst of the events, 'at' the heart of the emotion. Because of the closeness to Ribble's face and hands, and because of the swaying camera movement, the spectator perceives the beads of sweat on Ribble's furrowed brow, the tension in the grip of the two trapeze artists hanging in mid-air, and the hands slipping away. Then the hold is lost and Ribble falls. By means of a high-angle shot, the spectator sees the body falling, bouncing off the recovery net, and plunging to the ground. The impact with the ground is not shown: it is hidden by the re-establishing shot of the reaction of the spectators-*in*-the-film: they leap up, the orchestra stops playing, and the trapeze keeps swinging without the artist. After the fall, by means of a low-angle shot, the spectator sees the bleak image of the trapeze that swings in the air, now empty, the reverberation of a movement performed by an absent body, a dramatic failure, the futility of a fictional spectacle into which reality is tragically reintroduced, an action without an actor. These deep meanings are communicated by the film through a very powerful symbolic image that embodies a presence that is no longer visible. As in the Steinian model, the moment of detachment and objectifying interiorization completes the empathic process. Here a more complex stage of empathy is at work, one which has fed on all the previous stages and now stands out and culminates in a reflective interiorization, the 'comprehensive objectification' (Stein 1964, 10) of the other's experience, which nevertheless preserves distance.

The sense(s) of the void

Let us return to the initial example—*The Walk*—and consider it as an example of contemporary cinema that stresses some of the 'classic' strategies of cinematic empathy. Thanks to a complex ensemble of visual strategies, during the entire film—and in particular during the 20-minute-long take of the walk between the Twin Towers—the spectator experiences a vertiginous tension that literally holds her on the edge of her seat, which is enhanced by the depth effect provided by the 3D projection. The very special effect the film conveys is not so much the digital reconstruction of the now-disappeared skyscrapers as a background on which to place the walk of the rebel acrobat, but rather the realism of the sense of dizziness and vertigo.

This effect is achieved first optically: the displacement of convergence and focus (enhanced by the 3D projection, but not at all absent in the 2D, since three-dimensionality is evoked by the physiology of the eyes in natural vision), creates 'visual cliffs' (cf. *infra*, Ch. VI). Yet the eyes are not apart from the body: it is from the spectator's incapacity to place herself in the fictional space, while still feeling as though in the middle of it, that a sense of disorientation and estrangement emerges. The moments in which this particular impression emerges correspond to the *plongée* shots that show the 120-foot cliff below the character, as if the spectator were in precarious equilibrium on the wire.

The main point that should be considered in the analysis of the empathetic experience of *The Walk* is the incongruence between the character's experience and that of the spectator (and thus, the ways in which the film's visual and narrative elements enact that perceptual and affective mediation that allows the spectator to experience the character's perceptions and emotions). In fact, Philippe does not feel any sense of vertigo as his ability consists primarily of a sort of indifference to height, his ability to focus on action and goal and to enjoy the sense of freedom offered by the challenge of walking in mid-air. Thus, the spectator's experience is not empathic in the narrow sense of feeling the same inner state as the character: in this case the character does not suffer from vertigo. As far as we are concerned, however, what matters is the spectator's experience, the feeling of vertigo conveyed by the discrepancy between visual stimuli and kinaesthetic, bodily sensations—those reported in the newspapers and magazines mentioned at the beginning of this chapter. This effect does not depend on the conscious knowledge of the character's feeling, but rather on the film's capacity to evoke a physical reaction in the viewer.

A second empathetic walk follows the first and insists on the difference between the character's state and that of the spectator. Here too the optical vertigo experienced by the spectator contrasts with the psychological serenity and harmony experienced by Philippe, who now dances on the wire to the peaceful sounds of a piano playing Beethoven's *Für Elise*. It is necessary to raise the stakes in order to create tension in the spectator's nerves: the tightrope walker stops, puts the rod between the cable and one of the tie rods, kneels, relaxes, and performs other daring movements perceived by the spectator as extremely risky. It is the 'grace' of these new gestures in particular that begins to emerge from the pure execution of the stunt: the tightrope walker intentionally wants to offer a spectacle, he does not even need to concentrate. Moreover, the policemen arrive at the roofs of the Towers to stop him, but he turns around (passing the rod over his head with bold movements) and goes back again, moving in the other direction while performing other acrobatic numbers. The exhilaration of what happens on the Towers' roofs does not seem to distract the tightrope walker: his insistent and ecstatic serenity is even more strongly opposed to the apprehension experienced by the spectator. Here the gap between the character's emotions (characterized by great psychophysical balance) and the spectator's (extreme dizziness) reaches its apex.

At this point, even more energy is needed: the ending of the performance continues to be postponed and the difficulty of the manoeuvres increases, with the result of exasperating the spectator. The tightrope walker even slams back on the cable, but a seagull appears in the mist of the sky. Clouds and doubts begin to accumulate around the Towers and Philippe's mind—it is time to come back. The perception of danger returns drastically and increases. His previously injured foot bleeds visibly, the weather suddenly changes, a police helicopter ruffles his hair, the cables seem to be unable to withstand the weight and tension, the wire sways dangerously when there are only three steps left...

These energy-loading strategies are effective not only because of the actual precariousness of the situation and acrobatic movements of the tightrope walker, but also as a result of extensive narrative work that predisposes us to a sense of danger. In fact, the tension is increased by a series of cognitive clues disseminated throughout the film, which re-emerge during its climactic sequence. Philippe is not infallible, as indicated by some falls during the training phase shown previously in the film: just three feet from the platform, Philippe lost his concentration and slipped—he rescued himself only because he was able to quickly hang onto the wire. Given this prefiguration of the fall, the possibility that the incident could occur even at the final moment of the walk between the Towers is present.

The spectator therefore experiences the fear of the void not only optically, but also as a more general fear of falling—the concrete fear that the tightrope walker may lose concentration and balance. More important than the success (or failure) of the acrobatic number in keeping the audience 'suspended' is the tightrope walker's constant risk of falling. Here, emotion is certainly empathetic, as character and spectator share the same hesitation and physical and mental precariousness. Moreover, despite the spectator may know that historically Petit's performance was successful, the apprehension is real.

The optical vertigo and the fear of falling are therefore the main involvement strategies of *The Walk*; these are realized with precise shooting and writing techniques, with 'illusive' effects internal to the diegetic world, even if it is not separate from history. Indeed, despite the fact that there is no explicit and voluntary mention of them, the CGI reconstruction of the Twin Towers and Petit's enterprise inevitably refer to the tragic events of September 11, 2001. The dream of rebellion and freedom with which the tightrope walker horizontally joins two vertically erected lines—the two Towers—collides with the dramatically realistic image of their collapse, now crystallized in the eyes and consciousness of Western world. As impressive ghosts of steel and glass, the Towers are the nostalgic setting for the imaginary postponement of and memorial to a dizzying physical and symbolic fall.

The circuit of empathies

As the analysed examples help to clarify, cinematic empathy is a composite and multi-stage dynamic that is rooted in kinaesthetic and proprioceptive processes of the body. The cinema plays insistently with its ability to express tension and to communicate such tension through a combination of optical, cognitive, narrative, and symbolic components. An expressive-empathic circuit acts at all levels of perception, starting from a sensorimotor solicitation through which the spectator's body becomes an energy accumulator. Her tendons and muscles absorb the flow of energy emanating from the expressive potential of the image. Therefore, this 'loading' is not the result of a *projective* act through which the spectator empathizes with the character, but is instead the result of a *protrusion* through which the character and the environmental and relational conditions in which she is located communicate to the spectator in an intensified sensory form.

As in the filmological account of both motor and emotional empathy given by Michotte, a single movement depicted on-screen is experienced in two forms: the visual impression of the character's body in motion and the inner kinaesthetic feeling experienced by the spectator in her body. The 'bridge' between 'external' visual perception and 'inner' bodily perception supports the rise of emotional empathy, that is, a more complex relationship between the spectator's body and the character's *quasi*-body, both of which are to be conceived of as lived bodies in a phenomenological sense. According to Stein and Michotte (Case 3), the movements and emotions of the spectator's subjectivity remain extraneous to, or separate from, the character's *quasi*-subjectivity. Empathy implies an ontological separation that nonetheless represents the constitutive act of the film experience as a paradoxical 'proximity at a distance', sharing without fusion, a kind of intimacy in which one own identity is preserved.

The spectator's involvement takes place along the same spectrum of experience as the one described by the phenomenological and filmological approach to empathy. It starts from a basic neurophysiological layer of perceptual experience, that is, those processes of automatic and autonomic response to the sensory stimulation of the film that may affect motility but also affectivity. Empathy as such arises when mere motor synchronization or emotional contagion becomes a 'resonance' that allows the spectator to grasp, in an immediate and precognitive way, the emotions, intentions, and motivations of another subjectivity.

In addition, this simulation can also be carried out through the aesthetic aspects of the film as a technical and linguistic device capable of taking on a 'posture' and performing 'gestures', albeit in a qualitatively different way than a human. The 'bodily behaviour' of the film's body, in fact, shifts empathy from the spectator-character relationships to the spectator-film relationships. As I explained in the first chapter when summarizing Vivian Sobchack's notion of the film's body, this means that the point-of-view, the camera movement and the features of the filmic *mise-en-scène* are not mere discursive elements of the film as a linguistic system, but rather expressive means by which the film establishes a bodily engagement with the spectator, a set of 'gestures' that evoke corresponding response from the spectator's body. As Jennifer Barker (2009) writes, '[o]ur bodies orient and dispose themselves toward the body of the film itself, because we and the film make sense of space by moving thought it muscularly in similar ways and with similar attitudes' (75). The vertiginous 'bodily language' of *The Walk*, for example, clearly demonstrates that the film adopts our proprioception and deliberately perturbs our sense of equilibrium, which is a direct, pre-reflexive, bodily way of *embodying* our perceptual attitude. This expressive-perceptive dynamic is forged in the combination of 'muscular resonance'[7] and the film's intentional project, that is the involvement of the spectator in a narrative goal, as dangerous it might be (for example, performing an acrobatic walk in mid-air).

It is exactly the union of character-centred and film-centred empathy that leads to a higher level of experience, communicating a more complex and profoundly embodied meaning of intentionality. The acrobatic action is, in fact, a generator of tensive energy because it is pervaded by a force—gravity—that potentially alters the harmony of movement, the tendency towards a potentially dramatic outcome. The tightrope walker's action is not empathetic merely because it is a sporting and acrobatic performance, but because it is constantly exposed to the risk of tragic failure.

Bibliography

Agosta, Lou. 2004. *A Rumor of Empathy: Rewriting Empathy in the Context of Philosophy*. New York: Palgrave-Macmillan.

Balázs, Béla. 2010. *Early Film Theory: The Visible Man*. Edited by Erica Carter, translated by Rodney Livingstone. New York: Berghahn Books.

Barker, Jennifer M. 2009. *The Tactile Eye: Touch and the Cinematic Experience*. Berkeley and Los Angeles: University of California Press.

Batson, C. Daniel. 2009. 'These Things Called Empathy: Eight Related but Distinct Phenomena'. In *The Social Neuroscience of Empathy*. Edited by Jean Decety & William Ickes, 3-15. Cambridge, MA/London: The MIT Press.

Brain, Robert Michael. 2012. 'Self Projection: Hugo Münsterberg on Empathy and Oscillation in Cinema Spectatorship'. *Science in Context*. 25: 329-353. DOI:10.1017/S0269889712000166.

Bryant, Jennings, & Dolf Zillmann, eds. 1991. *Responding to the Screen: Reception and Reaction Processes*. Hillsdale, NJ: Erlbaum.

Carroll, Noël. 1999. 'Film, Emotion, and Genre'. In Plantinga & Smith, eds., 21-47.

7 According to Sobchack's notion of 'film's body', Barker (2009) writes, '[i]n any cinematic experience, we and the film have a muscular empathy for one another, which is derived from similarities in the ways the human body and the film's body express their relation to the world though bodily comportment, and similarities in attitudes and projects that both film and viewer in the world. The viewer's empathy with the film's body should not be confused with or reduced to identification with characters' (73).

Carroll, Noël. 1996. *Theorizing the Moving Image*. Cambridge: Cambridge University Press.

Chemero, Anthony. 2009. *Radical Embodied Cognitive Science*. Cambridge, MA: The MIT Press.

Chemero, Anthony. 2016. 'Sensorimotor Empathy'. *Journal of Consciousness Studies*. 23 (5-6): 138-152.

Child, Ben. 2015. 'Zemeckis 3D high-wire biopic *The Walk* "giving audiences vertigo"'. September 30. https://www.theguardian.com/film/2015/sep/30/robert-zemeckis-3d-the-walk-audiences-vertigo.

Clark, Adam, & David Chalmers. 1998. 'The Extended Mind'. *Analysis*. 58 (1): 7-19. DOI:10.1093/analys/58.1.7.

Coplan, Amy, & Peter Goldie, eds. 2011. *Empathy: Philosophical and Psychological Perspectives*. Oxford: Oxford University Press.

Coplan, Amy. 2012. 'Empathy and Character Engagement'. In *The Routledge Companion to Philosophy and Film*. Edited by Paisley Livingston & Carl Plantinga, 97-110. London: Routledge.

Currie, Gregory, & Ian Ravenscroft. 2002. *Recreative Minds*. Oxford: Oxford University Press.

Currie, Gregory. 1995. *Image and Mind: Film, Philosophy and Cognitive Science*. Cambridge: Cambridge University Press.

Curtis, Robin, & Gertrud Koch, eds. 2008. *Einfühlung. Zu Geschichte und Greenwalt eines ästhetischen Konzepts*. München: Wilhelm Fink Verlag.

Darwin, Charles. 1871. *The Descent of Man and Selection in Relation to Sex*. London: John Murray.

Eco, Umberto. 1994. *Six Walks in the Fictional Woods*, 75-96. Cambridge, MA: Harvard University Press.

Freeburg, Victor O. 1918. *The Art of Photoplay Making*. New York: MacMillan.

Gallese, Vittorio. 2007. 'Before and Below 'Theory of Mind': Embodied Simulation and the Neural Correlates of Social Cognition'. *Philosophical Transactions of the Royal Society B-Biological Sciences*. 362: 659-669. DOI:10.1098/rstb.2006.2002.

Goldman, Alvin I. 2006a. 'Imagination and Simulation in Audience Responses to Fiction'. In *The Architecture of the Imagination: New Essays on Pretence, Possibility, and Fiction*. Edited by Shaun Nichols, 41-56. Oxford: Clarendon Press.

Goldman, Alvin I. 2006b. *Simulating Minds: The Philosophy, Psychology, and Neuroscience of Mindreading*. New York: Oxford University Press.

Grodal, Torben, & Mette Kramer. 2010. 'Empathy, Film, and the Brain'. *Recherches sémiotiques / Semiotic Inquiry*. 30 (1-2-3): 19-35. DOI:10.7202/1025921ar.

Grodal, Torben. 1997. *Moving Pictures: A New Theory of Film Genres, Feelings, and Cognition*. Oxford: Clarendon Press.

Grodal, Torben. 1999. 'Emotions, Cognitions, and Narrative Patterns in Film'. In Plantinga & Smith, 127-145.

Grodal, Torben. 2009. *Embodied Visions: Evolution, Emotion, Culture, and Film*. New York: Oxford University Press.

Hildebrand, Adolf von. 1893. *Das Problem der Form in der Bildenden Kunst*. Strassburg: J.H.E. Heitz.

Hume, David. 1793. *A Treatise of Human Nature*. Oxford: Clarendon Press.

Husserl, Edmund. 1960. *Cartesian Meditations*. Translated by Dorion Cairns. The Hague: Nijhoff.

Husserl, Edmund. 1989. *Ideas Pertaining to a Pure Phenomenology and to a Phenomenological Philosophy*, Second Book: *Studies in the Phenomenology of Constitution*. Translated by Richard Rojcewicz & André Schuwer. Dordrecht: Kluwer.

Lanzoni, Susan. 2012. 'Empathy in Translation: Movement and Image in the Psychological Laboratory'. *Science in Context*. 25 (3): 329-353. DOI:10.1017/S0269889712000154.

Lee, Ashley. 2015. 'NYFF: How 'The Walk' Director Robert Zemeckis Shot Joseph Gordon-Levitt's "Painful" High-Wire Scenes'. September 26. http://www.hollywoodreporter.com/news/nyff-how-walk-director-robert-827442.

Lipps, Theodor. 1903. *Grundlegung der Ästhetik*. Hamburg/Leipzig: Voss Verlag.

Lipps, Theodor. 1965. 'Empathy and Aesthetic Pleasure'. In *Aesthetic Theories: Studies in the Philosophy of Art*. Edited by Karl Aschenbrenner & Arnold Isenberg. Englewood Cliffs, NJ: Prentice Hall.

Lipps, Theodor. 1979. 'Empathy, Inner Imitation and Sense-Feelings'. In *A Modern Book of Esthetics*. New York: Holt, Rinehart and Winston.

Locke, John. 1960. *An Essay Concerning Human Understanding*. London: The Buffet.

Lux, Vanessa, & Sigfrid Weigel, eds. 2017. *Empathy: Epistemic Problems and Cultural-Historical Perspectives of a Cross-Disciplinary Concept*. New York: Palgrave-MacMillan.

Mallgrave, Henry F., Eleftherios Ikonomou, & Robert Vischer, eds. 1994. *Empathy, Form, and Space: Problems in German Aesthetics, 1873-1893*. Santa Monica: Getty Center for the History of Art and Humanities.

Michotte, Albert. 1991a. 'The Emotional Involvement of the Spectator in the Action Represented in a Film: Toward a Theory'. Translated by Alan Costall. In Thinès, Costall & Butterworth, eds., 209-217.

Moran, Dermont. 2004. 'The Problem of Empathy: Lipps, Scheler, Husserl and Stein'. In *Amor Amicitiae: On the Love that is Friendship. Essays in Medieval Thought and Beyond in Honor of the Rev. Professor James McEvoy*. Edited by Thomas A.F. Kelly & Phillip W. Rosemann, 269-312. Leuven/Dudley, MA: Peeters

Münsterberg, Hugo. 2002. *Hugo Münsterberg on Film:* The Photoplay: A Psychological Study *and Other Writings*. Edited by Allan Langdale. New York/London: Routledge.

Neill, Alex. 1996. 'Empathy and (Film) Fiction'. In Bordwell & Carroll, eds., 175-194.

Perrett, David, Mark Harries, Amanda J. Mistlin, & Andrew J. Chitty. 1990. 'Three Stages in the Classification of Body Movements by Visual Neurons'. In *Images and Understanding*. Edited by Horace Barlow, Colin Blakemore & Miranda Weston-Smith, 94-107. Cambridge: Cambridge University Press.

Pinotti, Andrea, & Massimo Salgaro. 2019. 'Empathy or Empathies? Uncertainties in the Interdisciplinary Discussion'. *Gestalt Theory*. 41 (2): 141-158.

Pinotti, Andrea. 2016. *L'empathie: Histoire d'une idée de Platon au posthumain*. Paris: Vrin.

Plantinga, Carl, & Greg M. Smith, eds. 1999. *Passionate Views: Film, Cognition and Emotion*. Baltimore: Johns Hopkins University Press.

Plantinga, Carl. 1999. 'The Scene of Empathy and the Human Face on Film'. In Plantinga & Smith, eds., 239-255.

Plantinga, Carl. 2009. *Moving Viewers: American Film and the Spectator's Experience*. Berkeley/Los Angeles: University of California Press.

Plantinga, Carl. 2018. *Screen Stories: Emotion and the Ethics of Engagement*. New York: Oxford University Press.

Preston, Stephanie D., & Frans B.M. de Waal. 2001. 'Empathy: Its Ultimate and Proximate Bases'. *Behavioral and Brain Sciences*. 25 (1): 1-20. DOI:10.1017/S0140525X02000018.

Reynolds, Dee, & Matthew Reason, eds. 2012. *Kinesthetic Empathy in Creative and Cultural Practices*. Bristol/Chicago: Intellect.

Scheler, Max. 2017. *The Nature of Sympathy*. Translated by Peter Heath. New York: Routledge.

Shaw, Dan. 2016. 'Mirror Neurons and Simulation Theory. A Neurophysiological Foundation for Cinematic Empathy'. In *Current Controversies in Philosophy of Film*. Edited by Katherine Thomson-Jones, 148-162. New York/London: Routledge.

Smith, Adam. 2002. *The Theory of Moral Sentiments*. Cambridge: Cambridge University Press.

Smith, Murray. 1995. *Engaging Characters: Fiction, Emotion, and the Cinema*. Oxford: Clarendon Press.

Smith, Murray. 2017. *Film, Art, and the Third Culture: A Naturalized Aesthetics of Film*. New York: Oxford University Press.

Stadler, Jane. 2017. 'Empathy in Film'. In *The Routledge Handbook of Philosophy of Empathy*. Edited by Heidi L. Maibom, 317-326. New York: Routledge. DOI:10.4324/9781315282015.

Stein, Edith. 1964. *On the Problem of Empathy*. Translated by W. Stein. The Hague: Nijhoff.

Stein, Edith. 1991. 'Einführung in die Philosophie'. In *Edith Steins Werke. Vol. XIII.* Freiburg im Breisgau, Basel/Wien: Herder.

Stuart Mill, John. 1867. *An Examination of Sir William Hamilton's Philosophy and of the Principal Philosophical Questions Discussed in His Writings.* London: Longmans, Green, and Co.

Stueber, Karsten. 2006. *Rediscovering Empathy: Agency, Folk Psychology, and the Human Sciences.* Cambridge, MA: The MIT Press.

Tallis, Raymond. 2011. *Aping Mankind: Neuromania, Darwinitis, and the Misrepresentation of Humanity.* Acumen: Durham.

Tan, Ed. 1996. *Emotion and the Structure of Narrative Film: Film as an Emotion Machine.* Mahwah, NJ: Erlbaum.

Tan, Ed. 2013. 'The Empathic Animal Meets the Inquisitive Animal in the Cinema: Notes on a Psychocinematics of Mind Reading'. In Shimamura, ed., 337-367.

Titchener, Edward B. 1909. *Lectures on the Experimental Psychology of the Thought-Processes.* New York: Macmillan.

Turvey, Malcom. 2020. 'Mirror Neurons and Film Studies. A Cautionary Tale from a Serious Pessimist'. *Projections.* 14 (3): 21-46. DOI:10.3167/proj.2020.140303.

Vaage, Margrethe Bruun. 2010. 'Fiction Film and the Varieties of Empathic Engagement'. *Midwest Studies in Philosophy.* 1: 158-179. DOI:10.1111/j.1475-4975.2010.00200.x.

Vischer, Robert. 1873. *Über das optische Formgefühl: ein Beitrag zur Ästhetik.* Leipzig: Credner.

Vischer, Robert. 1927. *Drei Schriften zum ästhetischen Formproblem.* Halle: Niemeyer.

Walton, Kendall L. 1990. *Mimesis as Make-Believe: On the Foundations of the Representational Arts.* Cambridge, MA: Harvard University Press.

Warburg, Aby. 1893. *Sandro Botticellis 'Geburt der Venus' und 'Frühling': Eine Untersuchung Über die Vorstellungen von der Antike in den Italienischen Frührenaissance.* Hamburg: Leopold Voss. Then in 1932: *Gesammelte Schriften.* Leipzig/Berlin: B.G. Teubner.

Wölfflin, Heinrich. 1886. *Prolegomena zu einer Psychologie der Architektur.* Berlin: W. Hertz.

Wollheim, Richard. 1996. *The Thread of Life.* Cambridge: Harvard University Press.

Zahavi, Dan. 2014. *Self and Other Exploring Subjectivity, Empathy, and Shame.* Oxford University Press: Oxford.

Zillman, Dolf. 2006. 'Empathy: Affect From Bearing Witness to the Emotion of Others'. In *Psychology of Entertainment.* Edited by Jennings Bryant & Peter Vorderer, 151-181. Mahwaw, NJ: Erlbaum.

III Fall

Descent to equilibrium

Abstract
A common outcome of acrobatics, and a motif often combined with it, is the fall. The chapter 'Fall. Descent to equilibrium' discusses the recurrence of the motif of the falling human body in contemporary cinema, taking as a starting point Oliver Pietsch's found footage film *Maybe Not*. Relying on Torben Grodal's application of the notions of telic and paratelic to the film experience, referring to the use of cinema as metaphor for the mind proposed by Antonio Damasio, and interpreting several experiments on the perception of movement in film sequences whose temporality is manipulated, this chapter describes the modality through which cinema 'regulates' the fall by adopting a homeostatic process that reduces its traumatic character and, at the same time, enhances its expressive effectiveness.

Keywords: Falling, Homeostatic equilibrium, Slow motion, Telic/Paratelic, *Maybe Not*

> Our hopeless ambition to find the physiological equivalents of the items of consciousness.
> —Rudolf Arnheim, *Parables of Sunlight*, 1989 (335)

Maybe not

Maybe Not, a found footage video by German artist Oliver Pietsch (2005), opens with the final sequence of Takashi Miike's *Graveyard of Honor* (2002), a remake of Kinji Fukasaku's *Jingi no hakaba* (1975). After a sort of meditative dance atop a tower, the protagonist throws himself into the void. At this point a chain of cinematic falls (extracted from Western and, in part, Asian

D'Aloia, A., *Neurofilmology of the Moving Image. Gravity and Vertigo in Contemporary Cinema*. Taylor & Francis Group 2021
DOI: 10.5117/9789463725255_CH03

cinema) starts: the nightmare of Scottie and Madeleine/Judy's falls in *Vertigo* (Hitchcock 1958), Neo's first attempts to move in the world of *The Matrix* (L. & L. Wachowski 1999), the riding of the bomb in *Dr. Strangelove or: How I Learned to Stop Worrying and Love the Bomb* (Kubrick 1964), Peter Parker's training as a superhero in *Spider-Man* (Raimi 2002), the dramatic suicide in *Germany, Year Zero* (Rossellini 1948) and other falls extracted from *Oldboy* (Chan-wook 2003), *Lethal Weapon* (Donner 1987), *Strange Days* (Bigelow 1995), and others.

Formally, Pietsch's video consists of a juxtaposition of several variations on the same motif: the fall of a human body. Each fragment is the link of a chain perceived as unitary; although varying in direction within the frame, speed (however, slow motion unites almost all the fragments), format (for each the original is preserved), photography (black & white or colour), and despite being performed by different characters, the fall is a unique flow of movement gestaltically perceived as continuous.

In the montage, this motor continuity is associated with basic emotional continuity through the merging of visuals, sound, and dialogue. The elegiac pop song by Cat Power (which also serves as the title of the video) endows the work with 'conceptual unity' and gives it a melancholic tone. The chorus ('[w]e can all be free, maybe not in words, maybe not with a look, but with your mind') expresses the ambivalence—even the ambiguity—of human desire inherent in the fall. It serves as a gesture to the desire for freedom, and as an extreme intensification of, and a surrender to, the insuperability of human limits—a free fall that leads to death. The editing and sound mixing are designed to capture this sense of ambivalence, in both its poetic and symbolic aspects, thus involving both the motor and emotional spheres of the film experience.

Beyond these aesthetic and psychological aspects, *Maybe Not* testifies that throughout the history of cinema, especially in the wake of the 2000s, the fall of the human body, although used in different genres and with different narrative intentions—suicides, murders, accidents, gags, jumps, sports challenges, flights—is a recurring motif, almost programmatically inserted in topical sequences in order to generate that intensification of perception and search for bodily participation that I began to discuss in respect to the acrobatic gesture in the previous chapter. The vertigo and the sense of suspension that characterize the acrobatics in their ability to load an energy experienced internally and partly externally by the spectator are very often the result of a new and autonomous figure, a discontinuous movement through which energy begins to discharge and at the same time receives a new impulse (in the direction of what will in turn be a new tensive motif: the impact).

In this chapter I will study how this expressive discharging/recharging dynamic interacts with the spectator's empathic propensity to experience the same descending movement at both the motor and the emotional level. Even in this context, the analysis of the actual stylistic and formal modes in which the fall is represented will be closely linked to its psychological and philosophical implications. Like a new Icarus, the contemporary individual searches for the exhilaration of flight and altitude but approaches the sun too closely; his wax wings melt and the fall becomes inevitable. The ancient myth resonates dramatically in today's manifestation of trauma, in the painful and inevitable path of human bodies that rained from the Twin Towers of New York on September 11, 2001. In contemporary imaginary production, falling is a real obsession for both the individual and society. Its importance is so great that it appears with regularity and insistence in dreams. As Gaston Bachelard (1988) writes about the 'Imaginary Fall',

> If we were to make a balance sheet of metaphors of falling and rising, we could not help but be struck by the fact that those pertaining to the fall are much more numerous. Even before any reference to mortality, metaphors of the fall are fixed, it would appear, by an undeniable psychological reality. These metaphors all produce a psychic impression that leaves indelible traces in our unconscious: the fear of falling is a *primitive fear*. We find it as one component in fears of many different kinds. It is what constitutes the dynamic element of the fear of the dark. One who flees feels his legs giving way. Blackness and fall, the fall into blackness prepares facile dramas for the *unconscious imagination* (91).

I will delve into the (cinematographic) nature of this 'blackness' and its relationship with the fall in the next chapter, focused on the motif of impact. Here I just want to note one additional idea related to the dream of falling. Phenomenological psychiatrist Ludwig Binswanger identified in the dream of the fall an anthropological ancestry. In his essay *Dream and Existence,* written in 1930, more than a decade before Bachelard's *Air and Dreams*, Binswanger describes—as pointed out by Michel Foucault in his Introduction to the essay—'the vertical axis of the space in its meaning of existence' (Foucault & Binswanger 1993, 62), i.e. an alternation of euphoric and dysphoric states, of ascents and descents that are 'connected with the physical condition, especially breathing, in which case we are dealing with so-called body-stimuli dreams' (86). 'It is known', Binswanger writes, 'that in dreams flying and falling often are manifested by the hovering and sinking plunging of our own bodily form' (86) and this is even more evident when the flight is suddenly interrupted:

> When, in a bitter disappointment, 'we fall from the clouds,' then we *actually* do fall. Such falling is neither purely of the body nor something (analogically or metaphorically) derived from physical falling. Our harmonious relationship with the world and the men about us suddenly suffers a staggering blow, stemming from the nature of bitter disappointment and the shock that goes with it. In such a moment our existence actually suffers, is torn from its position in the 'world' and thrown back upon its own resources. Until we can again find a new, firm standing position in the world our whole Dasein [presence] moves within the meaning matrix (*Bedeutungsrichtung*) of stumbling, sinking, and falling (81-82).

These ideas, drawn from psychoanalysis and literary analysis, confirm that in human imagination the fall is a movement in opposition to flight and to ascendant movement. The fall offers a thrilling experience, and at the same time means abandonment to death. Because of this deep connection between the *sensorial* and the *sensate,* between bodily stimulation and cognitive reflection, the effects of trauma need be somewhat mitigated. As the cinema offers the spectator a mental and physical breakdown of ordinary balance (what I call the *disembodying phase*), forms of compensation and negotiation come into play in order to make the experience tolerable (the *reembodying phase*). It must be noted that the former is the result of the exceeding of the thresholds of embodied perception, and that the spectator is willing to accept this state; comparatively, the latter consists in the adoption, on the part of the film, of stylistic strategies that embody some of the biological functions of the spectator's body, which are carried out, in filmic form, on behalf of the spectator. In fact, this dynamic, which I consider of fundamental importance and which emerges in all of the tensive motifs, consists in the search for a homeostasis between excessive stimuli and the necessity of re-establishing of psychophysical balance.

Homeostatic disequilibrium

The concept of homeostatic equilibrium has been applied to film theory specifically in reference to the modalities through which the narrative is able to engender a state of cognitive tension in the spectator through the proposition of 'questions' that produce a cognitive and emotional accumulation and to which the plot development provides the 'answers', resulting in a soothing outcome. It should be noted that narratology uses the word 'equilibrium' to indicate, in respect to classical narratives, the initial state of staticity that is disrupted by an 'accident' through which a conflict (generally between opposing forces, incarnated by a hero and an anti-hero) that tends to resolve in the reconstitution of a new state of equilibrium arises (cf. Propp 1958; Greimas 1983). Each narrative film experience is characterized by a constant succession of stimuli and feedback, by events that cause disorder and events that seek to restore order, united by links of causality (Branigan 1992, 26-28) that promote a strong emotional involvement on the part of the spectator, especially if focused on a clear and effective character action. The film experience can thus be understood as an act of participation in a series of events unfolding over a relatively long period of time during which a character acts with clear motivation in order to reach a defined goal. In general, therefore, the narrative film is characterized by a *goal-oriented* structure.[1] This configuration works according to the principle of homeostatic equilibrium, although achieving this state is not at all to be taken for granted (and is less and less used in contemporary narrative cinema), precisely because of 'local' mechanisms which, within the 'global' narrative scheme, alternate tense states with soothing ones.

Some cognitive film theorists propose adopting the distinction (and interaction) between *goal-oriented* models and *process-oriented* models in order to differentiate between different forms of filmic narrative experience. Inspired by Nico Frijda's psychology of the emotions[2] and drawing from the 'reversal' motivational theory elaborated by psychologist Michael Apter (1982), Torben Grodal (1997) adopts the differentiation between *telic* dominant and *paratelic* dominant as a distinctive element of film narratives. In the case of a telic dominant, cognitive and muscular activations are *goal-oriented,* that is, aimed at achieving a specific objective, while in the case

1 di Chio (2011) identifies this form of 'strong' storytelling as a feature of 'classic' film experience: 'The progression that characterized it is centred on the *stimulus-motivation-action-goal* vector, whose elements are not only firmly linked with one another and linearly oriented, but also "well proportioned" and commensurate with each other. The action is therefore appropriate to the causes that move it, to the emotions that accompany it, and to the purposes that guide it.' (87, my trans.). ['La progressione che la caratterizza è centrata sul vettore *stimolo-motivazione-azione-obiettivo*, i cui elementi non solo sono saldamente incardinati l'uno nell'altro e linearmente orientati, ma anche "ben proporzionati" e commisurati vicendevolmente. L'azione risulta dunque appropriata alle cause che la muovono, alle emozioni che la accompagnano, agli scopi che la guidano.']

2 According to Frijda 1987, emotions are psychosomatic alterations that manifest the survival pulse characteristic of living beings.

of paratelic dominant they are *process-oriented,* or aimed at the pleasure of the action and movement in themselves. While the purpose of the paratelic mode is that of increasing the level of activation, the telic mode aims at reducing activation by reaching a goal (100-103). According to Grodal, the impulse to homeostatic equilibrium is activated in the spectator in different ways depending on the prevailing motivational system and is functional to a process of cognitive *labelling* of emotions dependent on the level of *arousal* (cf. 96-103). Strong excitement is experienced by the spectator as unpleasant in the telic system, while as pleasing in the paratelic one. Conversely, low excitement is experienced positively in the telic system and negatively in the paratelic one. The state of excitement can therefore be desirable or not depending on how it is labelled with respect to the dominant motivational system: a little excitement is considered a reason for relaxation in the telic system, though will be boring in the paratelic one, while high excitement is labelled as fun in the paratelic system, as is fear in the telic one.

Canonical narrative films are characterized, in general terms, by a *goal-oriented* motivational system, namely a telic dominant. Within this framework, the appearance of a tensive motif is a kind of interference in the narrative progression caused by a 'high voltage' of sensory stimuli deriving from the unusual movement of the character, a peak of energy charge that forces the spectator to enact a strong homeostatic regulation activity in a *process-oriented* system. A fall is an event characterized by a strong imbalance: it suddenly and dramatically raises the level of sensory stimulation and produces physiological reactions in the spectator, who attempts to rebalance that imbalance.

However, it is also true that the motivational system adopted by contemporary narrative cinema is hybrid. The spectator voluntarily seeks the risk, the danger, the vertigo. It might be said that even in the narrative film a certain dose of paratelic motivation is associated with telic motivation, since the spectator is willing to accept merely attractive and spectacular stimuli rather than voluntarily seeking these 'sparks' and 'shivers', provided, however, that they do not exceed certain limits and that the hyperstimulation does not become overstimulation. On the other hand, the tensive motif, usually placed in topical moments of narration (i.e. in the prologue, the climax, or the epilogue), serves to raise, from time to time, the average level of stress. For Apter himself, as for Grodal, there are thresholds beyond which these states become 'reversible' and not mutually exclusive. In the telic system, under a certain threshold of stimulation, relaxation can turn into boredom; in the paratelic system, over a certain threshold of stimulation, fun can turn into fear. This means that in the telic system, the tensive motif is an absolutely necessary means to maintain the spectator's participation. However, it also represents the risk of excessive excitement that can potentially go beyond the pleasure of a momentary shiver and turn into an annoying perceptual element, with the result of compromising the spectator's pleasure. It is to avoid exceeding these thresholds that, as we shall see, the cinema puts homeostatic regulation strategies and shifts of motivational systems into play on behalf of the spectator, so that the level of excitation remains (or returns) within acceptable boundaries.

Grodal's emphasis on the paratelic system, however, allows us to overcome a pure cognitive and disembodied account of homeostasis related exclusively to narration as a metaphor for the organism. My proposal is instead to enrich this perspective and broaden the notion of homeostasis to its fundamental biological meaning. In physiology, homeostatic equilibrium is the capacity of a living organism to maintain an internal biological balance in response to changes in external environmental conditions.[3] The tendency to homeostatic equilibrium would provide just the right combination of tension and relaxation, excitement and repose, spectacularity and narrativity. The tensive motifs, including the fall, are clearly special paratelic moments within the general framework of goal-oriented experience, moments that crush cognitive continuity through sensory radicalization. The analysis of the tensive motif shows that narration is not just a metaphor for the biological functioning of the human body. Through the production and management of stimuli, the film 'forces' the spectator to an intuitive biological regulation activity, a kind of compensation of 'body temperature' in respect to a sudden 'thermal excursion' in the external environment. Homeostatic regulation creates a continual and reciprocal influence between the internal and the external aspects of the organism: 'The "internal environment" of the body, which functions homeostatically and automatically, and is constituted by innumerable physiological and neurological events, is simply an internalized translation and continuation of the "external" environment', so that '[c]hanges in the "external" environment are always accompanied by changes in the "internal" one' (Gallagher & Zahavi 2007, 138). It is not surprising that a biologist like Antonio Damasio turns to the cinema to explain the nature

3 The term 'homeostasis' was introduced into physiology and medicine in 1925 by Walter Cannon (1926; 1929; 1932) and is borrowed from the concept of *milieu intérieur* proposed in 1854 by physiologist Claude Bernard (1949) in reference to the ability of the extracellular fluids of living beings to ensure the stability of tissue and organs. In turn, Bernard probably borrowed the expression from his contemporary, histologist Charles Robin (1853), who uses the phrase *milieu de l'intérieur* as a synonym for the ancient Hippocratic notion of 'mood'.

of certain aspects of consciousness. Damasio (1999) refers to the concept of homeostasis and *internal milieu* as a biological mechanism activated as a means for survival and inherent to living beings (which are equipped with a nervous system and therefore with consciousness). 'In a curious way', Damasio writes, 'life consists of continuous variation but only if the range of variation is contained within certain limits' (137).[4] As I said, the overcoming of limits occurs when a tensive motif breaks the moderate and constant flow of the narrative. In such cases, the spectator's body is instinctively engaged in the delicate process of restoration of the lost balance.

Too close, too far

Let us start the analysis from a limit case. In the curious prologue to *Magnolia* (Anderson 1999), the narrator recounts a singular 'suicide attempt': on March 23, 1958, the 17-year-old Sydney Barringer throws himself from a building in Los Angeles but is accidentally killed by a shotgun fired inside the building at his father by his mother during a domestic quarrel. Sydney himself loaded the rifle, which usually remained unloaded and was only used as a threat. The rifle bullet misses Sidney's father and hits the window just as the boy moves in front of it, piercing his chest. In fact, Sydney would have been saved thanks to the safety net installed a few days ago by a washer company—a safety net that, unlike the one in *Trapeze*, analysed in the previous chapter, would have been effective, had it not been for the twist of fate that rendered it useless.

The interesting thing is that the same event is replicated three times in different perspectives and representations. In the first exposition, the story starts by showing Sydney on the roof of the building. A tracking shot approaches the legs of the jumper, who drops into the void. At this point, a succession of four fast-paced shots shows the boy's falling body, but without ever focusing on his face clearly: 1) overhead shot from the building's edge, 2) frontal shot from outside the broken window, 3) a shot overturned by 180° showing Sydney's body as it is pierced by the shotgun, 4) low-angle shot of the safety net as Sidney approaches it. This succession of shots culminates, at

4 Here is a descriptive definition of the homeostatic process proposed by Damasio (1999): 'even when large variations occur in the environment that surrounds an organism, there is a dispositional arrangement available in the organism's structure that modifies the inner workings of the organism. The dispositional arrangement ensures that the environmental variations do not cause a correspondingly large and excessive variation of activity within' (136).

the height of an intensifying dissonant chord, with a still image that freezes the movement a moment before the boy reaches the net.

Here begins the second version of the story, this time told from the inside of the building and, at least in part, showing 'from within' the motives that pushed Sydney to such a dramatic gesture. The approach to the boy's legs on the building's edge starts from closer than it did in the first version, until it shows a farewell letter that protrudes from the pocket of his pants. A series of cross-fades shows some of the words of the letter ('I'm sorry...'), while the voice-over continues to explain what happened: the parents' quarrel, the woman who shoots, etc. This sequence too ends with a freeze-frame, this time of the two parents during the quarrel. At this point the spectator really begins to better understand the situation. The narration of the facts proceeds with the arrival of the police and the arrest of the parents, intercut with flashbacks that finally show the face of Sydney in his room, meditating on his suicide plan. But everything is in twilight, and even the portions of his face that are shown are inexpressive: despair over his parents' constant fighting has made the boy apathetic and depressed.

After this second version, full of 'explanatory' details, a third version of the event begins. In this case, it is a detailed analysis of a single full frame still image of the building from the other side of the road. The spectator sees Sydney dive off the roof, but as he passes in front of the window of the apartment where his parents are quarrelling, a third freeze-frame halts the action. The screen turns into a sort of blackboard on which a yellow marker tracks and analytically explains the phases of the incident: lines and circles point out the path and the stages of the fall, to the point where the boy was hit by the shotgun. The movement then resumes until the dead body of Sydney reaches the safety net that would have saved his life.

We find three very different accounts of the same facts, and yet all of them are *anempathetic*, since they clarify the course of events without giving them any broader context. Faced with the desperation of a teenager overlooked by his parents, the film chooses to progressively 'cool' this story (which is as a simple anecdote, external to the film narrative, used to support the general hypothesis of the movie: the bizarre power of chance.) This 'system of falls' exemplifies the use of strategies that weaken or even neutralize the classic strategies for spectatorial involvement.

In the first version, the very rapid succession of the shotgun fire, the close-up of Sidney's chest, the still final shot from underneath the safety net, and the body of the character, which seems to literally plunge onto the spectator as though he were a passer-by on the sidewalk, confront the spectator with a barrage of shocks that activate participation at a basic level. The spatial and temporal modes of representation—too close and too fast—leave no room for emotional involvement, especially since the face of the character is semi-hidden, and therefore the access to a well-defined subjectivity and a perspective to align with is denied. The classical dynamic of gazes is reduced to multiple perspectives: overhead shot, frontal shot and its reversal, and a low-angle shot.

In the second version, despite the fact that it is articulated in a more 'classical' style, the process of perceptual, cognitive and emotional subjectivation/objectification is weakened and largely ineffective. In particular, the use of the voice-over and of lighting continue to deprive the spectator of a real emotional attachment to the character. The spectator is not invited to share the pain of Sydney and the reasons for his decision, but rather he is invited to note the bizarre coincidence of the events that lead the young man to be blamed for attempted murder and his mother for manslaughter.

In the third version, everything is scanned and analysed 'scientifically' in detail, almost as though in a study session, through a dissection of space and a repeated crystallization of time. This excessive *distance* and this freezing of action undermine the possibility of any emotional involvement.

In the case of *Magnolia*, therefore, the motif of the fall is used in way that operates outside of the cooperative logic characteristic of the classic alignment mode: the body is too close or too distant, in both cases with no emotional proximity. This programmatic denial of empathy is symptomatic not only of the search for a mere sensory hyperstimulation or, on the other extreme, of 'anaesthesia', but also of the propensity of the contemporary individual, reflected by the cinema, to reject forms of deep sharing. Multiple perspectives, repetition, and fragmentation reveal uncertainty and the inability to make motivated choices. Faced with an existential dilemma, on the one hand we tend towards emotional distancing; on the other, we prefer to explore many possible paths. The first results from the excess of fast-paced editing (first version), the second from the excess of analytical breakdown of continuity (third version). In the middle, the complex narration of events (second version) stands as a kind of point of mediation between the two extremes.

The most important aspect is that when presenting the same event in three different stylistic variations, *Magnolia*'s prologue not only offers the spectator three different forms of experience but makes the equilibrium adjustment process itself explicit. This limit case allows us to identify some fundamental expressive elements that are put in place in order to weaken the empathetic system. These elements consist mainly of different ways of managing emotional alignment through the character's close-ups and the spacetime dimension of movement. In respect to the first factor, *Magnolia* proposes a dissociation of different forms and levels of empathy; in respect to the second factor, a temporal manipulation of representation is proposed. This trend, however, goes well beyond this specific case.

Empathy for the devil

In *American Gigolo* (Schrader 1980) Julian Kay's revenge against his pimp Leon takes place in a fit of madness. First of all, through an exchange of close-ups, we see anger mounting in Julian's face and Leon's hatred towards him. Julian pushes Leon off the balcony of his apartment, and suddenly the two men are in a state of precarious balance and strong tension: Leon finds himself hanging upside down on the balcony as Julian holds his feet. Realizing his guilt, Julian desperately tries to hold Leon, but the latter's boots slowly slip off of his feet… and Leon takes a fatal fall. At the level of the representation, the angles and the shot sizes are multiple: establishing shots and close-ups alternate rapidly, providing the spectator with an overview of events and at the same time focusing on the characters' emotion. A series of objective shots shows Julian's expressions and in particular the grimace that, through the effort being made, tenses his facial muscles. But it is Leon's point of view that is essential. Just after Julian's push, the spectator is optically aligned with the 'negative' character's perspective and sees the city's panorama outside the window, in a few and indistinct frames that embody the abrupt movement that brings Leon upside down over the parapet. The same effect of confused movement and alteration of perception is used to represent the early moments of the fall when Julian's grip slips away.

The entirety of Leon's fall is represented through a single point-of-view shot: the road approaches until the instant of total blackness which corresponds to the fatal impact. Julian's reaction is shown: his face expresses desperation at the gesture of madness he tried to remedy, in vain. The strategy is therefore twofold: on the one hand, the spectator is brought to align himself with Julian's emotional state, until the spurt that draws out the accumulated energy. From that moment on, the alignment is also very physical because his body and face are committed to holding Leon back. But at the same time, the spectator perceptually experiences Leon's dizziness and terror until he falls. Then Julian and his desperate realization of what has happened are shown.

As for Julian, the spectator is offered an alignment built on both his inner psychic emotion and his external physical tension, manifested objectively by the expression of his face and posture of his body, respectively. As for Leon, a strongly destabilizing optical subjective alignment is proposed, one that, through a POV shot, includes both psychic terror and the lack of physical coordination that characterizes the fall. This structure, which is typical of popular narrative films, can be used to draw some generalizations. Especially when the fall narratively functions as a conflict resolution between characters who are opposed in terms of their axiology, a division of alignment levels is offered through a double intensification. While a clear emotional (even ethical) alignment—linked to forms of sympathy developed in respect to the character's axiology—is proposed in respect to the positive character, the optical and kinaesthetic alignment is focused on the negative character.[5] At a precise point in the narrative, the tensive motif of fall creates a 'cooperative interference' of axiological and perceptual alignments.

Re-distancing

The 'cooperative conflict' between differing forms of alignments can also be found, for example, in the final sequence of *The Untouchables* (De Palma 1987). In order to avenge the honour of his murdered friend (so again, an act of pride that aligns with the sympathetic propensity of the spectator), Eliot Ness pushes Frank Nitti off the roof of the courthouse. Again, a complex system of point of view and motor and emotional alignments is proposed. At the end of the first part of the sequence, characterized by acrobatic actions represented by a vertical articulation of shots, Ness arrests Nitti after having rescued him from nearly falling into the void. The two make their way to the door of the stairs to the roof. A shot shows them in the vicinity of the door. Nitti's joke about Ness' friend's death triggers the latter's impulse for revenge. In this precise moment, a *re-distancing* from the door is realized: a shot from Nitti's point of view shows the door as a few meters more distant from the camera than it was in the previous shot. What may appear as a positioning error of the character is in fact a spatial repositioning functional to an energy reloading: a 'run-up' that gives more room to the movement of the characters in the profilmic space. This new and more energetic approach

5 On empathy as an independent and eventually opposite psychological dynamic in respect to moral attitude and the ethics of spectator's engagement, cf. Vaage 2016; Plantinga 2018.

(which corresponds to the violent thrust that Ness is imparting to Nitti) is shown subjectively and realized via a fast zoom that is directed first towards the door but at the last moment turns sharply to the right, towards the void over the edge of the building.

At this point the representation of the fall starts, according to a particular stylistic mode. A long shot shows Nitti pushed by Ness and the first part of the fall. Then a closer frontal shot shows Nitti screaming and flailing his arms as he falls down. The long shot that shows the fall is interspersed with both Ness' and Nitti's close-ups. Also in this case, with each shot the descending movement seems to resume from a point of space in which the character has already been shown in the previous one. Moreover, his movement is slowed down by a progressive *ralenti*, while his scream turns into an echo that merges with the crescendo of a dissonant chord. The fall is therefore represented in a highly unrealistic mode. Above all, Nitti's descent takes a much longer time than would actually be needed to cover the distance between the roof and the street below. The artifice of time dilation here is very marked and consciously experienced by the spectator. The multiple spatial re-distancing, the temporal manipulation, the multiplication of points of view and the acoustic treatment of the representation contribute to slow down the fall of the character both physically and perceptually, and to postpone the moment of impact. By acting as a means of homeostatic balance adjustment, this strategy results in the expansion of energy and in the weakening of the charging tension of the fall. Moreover, the fall ends with the impact of the character on the roof of a car parked in front of the court.

Importantly, the close-ups that characterize the sequence are functional to a clear presentation of the characters' emotions and intentions, which are strongly opposed in term of their axiology. Determination, anger, revenge, hatred, and satisfaction transform Ness' facial expressions during the course of the events (the arrest, the offense, the thrust, the fall, the impact). On the contrary, Nitti's face shows meanness. In sum, while the value alignment is clearly oriented towards sympathy for Ness and antipathy for Nitti, on the optical-motor level it is primarily conveyed through the antagonist's perception and movements.

Slowdown

In *The Untouchables*, the manipulation of the temporal dimension has a purely spatial function, since it is a *re-distancing* that changes a character's position in space rather than a real *slowdown* of action. The alteration of the impression of naturalness of the passage of time—i.e. slow motion—is, however, also a recurring solution intimately connected to the figure of the fall. Take for example the fall in the finale of *The Million Dollar Hotel* (Wenders 2000), in which Tom Tom is revealed to be the murderer of Izzy Goldkiss. During the re-enactment of an imaginary encounter between the two characters, Tom Tom leaves Izzy falling from the roof and decides to go the same way, yielding to one last flight. The first part of the sequence, in which Tom holds Izzy by the collar on the edge of the building, is characterized by a circular movement of the camera around the two characters. After dropping Izzy, Tom takes a long run-up towards the edge of the opposite side of the roof. The entire run is shown in slow motion from a lateral perspective and is interspersed with medium shots of Eloise, who meanwhile appears from the door to the stairs (she is the reason behind both Izzy's murder and Tom Tom's suicide). Tom sees and waves for the last time to the woman without interrupting his run, before jumping towards the street and his death. The descent, still in slow motion, is shown through Tom Tom's POV shot and a slow rotational motion. The impact with the asphalt is represented by an intense white light. The clouds, the roof and the hotel sign appear as viewed from below, as Tom Tom's POV shot from a reversed angle.

This 'first-person fall' is definitely different from that of Leon in *American Gigolo*. Here nothing happens in a gory or sudden way, nor is the spectator led to react instinctively to stimuli, the intensity of which is quite diluted in time and space. The problem, if anything, is being able to make one's own emotion correspond to what is expressed by the characters' faces and movements. Wenders interprets the fall not as revenge, an accident, or a suicide for which the motivation is unknown, but rather as a motivation without a body, or with a body rarefied by the expressive potential of images and sounds. Here the fall means liberation (and in fact constitutes one of the fragments of *Maybe Not*) and does not lead to black and to nothing but rather to a glow that opens onto a new and inverted view of the world—the perspective of a mortal, or already dead, body. In *The Million Dollar Hotel* slow motion is used not so much to emphasize the virtuosity of the character's movement or, reflexively, of the camera movement, but rather to obtain an extended 'temporal space' that, by slowing down or even suspending the natural flow of time, provides a place for the development and deepening of character interiority.

Writing on *photogénie*, Jean Epstein saw the alteration of speed as the decisive 'complication' of movement. Slow motion is a real emotional intensifier; it has represented an attempt, since its first appearance in *The Fall of the House of Usher* (Epstein 1928), to put the stability and the judgment of the spectator into crisis (cf. Epstein 1981; 2012). In the framework of classic Filmology, Étienne Souriau (1953) writes that

> it happens frequently that in certain sequences and sometimes throughout a film, the effects of slowed rhythm are sought. These, however, confer an 'eventual' density upon duration. In general terms, the accelerations or decelerations of this rhythm correspond with our need for excitement or rest, in order to provide us with the optimal psychic dynamics. The pace of this universe is a *psychic rhythm*, calculated as a function of our emotions in order to keep them in a state of constant stress (15, my trans.).[6]

Not surprisingly, Grodal (1997) used slow motion to demonstrate how the temporal manipulation of a film sequence moves the character's action and participation from the telic to the paratelic mode and has an impact on the degree of the spectator's identification (47). Drawing from Grodal, however, I have argued that the tensive motifs are perceived, although in the overall framework of a telic system, within a sub-local paratelic system, by a spectator willing to label the sensory excess as positive and pleasurable. The *slowdown* thus produces an energy modulation, a mitigation of the tension which has the purpose (and effect) of bringing the represented action into the telic system in order to make intelligible an action which would otherwise be only experienced as a physical stimulation. At a psychological level, in fact, the *slowdown* of the fall shifts the focus and the sensitivity of the spectator from action to reflection, restoring teleological tension to an action charged with a purely physical tension. The transition from 'exterior' fall to 'interior' fall is aimed at obtaining a lyrical effect and at digging deep into the character's motivations and intentions. The manipulation of the temporal dimension of action produces a weakening of the energetic charge that brings the stimulation of the tensive motif under the tolerance and reversibility threshold. The excess of the speed with which the character falls can lead to a kind of spectatorial misalignment. In order to reconstitute kinaesthetic empathy, it is necessary for the character to 'wait' for the spectator. Again, we are therefore witnessing the *reembodying* of a *disembodied* alignment,

6 '[I]l arrive fréquemment qu'on cherche dans certaines séquences, et parfois dans tout un film, des effets de rythme ralenti. Mais il s'agit d'une "densité événementielle" de la durée. Et d'une façon générale, ses prestos ou ses andantes sont concertés par rapport à nos besoins d'excitation ou de repos, de manière à nous mettre à notre meilleure allure psychique. Le rythme de cet univers est un *rythme psychique*, calculé par rapport à notre affectivité de manière à l'entretenir dans un état d'incitation constante'.

or the realignment of bodies whose relationships had been disrupted by excessive sensory intensification.

The bearable lightness

Experiments conducted by Belgian experimental psychologist Albert Michotte on the functional relations between motor stimuli and emotions discovered that the qualitative impression of an emotion depends on certain structural features of the movement, such as its speed. 'Rapid movement', writes Michotte (1991b), 'gives the impression of "violence" as opposed to the "gentleness" of slow movement' (107). As Michotte argues, 'the principles which govern the structural organization of perceptions come into play, and the emotional reactions of the agent evoke specific kinetic structures in the observer, the characteristics of which correspond at least partially to the emotions of the former' (110). Therefore, it can be argued that the intensity elicited by the depiction of a falling human body derives from the unusual, uncontrolled nature of the movement resulting from increasing gravitationally induced momentum and the inevitable impact. A falling body is perceived to be subject to the force of attraction exerted by the ideal point of impact—the final point or the goal to which it is directed. In other words, the extreme stimulation and the violence of impact are charged progressively over the course of the movement preceding it as a result of its being perceived as the point of culmination at which accumulated energy discharges instantly.

The researchers of the Institute for Visual Studies at James Madison University, directed by psychologist Sheena Rogers (2013), conducted experiments to study the perception of the performance of particular actions. Video clips representing impactful events (performed by 'anonymous agents' whose face was hidden from subjects) and lasting a few seconds were shown to a group of 20 observers. The events included hands clapping, people jumping, a boxer pounding a punching bag, Jell-O dropping on to a tabletop, a light plastic and a heavy metal baseball bat striking a pillow topped with loose leaves or with flour, and a hammer striking a light bulb gently until it breaks and then striking another lightbulb more forcefully. Each of these actions was presented, in random order, at different speeds: normal, slightly fast (twice normal speed), slightly slow (half normal speed), and slow (a quarter normal speed). Subjects were asked to rate, on a scale of predetermined values, how strong the impact was, how soft or hard the material was, how much effort was exerted in the blow, and how natural the image appeared to be. The results showed a correlation between the speed of the images and the values *perceived* (force exerted, consistency of materials, effort exerted, naturalness of action). The slower the projection of movement was, the lighter the impact appeared and vice versa; similarly, the faster the images were presented the greater the perceived exertion and vice versa. Moreover, the slower the projected actions were, the lighter the materials appeared and vice versa. The most interesting aspect pointed out by Rogers is that the correlation between perception and presentation speed was not measured in accordance with so-called 'external' principles: 'image characteristics are entirely responsible for perception' (157). Regardless of the manipulation of playback speed, events appeared to have a 'true character'. According to Rogers, in fact, within certain parameters of manipulation it is not possible to establish *a priori* what the actual speed of an event is. Therefore, it was the perceived characteristics (strength, impact, effort) and not the speed of images that determined the perceived 'naturalness' of the events. As Rogers writes, 'the dynamics of the moving image are perceived in the same way a directly witnessed, real event would be perceived if the objects were moving at the speeds depicted in the video clips' (157). Thus, for example, the representation in slow motion of a stick hitting a man ensures that this gesture is perceived *objectively* as less violent than it is at normal speed (and, above all, in reality). The 'truth character' of images thus depends on internal dynamics, so that a movement whose natural speed is manipulated acquires its own authenticity and is almost never perceived as unnatural. This happens because these dynamics 'are not decoded or consciously interpreted by the viewer; they are perceived directly and they are irresistible' (157).

Let us return to the cinematic representation of the fall and its mode of perception. In the light of the reflections brought out by Rogers' experiments we can assume that the spectator perceives the movement of the character in slow motion as a movement that is *slow* in itself and not necessarily *slowed*. It is true that generally slow motion takes over when movement at normal speed has already begun, which makes manipulation even more apparent. In this case, cognitive factors of perceptual constancy act to restore, in the spectator's mind, the slowed movement to its 'normal' speed. Despite this compensation, however, the represented movement is *also* sensed as slow, or better, as at a modified speed. The manipulation of time does not affect the image speed, but rather its expressiveness. The *slowed* movement (in relative terms) is perceived as autonomous (in absolute terms). Tom Tom's fall in *The Million Dollar Hotel*, for example, is perceived as a *slow* fall, rather than a *slowed* one. In this way, rather than merely being represented, the symbolic value of this fall is directly experienced by the spectator.

Filling a fall

Another recurring and complex form of strategic management of time dilation in the representation of the fall is what can be called 'memorial filling'. This strategy emphasizes the extreme introspective value and the intrinsic meaning of the descent. In this case inserts of the falling character's life are shown like a sort of 'a whole life that flashes before the eyes'. Whereas in *Wings of Desire* (Wenders 1987) the fall was not represented explicitly—the angel Damiel flies into the arms of his companion Cassiel and soon (with a temporal ellipsis) he awakens on the other side of the Berlin Wall—in its Hollywood remake *City of Angels* (Silberling 1998), the passage of Seth from the angelic to the human condition occurs through an explicitly represented fall, in a much less symbolic and in some way more *physical* form, yet richer with introspective cues. In fact, Seth's fall engages the spectator in a complex and articulated participation. With the usual alternation between high-angle and low-angle shots, the spectator both follows his descending movement in the environment and accesses his intentions: he jumps to become mortal and to love as a man. And, with the usual insertion of frontal medium shots and close-ups, the spectator can see his facial and postural expressions and focuses on his emotions.

At the climax of this first group of shots there is a close-up of the character's closed eyes. Then a series of images of his most significant memories begins, a sort of *flashback* composed of black-and-white fragments. The spectator has access to his mind and his memory and realizes the reasons that led him to the decision to turn his angelic condition into a human one. On closer inspection, this memorial flow consists in turn of images of movements of other falling bodies, of legs, arms, hands, tears, dives... These are all images showing the human body and referring to humanity through its body materiality. Seth's fall is shown entirely in slow motion, a form of intensification of movement filled with the externalization of the content of his mind: a temporal dilution that generates a psychic space, an empathetic journey into the affective memories of the character.

A similar example can be found in the finale of *Open Your Eyes* (Amenábar 1997). After discovering that everything he experiences is an oneiric illusion, César decides to jump from the top floor of a building and back to reality. Before the fall, the camera is behind César and approaches him, moving upwards and eliciting a sense of vertigo in the spectator. As César dives into the void, the spectator experiences the fall through a multiplicity of points of view and through formal techniques that show and embody the growing tension of the movement and the inner state of the character.

Let us compare *Open Your Eyes* with its Hollywood remake. In the last scene of *Vanilla Sky* (Crowe 2001) the protagonist David Aames greets his ghosts and launches into space to return to his real life. The fall, however, is represented in a very different way than in Amenábar's film. Even the way David jumps from the ledge (he runs) and in which he leans forward towards the void elicit a much stronger sense of vertigo in the spectator. By contrast, in his descent towards the soil, David does not scream as César does. Instead, a sweet and heavenly music accompanies (and contrasts with) his fast descent. The alternation of subjective and objective shots is similar to that of *Open Your Eyes*, but during the last few meters, the slow motion begins and the character's memories are introduced, like Seth's in *City of Angels*. We see snapshots of his childhood, the happy moments spent with the women in his life—Sofia and Julie—in increasingly rapid succession, until they become a barrage of barely perceptible frames. The image returns to show his face and finally, through a POV shot, the point of impact with the ground accompanied by illumination, as for Tom Tom in *The Million Dollar Hotel*, to symbolize the passage to another life. This mode of representation of the fall is much more emphatic on an emotional level and it is aimed at communicating the character's inner state, especially through the *slowdown* of the images, which leads directly into his memory and into his interiority.

Precipitation

Let us try to formulate some concluding remarks. The basic hypothesis is that the tensive motif of the fall constitutes a principle of homeostatic balance adjustment through a modulation between the telic motivational system and the paratelic motivational system. The sensory overstimulation that derives from the 'excited' movement of the fall is mitigated and contained within the threshold of 'experienceability' by the film itself on behalf of the spectator through strategies of spatiotemporal expansion and psychic 'filling'.

One of the formal constants in the representation of the fall is *multiple perspectives*. The movement of falling is generally shown from several points of view in order to make the view composite and comprehensive: high-angle, frontal and low-angle shots; long shots and close-ups; and point-of-view and objective shots alternate in a kaleidoscope of *positions* of both the character and the spectator. In order to meet the cognitive demand of narrative contextualization, the environment of the scene is shown in its entirety so that the height from which the character falls and the path that the latter performs can be also visually communicated. These contextual and informative factors affect the determination of the level of 'inevitability' of the fall and thus the pathemic investment that the spectators are willing to put into play.

The representation focuses in particular on facial expression, belonging not so much to the falling character (when he is not the protagonist), but rather to other characters present on the scene (usually the protagonist). The key factor for the 'emotional reading' of the featured events and for promoting spectatorial identification is, in fact, the expression on the face of the character that causes or witnesses the fall: for example, Julian's desperate effort in *American Gigolo* communicates repentance, and Ness' contentedness in *The Untouchables* expresses satisfaction with the accomplished vengeance. Particularly in cases in which the character's value system is opposite to ours, a split between axiological alignment and kinaesthetic alignment may occur. The spectator is led to experience the fall of the negative character on a sensorimotor level, while emotionally sympathizing with the protagonist.

A recurring and decisive stylistic means involves the rhythmic-temporal component of the representation of the fall. The fast pace of shots embodies the convulsion of the fall, which in fact begins to discharge the energy accumulated during its previous stages, but at the same time gains the energy generated by the acceleration of the body in a space dominated by the force of gravity. At this point, however, a *slowdown* occurs: the film carries out a manipulation of the temporal dimension in order to weaken the energy and to prolong the duration (and the effects) of the fall, thus modulating the balance between spectacle and narrative as a function of the homeostasis challenged by energy overload. The slowdown may consist of a spatial *re-distancing*, a kind of recoiling or reloading, often corresponding to a change of perspective, or, more significantly, a real extension or expansion of the psychological space of the character caused by manipulating the timing of the movement through slow motion. Through this move, the fall offers a passage to the inner state of the character that leads the spectator to experience the movement of descent not (only) as slowed down, but as slow in itself—a moment almost outside of time. This opening is in fact often *filled* with different intentions and strategies. For example, the emphasis aroused by slow motion can acquire a symbolic value or give space to memorial materials that externalize the interior of the character and his motivations. At least for a few moments, the force of gravity is weakened or even annulled. Slow motion allows the spectator to fully appreciate all the phases of the movement, making room for a multiplicity of perspectives and enabling a non-fleeting vision. Above all, it has the function of 'lightening' the fall's tensive charge by diffusing its energy and emphasizing its emotional and symbolic value.

Looking at the fall as though under a microscope and considering this motif as a 'punctual' moment of energetic intensification functional to narrative 'linearity', at least four phases can be identified. First of all, there is an initial phase of *establishing* in which the situation is described and the spectator is positioned. The alternation of close-ups and establishing/re-establishing shots that generally introduce, punctuate, and conclude the motif, has the function of offering, respectively, a focalized and close view and a comprehensive and distanced perspective. This combination of focalization and contextualization distinguishes the spectator of the film from any possible internal witness, whose perspective would be limited to one position in the environment and would not be facilitated by the 'omnipresent' gaze of the camera and the 'vantage point' it offers. At this point there is a more or less prolonged phase of *loading*, involving above all phenomena of motor synchronization. The extreme emphasis in the often 'verticalized' angles of the framings, images going out of focus, and the rapid, unstable, and oscillating movement of the camera, gives rise to perceptual and cognitive confusion. At this point a phase of *fulfillment* begins, in which there is a more or less sudden discharge of accumulated energy. The effect of this generation of energy continues to spread in a phase of energetic *reverberation* that leads the spectator to cognitive objectivation of the emotion, to reflexive re-elaboration or even interiorization that results from the connection between immediate sensorimotor and emotional experience and its symbolic, ethical, or moral valence.

The cinema thus addresses the tension of the fall by using it as an opportunity for reflection that embodies the need to better see—and *feel*—a movement that is too fast and too precipitous. Paradoxically, slow motion produces a state of suspension (and yet not a breaking) of narrative causality by acting on the *intentionality* of movement, namely on its being aimed at a *goal*. In the motif of the fall, slow motion, in fact, distances the moment from its inevitable outcome—the impact—and weakens its trauma by postponing it, though without erasing its ineluctability.

Bibliography

Apter, Michael J. 1982. *The Experience of Motivation: The Theory of Psychological Reversals*. London: Academic Press.

Arnheim, Rudolf. 1989. *Parables of Sun Light: Observations on Psychology, the Arts, and the Rest*. University of California Press.

Bachelard, Gaston. 1988. *Air and Dreams: An Essay on the Imagination of Movement*. Translated by Edith Farrell & Frederick Farrell. Dallas: Dallas Institute of Humanities and Culture.

Bernard, Claude. 1949. *Introduction to the Study of Experimental Medicine*. Translated by Henry C. Greene. New York: Henry Schuman.

Branigan, Edward. 1992. *Narrative Comprehension and Film*. London/New York: Routledge.

Cannon, Walter B. 1926. 'Physiological Regulation of Normal States: Some Tentative Postulates Concerning Biological Homeostatics'. In *A Charles Richet. Ses amis, ses collègues, ses élèves*. Edited by Auguste Pettit, 91-93. Paris: Éditions Médicales.

Cannon, Walter B. 1929. 'Organization for Physiological Homeostasis'. *Physiological Reviews*. 9 (3 July): 399-431. DOI:10.1152/physrev.1929.9.3.399.

Cannon, Walter B. 1932. *The Wisdom of the Body*. New York: W.W. Norton & Company.

Damasio, Antonio R. 1999. *The Feeling of What Happens: Body and Emotion in the Making of Consciousness*. New York: Harcourt.

di Chio, Federico. 2011. *L'illusione difficile. Cinema e serie tv nell'età della disillusione*. Milano: Bompiani.

Epstein, Jean. 1981. 'The Spirit of Slow Motion'. Translated by Tom Milne. *Afterimage*. 10: 34-35.

Epstein, Jean. 2012. *Critical Essays and New Translations*. Edited by Sarah Keller & Jason N. Paul. Amsterdam: Amsterdam University Press. DOI:10.1515/9789048513840.

Foucault, Michel, & Ludwig Binswanger. 1993. *Dream and Existence*. Edited by Keith Hoeller. Translated by Forrest Williams & Jacob Needleman. Atlantic Highlands, NJ: Humanities Press.

Frijda, Nico H. 1987. 'Emotion, Cognitive Structure, and Action Tendency'. *Cognition & Emotion*. 1 (2): 115-143. DOI:10.1080/02699938708408043.

Gallagher, Shaun, & Dan Zahavi. 2007. *The Phenomenological Mind: An Introduction to Philosophy of Mind and Cognitive Science*. London: Routledge.

Greimas, Algirdas J. 1983. *Structural Semantics: An Attempt at a Method*. Translated by Daniele McDowell, Ronald Schleifer, & Alan Velie. Lincoln: University of Nebraska Press.

Grodal, Torben. 1997. *Moving Pictures: A New Theory of Film Genres, Feelings, and Cognition*. Oxford: Clarendon Press.

Michotte, Albert. 1991b. 'The Emotions Regarded as Functional Connections'. In Thinès, Costall, & Butterworth, eds., 103-116.

Plantinga, Carl. 2018. *Screen Stories: Emotion and the Ethics of Engagement*. New York: Oxford University Press.

Propp, Vladímir J. 1958. *Morphology of the Folktale*. Bloomington: Indiana University Press.

Robin, Charles. 1853. *Traité de chimie anatomique et physiologique normal et pathologique, ou Des principes immédiats normaux morbides qui constituent et le corps de l'homme et des mammifères, Vol. 1*. Paris: J.-B. Baillière.

Rogers, Sheena, 'Truth, Lies, and Meaning in Slow Motion Images'. In Shimamura, ed., 149-164.

Souriau, Étienne. 1953. *L'univers filmique*. Paris: Flammarion.

Vaage, Margrethe Bruun. 2016. *The Antihero in American Television*. New York/ London: Routledge.

IV Impact

Experiencing the unrepresentable

Abstract
The fall tends inalterably to its completion: its inevitable end is the impact, a literally traumatic moment that is programmatically 'censored' precisely due to both the visceral and psychological violence that its explicit display would cause. Inspired by Alejandro G. Iñárritu's short film *11'9"01*, the chapter 'Impact. Experiencing the unrepresentable' describes the ways in which the film spectator experiences the *non-representation* of the cinematic human body hitting the ground, beginning with a reflection on the tragic events of September 11, 2001. A discussion of the amodal perception of occluded movements and its neural correlates will show that contemporary cinema adopts a series of formal strategies in order to negotiate with the trauma and make the 'unrepresentable' experienceable.

Keywords: 9/11, Unrepresentability, Intermedial imagination, Amodal perception

> It is the pleasurable experience of an insensate, animal superiority that allows us in the cinema at last to look things in the eye that would force us to look away if we saw them in reality.
>
> —Béla Balázs, *Visible Man*, 1924 (2010, 65)

Black flashes

The screen is completely black. After a few seconds, an array of melodious, obsessive, repetitive, and hypnotic voices—almost like a prayer—, progressively emerge. From time to time the sound of a thud can also be heard. Suddenly, for a short fraction of a second, an image brightens the black screen.

D'Aloia, A., *Neurofilmology of the Moving Image. Gravity and Vertigo in Contemporary Cinema*. Taylor & Francis Group 2021
DOI: 10.5117/9789463725255_CH04

Darkness lingers for another thirty seconds, while the volume of the noise increases and mingles with the sound of a dissonant chord. At this point a second flash briefly appears onscreen. The voice of a newscaster, some notes played on piano, the noise of an airplane, the rumble of an impact and an explosion, the frightened and appalled reactions of people, the opening of a TV news broadcast, the exclamations of a reporter, and an ambulance siren can be heard in quick succession. The third flash arrives a minute after the second, together with the noise of a thunderclap. This image is a bit longer than the previous and the eyes have enough time to better focus on its content: a falling body descends over the background of the grey and reticular wall of a skyscraper, accompanied by its shadow projected on the surface of the building. Then total blackness returns. The speaker's voice overlaps with those of the reporters, who speak various languages. After thirty seconds, a fourth flash, and then a fifth, follow—this time after only fifteen seconds. The image remains onscreen for at least an entire second: the vertical shape of one of New York City Twin Towers is now clearly visible. Two bodies wrapped in smoke fall. The situation is now definitively clear and one realizes that these are images of people trapped in the World Trade Center's top floors on September 11, 2001, those who preferred to throw themselves into the void rather than suffocate from smoke—a last, liberating flight into death's embrace. Then black again, and the noise of a thump, like the impact of a heavy body on a pile of plates; and a sixth image, and then a seventh, still slightly longer and with a shorter black interval between them than the previous ones. Finally, the excitement abates and leaves room for the emergence of emotion. The rhythm slows down; the eighth image remains visible for at least five seconds. Black reappears once more for a minute and a half. During this interval, the farewell phone calls of the passengers on the airplanes that crashed into the Towers and the crowd screaming in the street can be heard distinctly.

At this point, the same eight images reappear in rapid succession, separated only by a black fade. Then there is black again and the loud noise of the skyscraper collapsing can be heard for an endless minute. Suddenly the chaos breaks off and, for a few seconds in absolute silence, the images of the collapse appear onscreen. The screen turns black again and string music can be heard along with female voices, similar to those already heard in the opening. It is time for reflection and contemplation. The screen lights up slowly, until it becomes completely white. And on the white background a question in Arabic text appears, followed by the English translation: 'Does God's light guide us or blind us?'

Assembled from television images and videos shot by passers-by around the World Trade Center on that tragic day, the Mexican segment of *11'09"01*

– *September 11* (2002), directed by Alejandro González Iñárritu, draws from factual materials and recomposes them in a way that intentionally obscures visual perception of those materials. While on the level of sound the stimuli are literally crowded together, the most significant visual feature is the black screen. Slashed by short visual flashes, the image of the trauma is dosed—released a little at a time in unintelligible instants, becoming progressively clearer. What has been removed—it seems for Iñárritu—can only emerge through progressive fragments that burst into the visual void. The absence of the image is the only way that the *unrepresentable* can be represented. Unrepresentability seems to be the condition for the representability of the catastrophic and shocking event: the untold must be told through the impossibility of its telling.

Georges Didi-Huberman (2008) has written significant pages on the need to represent traumatic events. According to Didi-Huberman, despite the horror of certain unimaginable images (particularly of the Shoah), 'we must contemplate them, take them on and try to comprehend them. *Images in spite of all*: in spite of our own inability to look at them as they deserve; in spite of our own world, full, almost choked, with imaginary commodities' (3). The risk, Didi-Huberman points out, is twofold because of the 'double regime' of images—a dialectic between truth and darkness that makes images inadequate and inaccurate as we ask them to tell 'the whole truth' and, conversely, makes them simulacra as we take too little from them. The images of 9/11 seem to perfectly embody this dialectic, being at the same time too referential and too spectacular, or rather: too realistic to look real. As Slavoj Žižek (2002) wrote in relation to the collapse of the World Trade Center, '[t]he Real which returns has the status of a(nother) semblance: *precisely because it is real, that is, on account of its traumatic/excessive character, we are unable to integrate it into (what we experience as) our reality, and are therefore compelled to experience it as a nightmarish apparition*' (19).

The images of 9/11, we must say, seem to aggravate the readability of the archival image denounced by Didi-Huberman because of a double excess. First, there is a quantitative excess, which seems to add to the volume of 'imaginary commodities'. As Marco Belpoliti (2005) writes, '[t]he numerous images and words we have of this event—photographs, movies, audio recordings, written testimonies—[...] reveal the impossibility of representing the event and its enormity' (50, my trans.).[1] As infinite versions of the same

1 'Le numerose immagini e parole che possediamo—fotografie, filmati, registrazioni audio, testimonianze scritte—di questo evento [...] rivelano l'impossibilità di rappresentare l'evento e la sua enormità.'

horror, these overwhelming images fail to communicate the trauma. On the contrary, for Richard Grusin (2004; 2010) the mediatic reaction to 9/11 obeys to a logic of 'premediation' by which media offer a preventive negotiation and acceptance of the trauma implied in shocking events before they happen. This anticipation has the effect to diminish the level of anxiety for the uncertainty of the future.

Second, there is a qualitative excess that produces, so to speak, an aesthetic twist. In Iñárritu's minifilm, darkness is no longer an intrinsic limit, but a key feature of an intentional aesthetic principle and a new form of testimony: black is not a perceptual *absence*, but rather a perceptual *presence* as the result of an *affective saturation*. In this sense, many authors reflected on the critical nexus between the affective and spectacular quality of traumatic images after 9/11 (Baudrillard 2002, Sontag 2003), their testimonial value, and our reactions in front of 'intolerable images' (Rancière 2012). Luc Boltanski (1999), however, prophetically anticipated the issue: 'the presentation of the unfortunate in his horrific aspect is the only one which makes possible the communication of that unpresentable horror which overcomes the spectator and which is none other than the horror residing within him and which defines his condition' (116).

Reality and intermediality

In the wake of this philosophical reflection, from here on we will see how unrepresentability—conceived as a strategy for representing traumatic events—is an inherent element of the spectator's physiology and of the phenomenology of the film experience. Based on the interpretation of several neuroscientific experiments, which in turn confirm the intuitions of experimental psychology, I will argue that cinema actually incorporates basic 'removal' and 'censorship' mechanisms that are activated in the individual when violent events are shown. Furthermore, I shall argue that this reflects the perceptive attitudes of the spectator and often works in the same way as his brain and mind do in order to make the excess of events which are otherwise unbearable and unavoidable acceptable—in particular, the impact of the human body hitting the ground.

This argument seems to be more valid when the representation directly or explicitly refers to factual events that have happened historically in reality, and that therefore enter the imagination with reference to the real world and real history. It should be noted that this referentiality has to be understood not so much on the semiotic level (indexicality of the image), but rather on the level of the spectator's consciousness. The latter's awareness that the events have actually occurred has a decisive impact on the emotional level of the experience. This would seem to be true in the case of Iñárritu's minifilm on 9/11, since found footage materials (amateur videos of the attacks and their consequences) are deliberately used in order to elicit deep feelings and prompt critical reflection. However, as mentioned above, the referentiality of these images is perceived, as it were, retrospectively in the moment of the viewing of the film and was not perceived distinctly at the time of their generation: those images were not only too realistic, but also too *spectacular* to look real. Those catastrophic images seemed in fact to be taken from a Hollywood disaster film. As pointed out by Žižek, the factual *and* spectacular nature of images is a specific feature of media representation of historical events, particularly in the case of collective traumatic ones. In providing the images of the 9/11 attack and its immediate aftermath, Iñárritu offers a treatment that, although not a documentary, aims to restore the character of reality to events rather than to confer an imaginary character on reality. Representing 9/11 cinematographically, in fact, means mainly reflecting on the emotional effects of the trauma of that tragic day on Western society through an audio-visual form of thinking and dealing with loss.

In an essay entirely devoted to 9/11, Mauro Carbone (2007) refers to the Iñárritu minifilm primarily to indicate art's ability to reform an event in our imagination, to reduce its strength, its enormity, and its excessiveness to a more 'human' dimension, to transform the catastrophe into something more tolerable. Iñárritu achieves this purpose by refusing to succumb to the desire to narrate his version of events (17-18).

Another Italian philosopher, Pietro Montani (2010), refers to the cinematic representation of 9/11 to explain the notion of 'intermedia imagination', i.e. the reflux of reality in its different forms of discursive elaboration by the media (xii). According to Montani, the referentiality of the world is configured through the relationship between various technological image-making devices, as this affects the '*irreducible otherness of the real world*' (xiv, my trans.).[2] In this sense, it is no longer the authenticity of images that is at stake, but rather their ability to provide an *authentication* of the real. The intermedia process takes place as a critical remediation (Bolter & Grusin 1999), achieved by the cinema using amateur and TV images. By shifting the spectator's attention from content to representational modes—from referentiality to spectacularity—the cinema is able to suggest a reflective activity not so

2 '[*I*]*rriducibile alterità del mondo reale*'.

much on the catastrophe, but rather on the ability of different forms of the audio-visual image to 'recapture reality', specifically through the logic of intermediality rather than that of multimediality (Montani 2010, 8-9). As Montani writes, 'it is not so much in the relationship between the image and the world that the difference may be appreciated again, as in the relationship *between* images, or rather *between* the different media components and the various technical formats of the audio-visual image. It is this intermediate *space* [...] that is their very place of authentication' (24, my trans.).[3]

In another film on the subject, *Fahrenheit 9/11* (Moore 2004), cited by Montani, the reconstruction of the catastrophic event takes place indirectly, through denial or postponement: the image is replaced by a black background and perception is totally delegated to the soundtrack (screams, explosions, collapsing noise) and what is visually shown refers to the reactions of those who have witnessed the events (fleeing people and horrified faces). Iñárritu's minifilm adopts the same strategy but, according to Montani, in a more radical way, since it 'intends to use a generalized and distressing image of the visible' (38, my trans.)[4] and through work 'in which the image invoking the negation is systematic' (38, my trans.).[5] In both cases, however, the fundamental point is that, although 'censored', the event does not lose its contact with reality. The image, in fact, necessarily owes a *debt* to reality when it deposits its traces in the individual memorial archive: 'It is not enough that the imagination asserts its free constructiveness, it is also necessary that it comply with the *reality* of the trace (even if archived, as in the case of an erasure, in the form of removal)' (xii, my trans.).[6] The black screen then becomes the image of erasure and removal, the representation of the unrepresentable: 'The real escapes any direct viewing through images, but it is precisely in this escape that it affects the residual space in the archive—a rest, a wound, a deletion—for a deferred elaboration' (xii, my trans.).[7] Representation of 9/11 is the most obvious manifestation of the

3 '[N]on è tanto nel rapporto tra immagine e mondo che la differenza può farsi di nuovo apprezzare, quanto nel rapporto tra immagini, o meglio tra le diverse componenti mediali e i diversi formati tecnici dell'immagine audiovisiva. È questo spazio intermedio [...] il luogo proprio dell'autenticazione.'

4 '[I]ntende avvalersi di un'immagine generalizzata e angosciosa del visibile.'

5 '[I]n cui il ricorso alla negazione dell'immagine è sistematico.'

6 'Non basterà tuttavia che l'immaginazione faccia valere la sua libera costruttività, bisognerà anche che essa rispetti la realtà della traccia (quand'anche archiviata, come una cancellatura, nella forma della rimozione).'

7 'Il reale sfugge a ogni presa diretta delle immagini, è vero, ma è proprio in questo suo sottrarsi che esso incide nell'archivio lo spazio residuale—un resto, una ferita, una cancellatura—per un'elaborazione differita.'

obscurity that affects the status of the contemporary image. As Montani concludes,

> What the imagination *can show* [...] is precisely *its own collapse and its own limits.* In this way, that inadequacy turns [...] into a unique form of negative exhibition which allows the appearance, in the background of the represented, even of something that announces its *insurmountable difference* in respect to the representable (40, my trans.).[8]

The tunnel affect

The fundamental hypothesis of this chapter, also discussed in regard to fictional films, is that the spectator experiences the unexperienceable through physiological reactions based on brain mechanisms and psychological perceptual processes that ensure the automatic 'completion' of 'incomplete' experience, as in the case of the perception of a movement of which an intermediate stage is not shown. The basis of the argumentation are the psychological studies on *amodal perception* and its emphasis on its bodily characteristics and on 'sensorimotor understanding'.

Neurophysiological experiments have validated the hypothesis that the observer tends to complete a goal-directed movement at a neural level, even if the final stage of that movement is not displayed. Filion, Washburn and Gulledge (1996) determined that macaques could represent the unperceived movements of a stimulus. These findings were the product of subjects being tested on tasks in which they needed to chase or shoot at a moving target, which either remained visible throughout, or became invisible during parts of its trajectory. The experiment demonstrated that this breed of monkey is both capable of extrapolating movement and of processing the fleeting disappearance of a stimulus. This capability has also been recognized in human beings. Additionally, Vilayanur Ramachandran and Stuart Anstis (1986) conducted a series of experiments on the perception of apparent motion and demonstrated that when an object is replaced by a larger object in the visual field, the observer continues to perceive the *existence* of the first object as if it were occluded rather than absent.

8 '[C]iò che l'immaginazione può mostrare [...] è precisamente il suo stesso collasso e il suo stesso limite. Con il che l'inadeguatezza si converte [...] in una peculiare forma di esibizione negativa che lascia apparire, sullo sfondo del rappresentato, anche qualcosa che denuncia la sua insuperabile disparatezza nei confronti del rappresentabile.'

This 'continuity of existence', studied relatively recently in both neurobiology and psychology of perception, was earlier investigated by experimental psychologists. Indeed, Filion et al. (1996) experiment provides the neurophysiological basis for the famous demonstrations of the tunnel effect on human beings already identified and described separately by Luke Burke (1952), Alan Glynn (1954), and Albert Michotte (Michotte, Thinès & Crabbé 1967), wherein a moving object is seen to pass behind an occluder before re-emerging as the same object. These results suggest that, even if hidden or implied, all the phases of a movement are experienced by the observer through both a neural simulation and a cognitive completion process. In psychological terms, the completion of movement could be explained by recourse to the notion of 'phenomenal permanence' (Michotte 1950). Movement, more than any other stimuli provided in media consumption, is connected to motor action and activates *amodal* perception. Even though partially occluded, the movement is *amodally* experienced as unitary. In perceptual terms, the mind experiences specific phenomena that correspond to fundamental notions underpinning a spontaneous, non-critical understanding of the physical world. These notions include the materiality of objects, humans' preservation of identity through substantial changes (movement, metamorphosis), the continuity of existence despite the presence of discontinuities in experience, and actions exerted upon each other (causality) or in relation to each other (escape, chase) (Michotte 1963).

In the case of Iñárritu's minifilm, the 'obscured' image is an intermediate stage of movement, and the spectator does not always experience the occlusion of the movement of the same body. However, the continuity of direction and the constancy of dimensions of different bodies (represented with different shots) perceived by the spectator give unity to the perception of movement. By virtue of the fact that individual physical bodies are too far away to be clearly identified, the object of perception is not the individual falls, but the discerned movement in the broad sense. Thanks to processes of perceptual unification and neural mechanisms of completion, the intermittent movement of the falls is perceived as *single and continuous.*

I must now point out another level of unrepresentability in the re-elaboration of 9/11 offered by Iñárritu. There are in fact some phases of the movement that are perhaps even more unrepresentable than those that are *materially* darkened. What the film *does not show,* and the audience *does not see,* are the initial and final moments of the fall. That is, the moment of the dramatic decision to die by throwing oneself into the void instead of suffocating or burning alive, and the moment when the flight ends, i.e. the impact with the ground, which is only evoked acoustically by a noise in an unspecified location in space. These are precisely the moments of the fall that amateur images of passers-by were unable to record—the departure and the arrival, the detachment and the impact.

On a deeper level of reasoning, it can be pointed out that what the film hides is not so much the fall as the despair of the decision and the horror of crashing onto the ground. How can cinema also incorporate these aspects into its formal solutions for dealing with the irreproducibility of traumatic events? The impact of the body on the ground, conceived of as a traumatic moment at both physical and psychological levels, is a tensive motif quite different from the fall. The impact is in all respects a motif that simultaneously intensifies and compensates for the perception of the spectator: a moment in which all the energy loaded over the course of the fall flows and instantly discharges, generating an energetic reverberation. The effect is that of producing, on the part of the spectator, a visceral 'defensive' response: we tend to close or cover our eyes in order to avoid seeing the excessively violent events shown onscreen. By mirroring the spectator's response, the 'darkening' of the visual field proposed by the film aims at mitigating the traumatic effects without precluding a complete experience, as the experiments suggest.

It is interesting to note that the '(self)censorship' of cinematic impact is also valid in respect to fictional events, since it is embedded in biological (but also psychological) functions that developed in human evolution. The need to *not see*—or see a little, or little by little—and the modes of representation of this necessity reverberate in cinematic fictional worlds in contexts that the spectator knows are not real. In order to question how fiction cinema uses the tensive dynamic of the impact to give the spectator the experience of a *non-experience*, let us return to *Maybe Not,* a case discussed in the previous chapter. This video provides an overview of falls in contemporary cinema. In the first part of the video, the impact is repeatedly postponed in order to leave room for the chain of falls. Only in the third part is the impression of continuity of motion given by the juxtaposition of the falls broken and impacts shown, but through special modes. In the first case (from *Graveyard of Honor*) the impact is represented indirectly through a splash of blood (deliberately exaggerated in quantity, as is typical in Miike's films) on the external wall of the building, in front of the point of impact. Thus, the spectator does not see the body as it hits the ground; rather, the material consequences of the impact are shown. In the second case (from *Old Boy*), the character falls on a car roof in the background, while the focus of attention is directed towards the character's face as he walks towards the camera. In the third case (from the opening of *Graveyard of Honor*), the fall is represented through a progressive series of blood spatters on various surfaces. Here, too, an improbable amount of blood is released and the slow motion increases the symbolic emphasis at the expense of realism. The last fall (from *Lethal Weapon*) is shown from the inside of a car: the hood is dented as the body of the character falls from above.

As *Maybe Not* illustrates, when presenting an extreme experience, such as the impact of a human body, filmmakers employ technical and aesthetic means to make the stimulation of the senses and meaning both acceptable and experienceable. In order to illuminate the correlation between neural and cognitive processes, a more systematic analysis of the stylistic devices used to represent impact in such a way that engages the spectator's brain and mind activity is required. This analysis involves the identification of a series of approaches used to negotiate the representable and the unrepresentable by filmically embodying some basic human perceptual and visceral physiological reactions.

Unrepresented impacts

A first common strategy is to completely avoid the presentation of the impact. The latter is 'censored' via a variety of strategies, especially where the pact between the spectator and the film requires that the world of film function, predominantly at least, in accordance with the physical rules that govern the natural world (that is to say, in cases in which the fall would cause the character serious injuries or even death).

The most frequent specific mode of this strategy is the *replacement* of the impact with another shot, i.e. cutting away before the character hits the ground. At least two variants may be identified.

The first is replacing the impact with its *emotional effect on a witness*. Usually, the shot that would feature the impact is omitted in favour of a shot depicting the reaction of a character that witnesses the fall. It should be stressed that this reaction shot showcases a response intended to echo the one provoked in the spectator-*of*-the-film. Examples can be found in both classical-era and post-classical Hollywood films including *Trapeze* (1956), an example discussed in Chapter I, where the dramatic result of Mike Ribble's stunt is replaced by a re-establishing shot of the reaction of the circus audience. Even in the prologue of Alfred Hitchcock's *Vertigo* (1958), evoked several times in *Maybe Not*, the impact of Scottie Ferguson's colleague hitting the ground is replaced by a close-up of his acrophobic expression while he is hanging from the eaves of the building from which his colleague has fallen in the attempt to rescue him.

A second method consists in replacing the impact with the *material effects on the surrounding environment.* As noted above, in *Lethal Weapon* a car roof is smashed by the impact, in a shot taken from the passenger seat. In *Graveyard of Honor,* the blood spatter on the window replaces the impact.

These two replacement strategies are often combined with one another. A particularly interesting case is the fall of Captain Oliver Queenan in *The Departed* (Scorsese 2006). The slow motion and acoustic suspension through which the fall is represented oppose the excitement of the events and the heightening sound. The body falls outside the entrance of the building, right in front of undercover agent Billy Costigan, with a splash of blood that stains his hands. Costigan's abrupt and involuntary reaction is intended to reflect that of the spectator turning her head quickly, as though to express horror and despair.

Another widely used concealment strategy is *obscuration,* i.e. the replacement of the moment of the impact with a monochromatic frame, signifying the character's death or the interruption, even temporarily, of his perceptive faculties.

The first and most common obscuration strategy can be defined as *subjective black.* The falling movement is displayed, at least in part, by POV shots of the character falling, thereby enabling the moment of impact to coincide with total visual obscuration as the screen turns abruptly to black, as for example with Alex DeLarge's suicide attempt in *A Clockwork Orange* (Kubrick 1971), or in the finale of the already cited *Open Your Eyes,* in which the protagonist jumps from the top floor of a building and falls until his vision is blocked (represented by total blackness) after he puts his arms in front of him immediately before impact.

The second strategy can be defined as *objective black*: the insertion of black frames to stand in for the impact also characterizes cases in which the body lands directly on the camera lens, thus covering the visual field—an example is Richard Brown's suicide in *The Hours* (Daldry 2002). To realize this type of 'blackening', the camera location (i.e. the spectator's optical point of view) needs to be on the ground level, in correspondence with the expected point of impact.

Extreme over-illumination (rich in symbolic value) is another variant of obscuration: it can be called *whitening.* In *The Million Dollar Hotel,* for example, blinding white concludes Tom Tom's slow-motion suicidal fall. A similar effect is used during the final scene of *Vanilla Sky,* in which David launches himself into the void to return to his real life. The inclusion of white frames symbolizes the achromatic transition from one form of life (dream) to another (reality). Similarly, in *City of Angels* Seth decides to leave his angelic eternal life to become human. In this case, darkness is broken by a transition from the black-and-white photography used to convey the character's life as an angel to the colour imagery employed to express human existence. This transition is also used in Wenders' *Wings of Desire*, on which *City of Angels* was based.

Obscuration is also sometimes combined with replacement. In *American Gigolo*, another film analysed in the previous chapter, Leon's fall is presented through POV shots, with the moment of impact conveyed first by black frames, before being underscored by reaction shots of Julian, who caused Leon's fall.

Both replacement and obscuration eschew the presentation of impact but differ in terms of their psychological effects. Replacement mirrors the ideal reaction elicited from the spectator. Conversely, obscuration is an expressive perceptual representation of the occlusion: at the exact moment of impact, the film exploits the spectator's desire to *not* see. The screen may turn to black so as to occlude the 'unrepresentable', yet in doing so makes the unrepresentable 'experienceable' (at a more than merely neurophysiological level).

Lastly, it is also possible for the impact's representation to occur only acoustically. Not by chance, the process of the disambiguating and emotional interpretation of fragmentary information that is progressively released in Iñárritu's *11'9"01* is delegated to acoustic perception. As Michel Chion (1994) notes, the eye is characterized by its ability to select, exclude, and particularize; the ear, however, can only plunge into a continuous space that is hardly definable or controllable. Whereas the spectator can close her eyes when she does not want to see, it is more difficult to avoid hearing and it is less common to stop one's ears. In this sense the voices of witnesses, reporters, commentators, and victims, and the noises of bursts, blasts, explosions, and music in the finale are stimuli that allow the spectator to succeed in clarifying the content of the film and gain consciousness of the formal intent of the deliberate choice to not represent the trauma visually.

Cushioned crashes

In physically realistic fictional worlds there are also cases in which the impact is not censored, at least not totally. The impact is fully or partially visible on the screen, although in representational forms that attenuate its violent effects, so as to make it acceptable to the spectator.

The opening of *The Happening* (Night Shyamalan 2008) offers an interesting case of weakened impacts. The camera rotates around four workers at a construction site in Manhattan while they joke during a break. Suddenly, a body falls on a pile of material behind them, in the background of the frame, at a point partially covered by the shoulder of one of the men in the foreground. The four men approach the site where the body has crashed to aid to their colleague, who has fallen from the scaffolding. Moments later a thud and the sound of fracturing bones can be heard, at the height of a dissonant chord that increases the drama of the circumstances. While a long shot from above shows the four men turning towards this second fallen body, a hand appears and disappears rapidly in a corner of the frame in the extreme foreground. It is a third worker who has fallen. Shocked and incredulous, the team leader moves slowly between the scaffoldings, followed by a pan. In front of him other bodies fall, committing suicide, this time clearly visible in the background. The man looks upwards; he is shocked and terrified; a match cut to his gaze shows a 'flock' of human bodies literally raining from the top of the building in slow motion and to the rhythm of thumping music.

This sequence is littered with impacts without falls and falls without impacts. On the one hand, at least before the last image, the suicidal workers' impacts on the ground are (increasingly less) unexpected; on the other hand, the mode of representation of the impacts exploits various weakening strategies.

One type of weakened impact directs the spectator's attention away from the point of impact towards another area of the frame, or to another point of depth within it: the impact appears on-screen, but its prominence is diminished by virtue of its being located at a peripheral point in the spectator's field of vision.

A first specific strategy is that of diverting the main attention point *to the background*. In the opening sequence of *The Happening*, before the first impact, the spectator's attention is drawn to the characters' faces while suddenly something falls behind them. This impact occurs in the frame, but it is placed in the background both literally and figuratively. Moreover, the nature of the falling object remains unknown due to the speed at which it enters into the frame.

The impact may also be placed too close *in the foreground* to be fully discernible. For example, in the prologue of *Vertical Limit* (Campbell 2000), recreational rock climbing turns deadly, leaving Peter Garrett, his father Boyce, and his sister suspended above a void—the weight of three people on a single anchor. Boyce asks his son to cut the rope and let him fall, so that both Peter and his daughter may survive. Peter is faced with a terrible dilemma and close-ups of his face show his growing sense of tension. The following shot is an extreme long shot of the canyon replete with sunshine and an eagle flying quietly in the bright sky, providing formal and emotional contrast to the previous tension-filled shot. In this way, the spectator is led to think that the resolution to whether Peter cuts the rope or not has been deferred. However, Peter's father's body falls suddenly in the foreground, producing a cloud of dust as it lands. The spectator is prompted to experience surprise, having been distracted by imagery of mountains and the flight of the eagle. Clearly, Peter has decided to cut the rope and thus save his own life and that of his sister at the expense of his father, whose body falls unexpectedly under the nose, so to speak, of the spectator. Both perceptual and cognitive factors cooperate in this temporary dissimulation in order to provoke the surprise effect.

There are also cases where the collision with the ground is concealed or hidden via *interposition* of surfaces, objects, or human bodies, so that the effect of the impact becomes strongly weakened. This is the case of the first and last fall in the aforementioned opening scene of *The Happening*.

A second option for the representation of impact employs strategies that are aimed at softening its violence. 'Cushioning' surfaces, such as car roofs, are typical. Cases in point are the deaths of Frank Nitti in *The Untouchables* and Max Peltier, who falls from a skyscraper in Los Angeles at the end of *Strange Days*. In *The Fifth Element* (Besson 1997), after her long hibernation, Leeloo jumps from a building to escape the police. The jump and the first part of the flight are shown from above and in slow motion, while the vertical fall is shown by a POV shot, until the impact with the hood of Korben Dallas' taxi.

Another interesting type of softening uses a natural element as surface of impact, in particular, water. In *The Sea Inside* (Amenábar 2004) Ramón Sampedro recounts the incident that caused his quadriplegia, a dive into the sea at a place where the water was too shallow. The impact is visible but occurs underneath the water's surface and is hidden by a cloud of sand. The sequence is also significant because it works simultaneously on a sensorimotor and at a cognitive level. The spectator *knows* in advance that the plunge will cause a severe injury, and this tension towards the dramatic outcome is preceded by a series of clues positioned, so to speak, on Ramón's body and in his movements. The back of his head, which will soon crash against the ground, is shown with insistence before the dive: Ramón caresses his neck and the shadow of this gesture is shown over the hard surface of the rocks. In this sense, a relationship between surfaces is suggested insistently: Ramón's body, the rocks, and especially the inviting body of water.

There is also the possibility of *curbing* or *slowing down* the fall in order to make it less violent and non-fatal. This occurs, for example, via the use of parachutes, as in the climax sequence of science fiction and action movies such as *Stealth* (Cohen 2005) or *Star Trek* (Abrams 2009).

Innocuous tumbles

The examples considered thus far have been narrative fiction films in which the rules that govern the fictional world are similar to those governing the real world. In such cases and genres the spectator recognizes that the fall and the impact have plausible consequences: serious injuries or violent death. Moreover, in these cases, filmmakers tend either to not depict the impact or to show it discreetly. However, in other cases, wherein the rules that govern the fictional world differ from those that apply in the real world, the impact is rendered clearly and in full. Here, an industrial and spectatorial fiat determines the partial or total suspension of physical laws, such as those of gravity and temporal continuity, which in turn can facilitate the presentation of impact, albeit usually in a way intended to undermine intense reactions on the part of the spectator. Death or injuries do not ensue. The range of possibilities is wide.

Think of slapstick comedy, where the fall never has serious physical consequences for the character. In fact, the grotesque and caricatured body, which is that of *vaudeville*, *burlesque*, and the acrobatic circus, redefines the physical environment's rules. From the very origins of silent (and therefore more physically expressive) cinema, the body that gives life to a *gag* performs basic movements but is always able to unleash chaos.

The heroes of contemporary sagas seem, at least in part, to have inherited the characteristics of the comic body. The impact does not violate the physical integrity of heroes provided with superpowers and 'superbodies'. This is the case of Peter Parker in the *Spider-Man* saga, or of Bruce Wayne in *Batman*, but also of Ethan Hunt in the *Mission: Impossible* franchise. In *Spider-Man 2* (Raimi 2004), for example, the disastrous fall of the superhero into an alley in New York is also depicted using the softening strategies employed in realistic movies: the impact is fragmented and cushioned by a dumpster and a puddle, by the sunroof of an automobile, and so on. In these moments, the movie is, in fact, a slapstick comedy.

Animation cinema is inhabited by *animated bodies*. Freedom from physical rules is extremely sought after (and justified) in this genre and is the ideal terrain for the process of dematerialization and re-anthropomorphization characteristic of postmodern cinematic bodies. One particular example will suffice: in the live action-animation hybrid *Who Framed Roger Rabbit* (Zemeckis 1988), detective Eddie Valiant's 'flesh and bones' body falls and tumbles into the arms of an *animated body*.

In a fantasy or science fiction worlds almost everything is allowed. In one of *The Matrix*' slapstick scenes, Neo is testing his capacity (mental, rather than physical) to move from the roof of one building to another for the first time. The attempt fails and Neo falls on the asphalt of the street below. The asphalt is, however, an elastic surface that absorbs the impact and makes him bounce back. In the aforementioned *Star Trek*, Kirk and Sulu's landing on Vulcan becomes potentially fatal after the accidental loss of the parachute while trying to return to the base. But an instant before the fatal impact, the two characters are teleported to the Enterprise and rescued. The formal construction of the sequence creates extreme intensity through the bodily tension induced through the posture of the two characters (intertwined with each other) and their facial expressions deformed by speed, and through the suspense generated by the cross cutting between the fall and the transporting procedure performed by their colleagues on the Enterprise. Sensorimotor and cognitive voltage cooperate in creating an increasing energy which is then suddenly dissipated as they 'land' on the ship.

Sometimes filmmakers resort to *temporal manipulation*. In the fantastic world of *The Hudsucker Proxy* (J. & E. Coen 1994), the passage of time can even be blocked. On New Year's Eve, Norville Barnes falls from the ledge of his office at the top of the Hudsucker Industries skyscraper, but suddenly time magically stops and the character remains suspended in mid-air. It is not exactly a freeze-frame because Norville can keep moving and can communicate with the company's late founder Waring Hudsucker, who manifests as an angel to deliver a letter with his last wishes. The clock starts again and Norville's fall resumes but stops again a meter from the ground, allowing him to get out of the situation safely when time resumes once again to flow regularly.

The impact factor

This review shows that in contemporary cinema impact is often conveyed without actually being shown onscreen. Even when it is clearly shown, a deliberately exaggerated style of representation, with an unrealistic effect that causes the spectator to consider it implausible, is adopted. In fact, an invariable aesthetic policy seems to characterize the representation of the fall on the cinematic screen: whether the negative outcome of a stunt or a climb, a tragic accident or a suicide, the fatal impact with the ground—i.e. the high point of this movement, its natural and inevitable outcome—is not shown or, if it is shown, is hidden through the use of different strategies. The object towards which the motor and emotional crescendo and all expressive elements of the representation are addressed and directed is censored, kept out of frame.

If this way of (not) representing the impact is typical of a trend in contemporary cinema, it is worth considering the reasons behind such concealment. One explanation would be to cite technical and budgetary limitations; the impact of the falling human body is not depicted because it would be too technically complicated or prohibitively expensive to achieve. These problems, however, can be affordably overcome by the employment of digital special effects. Financial restraints may, however, coincide with concerns over certification or censorship. Here the depiction of corporeal damage may risk a restricted film-rating, especially in respect to younger audiences, and this leads to a preventive self-censorship. The actual reason for this concealment, however, is not due to production practices and policies, but rather to the need to weaken or even to avoid the concrete psychophysiological effects that the explicit representation of the impact would generate in the spectator. The impact is a potentially traumatic event and has to be kept off screen or presented under certain conditions. Because impact is *unrepresentable*, filmmakers employ alternative strategies to make impact nevertheless *experienceable*.

These strategies consist in the embodiment, by elements of the film, of the modalities through which the spectator avoids the impact by adopting 'adverse' autonomic responses. In spite of being acutely aware of the fact that they are watching fictional events, which have either been performed by actors who have not sustained actual injuries or have even been generated digitally, spectators nevertheless tend to avoid the sight of cruel and violent events. The clearest evidence of this phenomenon is provided by cases of spectators jumping, grimacing, closing or covering their eyes, or looking away at the precise moment at which a fall culminates in an impact. Although predictable, although patently fictional, and although not shown on screen, the impact is experienced by the spectator in terms of sensorimotor activation. Even though the impact is not materially present or visually perceivable, it generates an instinctive and strongly adverse reaction. The falling motion, in this sense, reaches completion even though its culminating point may not be shown on the screen.

A detailed categorization provided by Julian Hanich (2010) in a study of horror films helps to clarify the 'somatic' layer of empathy in the film experience as a physical and automatic dynamic, rather than an imaginative one. Hanich implicitly refers to a series of connected phenomena that I have briefly described in the paragraph on the cognitive account of empathy in Chapter II—in particular, *affective mimicry*, the automatic tendency to mimic and synchronize with others' expressions, postures, and movements, as emotional contagion inductors. 'Somatic empathy is a form of *Einfühlung* that describes a more or less automatic, but no more than partial parallelism between a character's and my own body's sensations, affects or motions' (103). This kind of basic and 'preliminary' empathy (I use the expression *pre*-empathy to describe Albert Michotte's case 2 in Chapter II) arises from the three distinct varieties of mimicry: motor, sensation, and affective. The first involves some muscular effort performed by the film character; the second involves, for example, a stimulus on the skin of the character; and the third involves some kind of appreciation or aversion for a pleasurable or unpleasant emotion. This somatic reaction entails automatic mimicry that does not depend on a strong character engagement or allegiance, but rather is 'a particular carnal response that makes us feel ourselves feeling and thus enables a strong awareness-of-oneself as an embodied viewer' (104). Somatic empathy is possible precisely because the spectator is in a position different from that of the character and is a sort of balance of the experiential disproportion of position. As Vivian Sobchack (2004) (cited by Hanich) explains,

> my body's intentional trajectory, seeking a sensible object to fulfil this sensual solicitation, will reverse its direction to locate its partially frustrated sensual grasp on something more literally accessible. That more literally accessible sensual object is my own subjectively felt lived body. Thus, 'on the rebound' from the screen—and without a reflective thought—I will reflexively turn toward my own carnal, sensual, and sensible being (76-77).

Accordingly, in case of the cinematic impact, the spectator experiences a *reflexive-bodily* reaction rather than a *reflective-cognitive* understanding; the *sense* emerges first by means of somatic empathy rather than of a deliberate act of acquiring knowledge.

An alternative account of perception—yet one not distant from the Merleau-Pontean and Sobchackian perspective—is the enactive approach. According to the enactive philosopher Alva Noë, perception is an active phenomenon that involves the whole organism insofar as it consists in the establishment of appropriate patterns of sensorimotor dependence: to perceive is to implicitly understand the effects of a movement based on such patterns. As Noë (2005) claims, '[p]erceiving is *exploring the world*' (244) 'perceiving is not a way of representing, it is a way of gathering or assembling content' (244). 'Perceiving is a relation between the perceiver and the world. Perception in nonrepresentational in the sense that perceivings [...] are not *about* the world, they are episodes of contact with the world' (256). Accordingly, perceptual constancy is not (only) a matter of *sensation* (i.e., how the world appears), but rather of our corporeal experience of the world. Our perception of the cinematic impact does not depend on what we (do not) see, but rather on how we experience the impact, which is a complete experience despite the partial occlusion. It depends on the kind of corporeal and sensorimotor relationships between the spectator and the character situated in a particular ecological condition. As Noë states, 'sensorimotor understanding belongs to the complicated adjustments necessary for attaining and maintaining perceptual contact with the world' (257). This non-representational stance leads to the idea that '[s] ensorimotor understanding, like computational or neural processing in the brain, enters into perceiving not by giving rise to representations of what is seen is us, but by enabling us to occupy a vantage point from which it is possible to see' (257). According to the enactive direct realism that Noë adopts, 'there is no perceptual experience of an object that is not dependent on the exercise, by the perceiver, of a special kind of knowledge. Perceptual awareness of objects [...] is an achievement of the sensorimotor understanding' (256). In this sense, the cinematic impact is present in its absence; it is experientially available in spite of its visual unavailability. As amodally perceived, the censored impact is present in the spectator's experience as a whole. As a film spectator, I move with the character: I fall with him/her and hit the ground, although at the last moment I tend to avoid this experience.

Along the same lines, philosopher of perception Robert Briscoe maintains that amodal perception includes both top-down or cognitive completion (C-completion) and stimulus-driven or 'non cognitive' completion (NA-completion), where the former involves a variety of representational resources and processing mechanisms (such as mental imagery and beliefs) and the latter is non-representational.[9] Representations of object-directed bodily actions play an important role in amodal perception. As Briscoe (2011) writes,

> When we engage in visuomotor actions targeted on an object, the kinematic parameters of the movements that we perform are often determined not only by the spatial properties of the object's visible surfaces—in particular, their orientations and distances in depth—but also by the spatial properties of the object's currently occluded surfaces (167).

This seems to be consistent with Merleau-Ponty's assumption that the body is an organ of *complete* perception: 'when we reach for an object, our grasping hand has 'knowledge' of the object's hidden features that our eyes do not have. This knowledge is displayed in our practical awareness of how to engage in actions that are kinematically appropriate to the object as a 3-D whole, and not just to its visible surface geometry' (167). In fact, what Briscoe (2011) called 'motoric completion' is a kind of completion in addition to NA-completion and C-completion and describes cases in which '[a]n object's currently occluded features are motorically completed when they figure in the contents of 'action representations' [...] that underwrite our abilities to interact with the object in ways that are appropriate to its 3-D, volumetric shape' (168). Motoric completion in fact 'plays an important role in conferring a sense of real, if unseen, presence on the occluded features of the objects that we perceive (168). Briscoe's theory of motoric completion supports the 'sensorimotor understanding' that the enactive account of perception uses to explain the perception of occluded actions and the 'bodily knowledge' by which we 'grasp' the meaning of object's movement, such as the final, occluded part of a cinematic falling body. As I recalled in Chapter I in regard to the notion of 'surrogate body' that Christiane Voss (2011) recovers from Sobchack's phenomenology of the film experience, it is precisely the body (and the bodily grounded perception) that provides the third dimension of the bidimensional illusion of film. As Voss writes, 'it is only the spectator's body, in its mental and sensorial-affective resonance with the events on- screen, which [...] 'loans' a three-dimensional body to the screen and thus flips the second dimension of the film event over into the third dimension of the sensing body' (145).

9 For a synthesis of the current debate on amodal completion in perception, cf. Calabi 2016.

Neural impact

In an experiment on the neural correlates of occluded objects, Oliver Hulme and Semir Zeki demonstrated that certain areas of the brain activate systematically, irrespective of whether an object is visible or whether it is blocked from sight when it vanishes behind an opaque surface. As Hulme and Zeki (2007) report, 'when objects are directly viewed, activity within object selective regions may reflect the awareness of presence, not the direct perception of the object' (1197). In other words, the brain responds when objects are known to be present but are obscured, meaning that awareness of presence both precedes and influences the neural activation that allows the subject to experience an absent stimulus. This experiment suggests that the spectator is subject to the same dynamic when she encounters a directed movement (the fall), the final stage of which (the impact) is occluded from sight and when movement is therefore merely suggested. This phenomenon shows that the spectator's response is grounded in brain function mechanisms.

If there was no difference in brain activity between viewing a fully presented impact and an impact that has been merely suggested, then it would seem to matter little whether or not the fall is depicted plausibly or in a realistic manner. But on the contrary, in each act of engagement with a film, a range of preliminary factors influence the spectator's understanding of the events being presented or alluded to. These factors precede and affect the sensorimotor and basic neurophysiological activation—usually weakening it—and are generally conventions which constitute the pact forged between filmmakers and spectator, and thereby establish the general cognitive framework in which the film experience takes place. Factors that cannot be neglected include: genre conventions, verisimilitude, the location within the individual film of a specific fall/impact sequence, and the spectator's emotional investment in the characters involved in the sequence. Therefore, comprehension cannot be limited to local motor activation and to physiological mechanisms of the spectator's body or brain. Rather, it must concern those more or less conscious and deliberate mental processes (psychological, rather than physiological) that allow the spectator to experience the cinematic fall and impact of the human body within the broader context of each individual film experience.

Cinematic falls come in many forms, all of which differ qualitatively according to their formal and stylistic presentation. Therefore, when analysing them, attention should also be directed to stylistic features generated by cinematography, *mise-en-scène*, editing pace, and diegetic time, in other words to the 'film's body' and the way in which this pseudo-organism interacts with the spectator. Different uses and combinations of these devices generate fairly intense sensorimotor activations and qualitatively diverse emotional effects. Similarly, the effectiveness of impact as a tensive motif will depend on the specific modalities of management of the energy loaded during the fall. If the intensity aroused by the representation is derived from the unusual, uncontrolled, and authentic nature of movement, the impact depends on the force of attraction exerted by the ideal point of impact of the falling body. In other words, the extreme and violent stimulation of the impact is loaded progressively during the course of the movement that precedes it; it is the result of its being perceived as a point of culmination and accumulation of the energy—an energy that discharges instantaneously at the exact point of impact, and that reverberates just after that. Accordingly, in regard to the relevance of neuroscientific findings on the mirroring of observed intentional actions, we can assume that the impact is the precise goal to which the action is directed. The withholding from the spectator of the final stage of the fall or of some of its later stages indicates that a goal-oriented action is understood ideally in terms of its intentionality, rather than in terms of its fulfilment.

An experiment conducted by Umiltà et al. (2001) demonstrated a correlation between a type of neuron found in the premotor cortex of the macaque and the response to observing object-directed action when the object is occluded. As I discussed in Chapter I, brain cells called 'mirror neurons' fire both during the execution of goal-related motor action and when observing other individuals (monkeys or humans) executing similar acts. The study shows that a subset of mirror neurons fires during the action's presentation and also when the final part of the action—crucial to triggering the response when full vision is available—is hidden and can therefore only be inferred. As Umiltà et al. (2001) report, '[t]his implies that the motor representation of an action performed by others can be internally generated in the observer's motor cortex, even when a visual description of the action is lacking [and] these findings support the hypothesis that mirror neuron activation could be at the basis of action recognition' (155). In other words, 'even when an object, target of the action, is not visible, an individual is still able to understand which action another individual is doing' (155). As they explain, '[f]ull visual information about an action is not necessary to recognize its goal'; '[a]ction understanding could be based on a mechanism that can trigger the internal motor representation of the action' (155).

As mentioned in Chapter I, in neurophysiological terms the mirror neuron system generates an internal representation of the observed movement and entails an embodied simulation of that movement; in other words it is a functional mechanism that 'mediates our capacity to share the meaning of actions, intentions, feelings, and emotions with others' (Gallese 2009a). Accordingly, I would suggest that the impact is experienced by the spectator because he empathically experiences the meaning of a falling body by simulating its movement internally. In light of neuroscientific research on the link between motor simulation and action recognition, one can hypothesize that the instinctive fulfilment of a partial action is connected to an immediate and empathetic understanding of the meaning of that action. Insights gained by experimental psychologists in conjunction with neuroscientific evidence confirm the hypothesis that the meaning of a goal-directed action depends on the empathetic comprehension of the intentionality implied in the action. As far as we are concerned, the movements of the human body on the cinema screen are conceived as goal-oriented actions, the intentionality of which is experienced through the tension that pushes the body towards the goal.

Blind gazes

The spectator's emotional response is tied to the concrete ways in which cinema has carried out its intermedial re-elaboration of history. In Iñárritu's episode of *11'09"01*, the emotional connotation depends not so much on the character of the images as *factual*, but rather on the 'sensory script' onto which these images are grafted: here impacts are not featured at all. The black screen is used partially to obscure the movement that precedes the impact, which is therefore only evoked as the dramatic and inevitable conclusion to the falls, resulting in a reduction of the tension accumulated by the spectator over the course of the fall. As noted above, the intensity of the response provoked by the image of a falling human body derives from the increasing gravity-induced speed of a fast and uncontrolled movement leading to an inevitable impact. If the point of impact, although not presented on-screen, is perceived as being too distant, then the spectator's sensorimotor activity will be significantly less intense or may even be absent.

Iñárritu's film not only reflects the spectator's reaction to the impact, but also the development of the entire perceptual process. Here, the cognitive framework of the film experience and the aesthetic and formal rendition of events coincide. The spectator's involvement may be influenced by the foreknowledge that the images captured actual events. Iñàrritu's segment uses formal and stylistic devices to maximize the emotional responses of spectators assumed to be fully aware of the authenticity of the featured events. The presentation of the images against a cacophony of noises, voices, and sounds takes place alongside a recognizable rhythmic 'score', with a progressive release of emotion making the shock palpable. A few months after 9/11, filmmakers like Iñárritu had begun to reinterpret the 'unrepresentable' events of that day. Nevertheless, stylistic devices were used to weaken the effect of such traumatic material. Due to the extreme long shots employed by the amateur videos used in the film, spectators are unable to clearly see the faces of any of the people falling. Instead, small figures, which are barely recognizable as human beings, are visible. So from where, then, does the spectator's pity and consternation arise? What is it that disturbs and worries the spectator, even though she is unlikely to have been involved directly in these events and even though an absence of close-ups prevents her from glimpsing despair, fear, and resignation on the victims' faces?

The experiments described above indicate a relationship between perceptual interference in motion continuity and emotional involvement. The core of this relationship may be the reliance on the whole *sui generis* structure of the movement as amodally perceived by the spectator. In Iñàrritu's minifilm, the black screen represents a darkening of both the visual field and of consciousness. The distant sight of desperate, defenceless falling bodies is experienced immediately and emphatically by the spectator because of the precarious nature of its representability. The unwatchable, the unbearable, the unrepresentable is therefore encapsulated in metaphorical form in the 'blind' gaze of the black screen. Deferring, fragmenting, rationing, and partially blacking out the movement, Iñàrritu tries to keep us at a *safe distance* from horror and pain in order to make those piteous images acceptable and bearable. An *emotional distance* aims at compensating for the traumatic hyper-reality and spectacularity of the intermedial event, and above all for the irrevocability of the real. The film embodies both a perceptual and an interpretive approach. The unsensory (i.e. the negation of perception) communicates the insensate (the inconceivability of the events). The physical and the psychic are bound together in an empathetic process of understanding.

Even in spatial terms, in Iñárritu's minifilm representation respects the principle of distancing by renouncing the use of the close-up (i.e. one of the main means for filmic empathy). In fact, the spectators do not have visual access to the facial expressions of the falling people, which would allow them to see their despair, fear, and resignation more closely. What can be seen are only small bodies, hardly recognizable as humans, that appear to be almost like falling debris. The compassion that the spectator experiences is therefore not achieved through the proximity of the spectator's body to that of the 'characters', but rather through the proximity to the sensory elements of the film (the progressive release of the visual fragments, the audio track of farewell phone calls, the intense string music in the finale), carefully designed and assembled to make that unacceptable pain more closely felt by the spectator.

Taking the fall not only and not so much a physical element as a symbolic one (the fall of bodies in fact anticipates the collapse of the Towers, which symbolizes the fall of a Western and capitalist symbol and, ultimately, a moral abatement), the minifilm actually reflects the cognitive process and embodies the perceptive attitude of the spectator in its formal components. Perceptions are literally and deliberately hampered by visual and acoustic interference (a perceptual impediment that at first glance can even annoy the viewer or be interpreted as a projection or playback device malfunction). By offering images at first so briefly as to not allow a clear understanding of their content, and then by increasing the duration of each single exposure and the frequency of their appearance, the film reflects the same interpretative effort carried out by the spectator.

Thus, the empathic relationship does not occur through the proximity of the spectator's body to those of the falling victims, nor through the display of the victims' facial expressions; rather, it occurs through the expressive qualities of on-screen events: the film is operating literally on the edge of visual perception, working to bring into focus bodies that are almost indistinguishable from the rubble—falling debris, souls in search of liberation, as in the sequence from *Maybe Not* described in the opening paragraphs of this chapter. Verticality is ineluctability; the fall is a decline. The power of the expressive qualities of image and sound affects the neurophysiological basis of the spectator's emotional experience, while reaching a higher, symbolic level: movement in space offers a sense of the void—the spectator feels that she is plummeting. These emotions heighten not only the recognition of the bodily conditions of the falling bodies and the empathy that arises from awareness of the spectator's human similarity to those people, but also from the 'expressive shape' of the movement. The representational forms and expressive dynamic have—or rather, they are—expressive means that refer to figurative concepts (the fall as a sense of emptiness, decline, decay, human weakness, dizziness as instability, fear; speed as an uncontrollable, inevitable force) and thus arouse emotions empathetically, i.e. in the form of an immediate understanding of the meaning of the fall.

In sum, in Iñárritu's minifilm emotional distancing is mainly based on a darkening and a visual distancing. The black screen embodies the denial of visual perception: eyes are closed because the pictures are too shocking. You can open them only from time to time and only for a few instants. The most significant moment is when the eight visual fragments are presented consecutively, separated by black fades that seem to reproduce the spectator's blinks; the viewer progressively reopens her eyes to reality. Thus, the film's *not-showing* corresponds to the spectator's *not-watching*; by *not showing*. The film *shows* the mental and physical dynamics of a spectatorial *not-watching*.

The spectator's instinctive inclination to not see and the tendency of film practitioners to not show the impact clearly indicate that any given film visualizes the spectator's physical and psychical disposition; film functions like the spectator does, or rather would, if she had experienced the event first hand. However, rather than a mere physiological autonomic reaction, the *unrepresented* impact elicits a more complex and stratified response. This response cannot be interpreted only in terms of the activation of motor and physiological mechanisms of reaction to the observed actions, it must also entail a more or less conscious biologically developed manifestation of an intimate and deeper aversion to violence and death. By 'representing the unrepresentable', the cinema offers a seemingly paradoxical experience involving the superficial excitation of the senses together with the embodied expression of deep meanings. Images such as that of *11'09"01* are able to construct a perceptual and emotional 'common black', a shared area that is not a disembodied elaboration of loss, but rather an opportunity to feel compassion and vulnerability and to share empathetically, through the medium of cinema, as though we 'die together because the death of others has been lived together' (Carbone 2007, 18-19, my trans.).[10]

Bibliography

Balázs, Béla. 2010. *Early Film Theory: The Visible Man*. Edited by Erica Carter, translated by Rodney Livingstone. New York: Berghahn Books.

Baudrillard, Jean. 1983. *Simulations*. Translated by Paul Foss, Paul Batton & Philip Beitchman. New York: Semiotext(e).

Belpoliti, Marco. 2005. *Crolli*. Torino: Einaudi.

Boltanski, Luc. 1999. *Distant Suffering: Morality, Media and Politics*. Translated by G. Burchell. Cambridge: Cambridge University Press.

10 '[*E*]*ssere morti insieme perché insieme si è vissuta la morte di altri*'.

Bolter, Jay D., & Richard Grusin. 1999. *Remediation: Understanding New Media.* Cambridge, MA: The MIT Press.

Briscoe, Robert E. 2011. 'Mental Imagery and the Varieties of Amodal Perception'. *Pacific Philosophical Quarterly.* 92 (2): 153-173. DOI:10.1111/j.1468-0114.2011.01393.x.

Burke, Luke. 1952. 'On the Tunnel Effect'. *The Quarterly Journal of Experimental Psychology.* 4 (3): 121-138. DOI:10.1080%2F17470215208416611.

Calabi, Clotide. 2016. 'Amodal Completion, Perception and Visual Imagery'. *Phenomenology and Mind.* 4: 170-177. DOI:10.13128/Phe_Mi-19599.

Carbone, Mauro. 2007. *Essere morti insieme. L'evento dell'11 settembre 2001.* Torino: Bollati Basic Books.

Chion, Michel. 1994. *Audio-Vision. Sound on Screen.* Edited and translated by Claudia Gorbman. New York: Columbia University Press.

Didi-Huberman, Georges. 2008. *Images in Spite of All: Four Photographs from Auschwitz.* Translated by Shane B. Lillis. Chicago/London: The University of Chicago Press.

Filion, Chrisine M., David A. Washburn, & Jonathan P. Gulledge. 1996. 'Can Monkeys (Macaca Mulatta) Represent Invisible Displacement?' *Journal of Comparative Psychology.* 110 (4): 386-395. DOI:10.1037/0735-7036.110.4.386.

Gallese, Vittorio. 2009a. 'Mirror Neurons, Embodied Simulation, and the Neural Basis of Social Identification'. *Psychoanalytic Dialogues.* 19 (5): 519-536. DOI:10.1080/10481880903231910.

Glynn, Alan J. 1954. 'Apparent Transparency and the Tunnel Effect'. *The Quarterly Journal of Experimental Psychology.* 6 (3): 125-139. DOI:10.1080/17470215408416658.

Grusin, Richard. 2004. 'Premediation'. *Criticism.* 46 (1): 17-39. https://digitalcommons.wayne.edu/criticism/vol46/iss1/3.

Grusin, Richard. 2010. *Premediation: Affect and Mediality After 9/11.* London/New York: Palgrave Macmillan.

Hanich, Julian. 2010. *Cinematic Emotion in Horror Films and Thrillers: The Aesthetic Paradox of Pleasurable Fear.* New York/London: Routledge.

Hulme, Oliver, & Semir Zeki. 2007. 'The Sightless View: Neural Correlates of Occluded Objects'. *Cereb. Cortex.* 17 (5): 1197-1205.

Michotte, Albert, Georges Thinès, & Geneviève Crabbé. 1967. *Les complements amodaux des structures perceptives.* Louvain: Publications Universitaires de Louvain.

Michotte, Albert. 1950. 'On Phenomenal Permanence: Facts and Theories'. *Acta Psychologica.* 7: 293-322.

Michotte, Albert. 1963. *The Perception of Causality.* New York: Basic Books.

Montani, Pietro. 2010. *L'immaginazione intermediale. Perlustrare, rifigurare, testimoniare il mondo visibile.* Roma/Bari: Laterza.

Noë, Alva. 2005. 'Real Presence'. *Philosophical Topics*. 33 (1): 235-264. DOI:10.5840/philtopics20053319.

Ramachandran, Vilayanur S., & Stuart M. Anstis. 1986. 'The Perception of Apparent Motion'. *Scientific American*. 254 (6): 102-109. DOI:10.1038/scientificamerican0686-102.

Rancière, Jacques. 2014. *Figures of History*. Translated by Julie Rose. Cambridge: Polity Press.

Sobchack, Vivian. 2004. *Carnal Thoughts: Embodiment and Moving Image Culture*. Berkeley: University of California Press.

Sontag, Susan. 2003. *Regarding the Pain of Others*. New York: Macmillan.

Umiltà, Maria Alessandra, Evelyne Kohler, Vittorio Gallese, Leonardo Fogassi, Luciano Fadiga, Christian Keysers, & Giacomo Rizzolatti. 2001. 'I Know What You Are Doing. A Neurophysiological Study'. *Neuron*. 31 (1): 155-165. DOI:10.1016/S0896-6273(01)00337-3.

Voss, Christiane. 2011. 'Film Experience and the Formation of Illusion: The Spectator as "Surrogate Body" for the Cinema'. *Cinema Journal*. 50 (4): 136-150. DOI:10.1353/cj.2011.0052.

Žižek, Slavoj. 2022. *Welcome to the Desert of the Real: Five Essays on September 11 and Related Dates*. London: Verso.

V Overturning

Upside-down dissimulations

Abstract
The chapter 'Overturning. Upside-down dissimulations' deals with the motif of the overturned representations of the human face and body in contemporary films and its effect on the spectator's vestibular system. The argument builds off of Maurice Merleau-Ponty's reflections on the phenomenology of the perception of space and Rudolf Arnheim's discussion of the artistic potential a film can derive from the relativity of point of view and movement. The analysis (in particular of Christopher Nolan's *The Dark Knight*) leads to the identification of a dynamic that moves from the disorientation produced by the representation of overturned faces to an 'un-overturning'.

Keywords: Upside-down image, Equilibrioception, *Phenomenology of Perception*, *The Dark Knight*

'This is what happens when an unstoppable force meets an immovable object. [...] You see, madness, as you know, is like gravity. All it takes is a little push!'
—The Joker, *The Dark Knight* (Nolan 2008)

In Wonderland

Alice falls downward. Wonderland is waiting for her, at the bottom of the infinite tunnel of her frustration and curiosity. As the girl reaches the bottom, she breaks through the ceiling of a room. When she recovers from the tumble, a point-of-view shot shows a chandelier oriented strangely upwards. A moment later, a close-up shows a strange expression on the girl's face; the shot enlarges to show her long blond hair dangling upwards, against the force of gravity. Suddenly, a quick rotating camera motion tilts the perceptual

D'Aloia, A., *Neurofilmology of the Moving Image. Gravity and Vertigo in Contemporary Cinema*. Taylor & Francis Group 2021
DOI: 10.5117/9789463725255_CH05

plane 180°. The spectator realizes then that the ceiling is actually the floor, and that the world into which Alice has plunged is organized according to a new, completely inverted orientation. This overturning, this 'revolutionary' camera movement in the opening scene of *Alice in Wonderland*'s (Burton 2010), is something that goes beyond a mere change of the inner spatial organization of the fantastic world into which the character has dropped. This filmic 'gesture' tells us something about our own status as film spectators, and therefore about the nature of the film experience.

The most interesting, albeit almost undetectable, aspect of the scene is precisely that brief moment of time during which Alice remains attached to what at first seemed to be the room's floor and what is soon to to turn into its ceiling. The world in which she has landed is overturned with respect to the world from which she has come, but for a moment her body continues to be oriented according to the physical laws of the latter. Alice does not undergo the effects of the new gravitational system—she does not fall—until the image itself is overturned. In this way, the world's overturning seems to be caused by the camera movement. The camera rotation affirms the *relativity* of the character-spectator reciprocal orientation system. The overturning is in fact an *adaptation* of the spectator's orientation system to that imposed by the onscreen world. In other words, the rotation accomplishes a reorientation that affects both the re-cognition of the environment and the proprioception of the spectator's body. The landing in a differently oriented world generates a gap and breaks down the 'ordinary' world's parameters of orientation. At the same time, it proposes a solution to such an unusual and estranging inversion by delaying the action of gravity in the new orientation system, consequently delaying the character's fall.

Watching a film is an experience of a relationship between bodies in space. Orthogonally oriented in front of the screen, the spectator sits (externally almost motionless, although internally extremely active) and relates to a series of landscapes, objects, and bodies displayed on screen. What is important is that, though different in nature, both the fictional world of the character and the real world of the spectator usually have the same basic orientation: head up, feet down, as in ordinary everyday life. The space in which the fictional character's body moves seems to be bound by the same laws that govern the real world (even if the film does not deal with realistic subject matter)—above all, by the law of gravity, the very force that controls the relationship between body and space. The character walks along a street that is *under* his feet; a car runs along a road that passes *under* its wheels; a superhero soars *upwards*; in the close-up, the forehead is *above* the chin, and the nose is *under* the eyes... In short, we see bodies and environments as we see them outside the cinema, on a plane that is orthogonal to our vision and that offers an orientation that can be called 'natural' because it is 'common,' 'usual', 'habitual', 'ordinary', 'normal', and readable without any effort, and because it obeys the laws of nature.

The power of cinema, of course, is that it can disregard physical laws. Cinema may make use of fantasy or artistic license: in some cases, the character may even walk *on* the walls or the ceiling, or his face may appear on the screen upside down. How does this exceptional case affect the spectator's experience? What if the 'standard' bodily orientation of the film experience were overturned? What happens if the spectator's head-up/feet-down orientation is placed in relation to the upside-down character's bodily orientation?

The film often creates a short-circuit between the perception and the recognition of the image thanks to its faculty to propose a multiplicity of 'unnatural' and therefore potentially expressive views. The fact that filmic perception is free from the limitations of natural vision, which is anchored to the body of the viewer, makes its point of view and movement necessarily *relative*. The cinema can orient the characters' bodies at its own discretion, upright or upside down (oblique orientations are rare). This flexibility is not affected by an obligation to respect the force of gravity: the film as a means of representation is always potentially non-gravitational (whereas the spectator's orientation is necessarily rooted in his position).

This chapter analyses a series of upside-down images (especially of the characters' faces) in different genres of narrative films. Even though this is not a very frequent occurrence in narrative cinema—we will also discuss why it is avoided—it can nonetheless be found throughout cinema history, with different aims and specific stylistic presentations. The fundamental argument here is that the upside-down image provides the spectator with an experience that operates in two opposing phases. In the *disembodying phase*, the narrative situations and formal solutions used in the film aim to perturb the spectator's usual perception and to elicit the pleasure of experiencing such an unusual and thrilling condition of perception. In the *reembodying phase*, the film restores the ordinary conditions of perception in order to avoid demanding that the spectator make a prolonged cognitive and perceptual effort. However, this process implies that the final 'straightened up' image and the initial 'upright' image are different and express different psychological meanings.

The theoretical framework of this study embraces phenomenology and psychology. In particular, the analysis draws on Maurice Merleau-Ponty's contribution to the phenomenology of perception and relies on a Gestaltic approach to the film experience. However, film theory has not yet approached the upside-down image systematically. This exploration may be even more productive if conducted within the paradigm of embodied cognition (as discussed in the Introduction). I will argue that the upside-down image establishes a conflictual relationship between the body and the eye, which in the disembodying phase interfere with each other, until the reembodying phase comes into play as a means of reorganization and reorientation. Although human perception, when confronted with an upside-down image, adapts to the inverted image and re-establishes an orientation automatically, the film provides a perceptual and cognitive adaption *on behalf* of the spectator.

Inverted inversion

In recent years, both cognitive psychology and neurocognitive research has investigated the psychic conditions and the neural correlates of upside-down vision (Linden et al. 1999; Richter et al. 2002; Yoshimura 2002). The phenomenon of retinal inversion and adaptation to upside-down spectacles attracted psychologists at the turn of the 19th century (Stratton 1896; Stratton 1897a; Stratton 1897b; Wertheimer 1961) and was subject to renewed interest in the 1960s (Kohler 1961; Smith & Smith 1962; Taylor 1962; Held & Freedman 1962; Kohler 1964; Harris 1965; Rock 1966; Welch 1978; Dolezal 1982). One of the philosophical foundations of these reflections can be found in Maurice Merleau-Ponty's *Phenomenology of Perception*. In the chapter 'Space', Merleau-Ponty (2002) recounts psychologists George Stratton and Max Wertheimer's experiments on vision without inversion of the retinal image in order to demonstrate that the human sense of space is primarily bodily and not reflective. 'Space is not the setting (real or logical) in which things are arranged, but the means whereby the position of things becomes possible' (284). The best way to demonstrate this insight is by analysing an 'exceptional case' (i.e. vision without retinal inversion) in which what we normally perceive through our ordinary experience is deconstructed and re-formed.

In one of the reported experiments, Stratton asked a subject to wear special glasses that correct the retinal images and invert the physiological retinal inversion so images are cast on the retina as if the whole field of view had been rotated 180° around the line of sight. The experiment lasted a week and during this period the subject's vision changed. During the first day, the landscape appears unreal and upside down; this is due to the conflict between tactile and visual perception. Yet, progressively, their vision becomes less unreal. The next day, in fact, 'the landscape is no longer inverted, but the body is felt to be in an abnormal position' (285). From the third day on, 'the body progressively rights itself, and finally seems to occupy a normal position' (285). In other words, what Merleau-Ponty aims to demonstrate is that human perception is capable of adapting to a new and inverted visual orientation to the extent that the latter becomes 'normal' (285). 'The new visual appearances which, at the beginning, stood out against a background of previous space, develop round themselves [...] with no effort at all, a horizon with a general orientation corresponding to their own' (285). This happens so much that, when the glasses are removed at the end of the experiment, 'objects appear not inverted, it is true, but 'queer,' and motor reactions are reversed' (285). The revealing moment of the experiment, therefore, is when the glasses are removed and the initial 'normal' situation is restored. The new 'image of the world' calls the old image into question: the new upright image does not correspond to the 'old' upright image, since the reversal has disturbed and re-formed the subject's sense of what is upright and what is upside down.

Is this theoretical framework applicable to the analysis of the upside-down film experience? Since the film experience does not share all the features of non-mediated experience, some preliminary remarks concerning the specificity of the film experience as a *sui generis* form of relational experience between bodies are required. The first consideration relates to the psychophysical condition of the beholder, in particular the peculiar kind of 'active passivity' in which he is involved; the second addresses the role of the camera and point of view as factors mediating that relationship. Both of these clarifications are necessary for a full understanding of the complex dynamic that creates a conflict between the spectator's and the character's bodily orientations and that leads narrative cinema to resolve it. As stated above, rather than rashly embracing embodiment as a general description of the film experience, my fundamental hypothesis is that narrative cinema offers a *disembodying* phase followed by a *reembodying* phase.

Let us reflect on how the conclusions suggested by Merleau-Ponty relate to the film experience. First, the perceptual act is not only a visual activity; the body is also involved. Second, the body and the eyes work differently, even in contrast with one another, but also with reciprocal adjustment: the conflict between tactile sensations and visual images tends to resolve itself. Third, it is exactly this discrepancy that makes the generation of 'new' images possible: once one is accustomed to vision through the glasses, the upside-down image is experienced as 'normal'. Once the glasses are removed, the 'normal' image is experienced as 'queer'. Therefore, we have

1) an initial image, the 'right way up' representation of an 'upright' figure; 2) an inverted image, perceived as unreal in respect to a sensation of the body still being perceived as though in its 'normal' position; 3) an inverted image no longer perceived as unreal in respect to a sensation of the body, which is perceived as 'abnormal'; 4) an upside-down picture now perceived as normal in respect to a body that is now also perceived as normal; 5) and a 'corrected' image perceived as abnormal in respect to a body that still continues to be perceived as normal.

Cinematic dictatorship

A classic case that helps us to understand this dynamic is the humorous dialogue between the Jewish barber and the Tomainian officer Schultz on the airplane in the opening sequence of *The Great Dictator* (Chaplin 1940). Schultz feels faint and abandons the controls, causing the plane to turn upside down. The two characters initially have an upside-down conversation; then, after a simple cut, the camera turns upside down and shows the scene with normalized orientation axes. The gag exploits both of these overturned images for comic effect, as in the first shot the barber looks *down* and sees the sun and, in the second, the watch comes out of his pocket and falls *up*, while the water comes out of the bottle *upwards* by itself.

Beyond its humorous dimension, this example highlights how perception and cognition can trip over each other, as typified in optical illusions: even if the spectator *knows* that he is observing the situation in a certain way, he continues to perceive it in conflict with that knowledge. In restoring the upside-down body to its normal orientation, the film has resolved the conflict on behalf of the spectator. What is interesting is the comic effect of the cinematic representation of this cognitive dynamic: in being surprised by the 'strange' gravity he is experiencing, the barber-Chaplin behaves as if he were upright. And in fact, even if he is oriented *physically* upright once the image has been 'corrected', he is still *perceptually* upside down. Looking closer we see that, in doing this, cinema generates another, inverse, interference: we perceive the characters as upright, but we must try to infer that they are upside down.

The expressive and comical element that makes this strategy interesting is that a state of affairs inferred (but not perceived) as being upside down is, however, different from the ordinary upright state of affairs, perceived without any cognitive effort. Adopting a Merleau-Pontean perspective, we are before a case of explicit filmic representation of the perceptual and conceptual shift from upright as 'double upside-down' to *downside up*, an 'inverted normality'. In fact, the *downside-up* image is impossible in physical terms (yet possible in perceptual terms), since the camera has moved to the other side of the plane and the characters have swapped position, but the airplane continues to fly to the right, whereas it should go to the left. This infringement of the rule of spatial continuity demonstrates that continuity of direction of movement prevails over correctness of orientation.

The novelty of this *inverted normality* lies in exploiting the same forces that regulate the real physical world and that, by extension, would regulate the physical world of the film. The pocket watch that floats upwards or the water rising upwards are effects caused by the action of gravity, but in a reversed visual field, and are thus unusual and therefore comical. The comic effect is achieved by the character's initial misunderstanding (represented by counter-reversal in the form of perceptual ambiguity): in being surprised by the 'queer' gravity of which he is experiencing, the barber behaves as if his head were in its normal upward position. Indeed, though *physically* upright, he is *perceptually* upside down.

Only at the end of the sequence does the force of gravity return to assert itself. In fact, the picture is once again oriented like the airplane—upside down—and the barber slips into the void *below* him. The plane crashes *down*, but with no physical consequences for anyone, of course!

In *The Great Dictator*, therefore, the 'ordinary' orientation is restored by the film itself through the editing process: the counter-overturning is implicit and extraneous to the narrative, but it is explicit as a *static* 'act of language'. The spectator needs just a moment to contextualize the orientation of the characters in space (through the alternation of close/medium shots and long shots) and to thereby grasp the comic effect of the gag. The film has only *represented* the 'normalization', rather than conveying it to spectators in a way that can be fully *experienced*. This disembodied strategy is less effective and less interesting than one in which the camera movement itself causes a perturbation of equilibrium that can be more directly felt by the spectator, as I shall discuss.

Chaplin's example leads us to a reflection on the psychophysical conditions of the spectator who sees the upside-down character's body, and in particular on the peculiar 'active passivity' of his involvement. As Merleau-Ponty clarifies, the progressive *bodily righting* experienced by the subject in Stratton's experiment is achieved 'particularly when the subject is active' (285). As the visual field is inverted, the

> mass of sensations which is the world of touch has meanwhile stayed 'the right way'; it can no longer coincide with the visual world so that the

> subject has two irreconcilable representations of his body, one given to him by his tactile sensations, and by those 'visual images' which he has managed to retain from the period preceding the experiment; the other, that of his present vision which shows him his body 'head downwards' (286).

The resolution of the conflict between tactile/motor sensations and visual images 'is the more successfully achieved in proportion as the subject is more active'. The fact that the subject uses his body to move into space assists with the progressive *righting* of perception. In other words, 'it is the experience of movement guided by sight which teaches the subject to harmonize the visual and tactile data: he becomes aware, for instance, that the movement needed to reach his legs, hitherto a movement "downwards", makes its appearance in the new visual spectacle as one which was previously "upwards"' (286). By contrast, when the subject 'is lying motionless on a couch, the body still presents itself against the background of the former space, and, as far as the unseen parts of the body are concerned, right and left preserve their former localization to the end of the experiment' (285).

An obstacle to the application of Merleau-Ponty's reflections to the film experience may be the (relatively) passive condition of the spectator, who sits almost motionless in front of the 'virtual' space of the screen, which depicts movements and gestures of foreign bodies, not of his own. How can the conflict between motor sensations and visual images be resolved if motor sensations exclusively depend on visual images, and the spectator's body is inactive and unable to counterbalance this effect?

As I have already discussed, relatively recent discoveries in neurocognitive research on the so-called 'bimodal' neurons provide scientific evidence that, in particular conditions, human beings are internally *active* during the mere observation of actions and emotions executed and expressed by other subjects. By applying the embodied simulation paradigm to the film experience, it can be hypothesized that, although the spectator's physical body remains still in front of the screen, he internally simulates the (intentional) actions and emotions that are represented on screen as if actually carrying out those actions and feeling those emotions. Moreover, according to the neurophenomenological approach to perception, the film experience is constitutively multisensory and cross-modal. Nevertheless, being confronted with an upside-down image entails a disorientation of the embodied perceptual patterns. The upside-down image causes a sort of displacement of perception (*disembodying* phase); it creates a gap that needs to be filled. As Merleau-Ponty suggests, even in the film experience, tactile and visual perception are potentially in constant conflict. The conflict can be resolved by the spectator on a cognitive level (through a perceptual adaptation), or by the film itself on an expressive level (i.e. what I call *reembodying* phase).

Relative absolute

As anticipated, if static shots and editing imply a disembodied participation, the formal element that most strongly solicits the spectator's corporeality is the movement of the camera: the virtual movement that manipulates and potentially alters the spectator's perception to a such an extent that it also affects his perception of his physical condition. The camera movement, in other words, activates the observer subject even at the motor level.

Consider a case where the frame remains static and the character moves in the environment in a way that violates the laws of gravity. In *Royal Wedding* (Donen 1951), Tom Bowen is in love with a beautiful woman and starts dancing on the walls and the ceiling. Here we have a subversion of the physical laws that, until that moment, seemed to govern the movement of bodies internally in the film space; the spectator's natural perceptual habits are thus disturbed. Suddenly, the character does not obey the laws of gravity that have governed the space in which he moved, and spectators need to reformulate their judgments of the validity of those laws. They immediately adjust their perceptual and cognitive patterns to adapt to the new state of affairs. It is less difficult here than in other cases, since we are in a musical, a genre that sometimes has the license to stray into the realms of fantasy. Moreover, the wide shot composition allows the movement to be fully contextualized. The film expresses and communicates to the spectator the character's state of happiness, light-heartedness, and gaiety on both a motor and an emotional level. This solution works because it thematizes the contrast between the fixedness of the external world (the frame remains static with the room in a 'standard' orientation) and the variability of the internal world (as the character's anti-gravitational movement expresses his emotions).

Let us consider a more complex example from the science-fiction genre. In some of the indoor sequences of *2001: A Space Odyssey* (Kubrick 1968), upside-down images are justified by the setting in outer space, namely in an environment where the force of gravity is naturally absent or severely weakened. Initially, the film adheres to the artificial micro-gravity induced by the rotation of the spacecraft: the character remains upright. Suddenly, however, the upside-down image appears on screen. A static shot shows the Aries 1B Moon Shuttle's hostess walking on a circular surface. From this point on, there is no floor, no wall, and no ceiling in the film. As in *Royal Wedding*, this effect was achieved by building the set inside a revolving steel barrel and mounting the camera and operator to the floor so they would rotate along with the room. The result is a static frame in which the character moves in opposition to the laws of gravity. The relationship between the character's circular orientation frame and the spectator's square, four-sided orientation frame (the screen) frees the film from the implicit 'gravitational pact'. This is easily achieved by the choice of static long shot, which continues to obey *a* law of gravity that applies to the audience (the spectator is 'kept still') but not to the characters.

The point that I want to make here is, again, the importance of considering this 'displacement' of the usual orientation in terms on its bodily implications and effects, in particular the 'proprioceptive revolution' elicited by the motif of overturning. As Annette Michelson (1969) noted in a famous article on Kubrick's film, '[t]he system of pre-suppositions sustaining our spatial sense, the coordinates of the body itself, are hereby suspended and revised' (60); 'one rediscovers, through the shock of recognition, one's own body living in *its* space. One feels suspended, the mind not quite able to 'touch ground'' (58); 'one becomes conscious of the modes of consciousness' (59). The spectator soon accepts that upending bodies is entirely justified in the world of the film, but he has to face the disorientation. In a gravity-free environment, the notions of up and down or horizontal and vertical lose meaning for the character, but not for the spectator, since the represented three-dimensional space depends on the point of view offered by the camera. As Michelson writes,

> A weightless world is one in which the basic coordinates of horizontality and verticality are suspended. Through that suspension the framework of our sensed and operational reality is dissolved. The consequent challenge presented to the spectator in the instantaneously perceived suspension and frustration of expectations, forces readjustment. The challenge is met almost instantaneously, and consciousness of our own physical necessity is regenerated. We snap to attention, in a new, immediate sense of our earth-bound state, in repossession of those coordinates, only to be suspended, again, toward other occasions and forms of recognition (60).

Michelson's analysis insists on reflexivity (as a paradigm of modernism in cinema) but also hints the bodily basis of this *revolution*. I will return to

Michelson and this issue in the next chapter. Here I want to underline that the analysis of *2001: A Space Odyssey* and Michelson's suggestions point to the need to more deeply consider, from a phenomenological philosophical perspective, the problem of relativity of movement and point of view. The issue is, more radically, that of establishing or pre-establishing a system of reference points of orientation. The right side up and the upside-down depend on the relationship to a reference point, but upon what does the reference-point system depend? As Merleau-Ponty (2002) says, 'mere presence is not enough to provide any direction whatsoever' (287):

> 'Inverted' or 'upright,' in themselves, obviously have no meaning. The reply will run: after putting on the glasses the visual field appears inverted in relation to the tactile and bodily field, or the ordinary visual field, which, by nominal definition, we say are 'upright.' [...] we have as yet only sensory fields which are not collections of sensations placed before us, sometimes 'head to the top,' sometimes 'head downwards,' but systems of appearances varyingly orientated during the course of the experiment (287).

The philosopher challenges both empiricist and intellectualistic psychology. The first 'treats the perception of space as the reception, within ourselves, of a real space, and the phenomenal orientation of objects as reflecting their orientation in the world'; for the second, 'the "upright" and the "inverted" are relationships dependent upon the fixed points chosen' (288) Merleau-Ponty chooses a 'third spatiality' and affirms the need for 'an absolute within the sphere of the relative', a space that 'survives (the) complete disorganization' (289) of 'up' and 'down'. The philosopher is not offering a *relativist* account of orientation, but rather an *embodied* account of human perception.

Wertheimer's experiment on repositioning the orientation parameters (i.e. up and down) while the subject sees the image of a room oriented obliquely through a mirror, suggests a solution that is consistent with a notion of the spectator's body as *active*. 'My body is wherever there is something to be done'. It is, phenomenologically, a lived body and, in fact, '[t]he reflected room miraculously calls up a subject capable of living in it'. As Merleau-Ponty states,

> This virtual body ousts the real one to such an extent that the subject no longer has the feeling of being in the world where he actually is, and that instead of his real legs and arms, he feels that he has the legs and arms he would need to walk and act in the reflected room: he inhabits the spectacle (291).

Grounded in the body is a *primordial level* of space, an 'already constituted' (293) space that represents the general system of orientation in respect to which we can identify the *sense* of 'up' and 'down', a sense that survives its perturbation. The 'correction' of the field (i.e. the '*new* normal' orientation) is understandable only if one conceives of the body as 'the subject of space', which is 'geared onto the world' (292): 'The perceptual field corrects itself and at the conclusion of the experiment I identify without any concept because I live in it, because I am borne wholly into the new spectacle and, so to speak, transfer my centre of gravity into it' (293). Rather than 'a process of thought', bodily orientation is something precognitively *lived*. It is an experience in which the body is a *centre of gravity*, a point of reference relative to which a relationship is established, and this relationship is between the body and the world, between the subject and the environment in which it moves.

However, the film spectator's condition of paradoxical 'active passivity' makes the matter more complex. It is not the real body of the spectator that moves in the film world, dwells in the environments, and touches objects. The spectator's experience takes place in the form of multisensory perception; the relationships with characters are, as we have seen in chapter on the motif of acrobatics, inherently empathetic and his positions and movements in the film world are mediated through the positions and the movements of the camera. With regard to the upside-down image, we must therefore wonder how the conflict between motor sensations and visual perceptions can be resolved if the first are generated by, as well as being totally dependent on, the latter. Is it possible to overcome the conflict between tactile sensations and visual images, between body and mind? How can an image create a space where a 'third subject' organizes the relationship between two different orientation systems—that of the character and that of the spectator—especially when they do not coincide, exactly as in the motif of the upside-down image?

Formative concealments

On closer inspection, this 'deficiency' of the *disembodied eye*, that is, the *relativity* of the spatial framework, may even be seen as an advantage for the artistic purpose of the film. For Rudolf Arnheim (1957), the gap between ordinary experience and film experience is not only a 'differentiating factor', but also a 'formative means' that can be used for expressive purposes: 'One of the factors that determine the difference between looking at a motion picture and looking at reality is the absence of the sense of balance and other kinesthetic experiences' (32). In the film experience, since there is nothing to suggest to the spectator what the camera angle is or whether it is upside down, '[t]he absence of any feeling of the force of gravity also makes a worm's-eye view particularly compelling' (104). In fact, 'a "defect" of photographic technique—the inability to realize the correct space coordinates purely from the appearance of a picture—would have been used to achieve an artistic effect' (106). Arnheim's words help us to focus on a second aspect that is closely connected to the previous aspect: the problem of the constitution or pre-constitution of a system of reference points for orientation. The interference between *recognition* and *perception*—the conflict between the spectator's assumptions and the 'real' orientation in the fictional world—seems to be very problematic if related to an embodied conception of the spectator.

Let us reflect on the cases in which cinema can exploit the interference between the eye and the body when perceiving overturned images in order to create an imbalance that can extend from a merely *physical* to a more *dramatic* and, to a certain extent, *symbolic* level. In the thriller *Cape Fear* (Scorsese 1991), Max Cady phones Danielle, attorney Bowden's daughter, to lure her into a trap. After a slow pan of his room, a close-up shows Cady on the phone, with hair hanging down (he is hanging from a door frame to train his abs). Suddenly there is a rapid, full counterclockwise camera rotation that upturns Cady's upside-down face, so that the character is now shown head up, although he continues to be physically upside down. The inversion is thus explicitly artefactual and clearly noted as such by the spectator, but it is not intended to hide anything. The reversal or normalization of perception through which spectators see Cady upright (despite his being upside down—this is what I call *downside-upness*) allows them to directly experience the character's mental instability. Cady's initial upside-down position embodies his own inner reversal, his thirst for revenge, his madness.

Let us take another interesting case, similar to some extent to *Cape Fear*, but that puts into practice a somewhat subtler strategy. In the crime-comedy *A Fish Called Wanda* (Crichton 1988), the dialogue between Otto and Archie, the lawyer, is represented through an apparently classic shot/reverse-shot dynamic. After a quarrel inside the building, we see Archie upright, with his back against a brick wall, finally apologizing to Otto. Suddenly there is a rapid 180° rotation of the camera on its axis, combined with an enlargement of the shot. We now see the whole situation: Archie is upside down hanging out of the window, and Otto is holding his legs, in a state of affairs quite different from the one initially suggested. The actual position of the character is hidden by the cut and by the initial narrow, decontextualized frame, which shows only some of the facts of the scene and the space. Contrary to *Cape Fear*, the contextualization is postponed in order to create an initial ambiguity.

The most interesting stylistic techniques are used in the initial shot: Archie's physical and facial composure, his quiet voice, the legal language (which we certainly would not use if we were in his perilous condition), the presence of a vertical support surface (the wall of the building), and the narrow framing. These elements are *partial,* in the sense of both 'incomplete' and 'partisan'. We are the victims of a double concealment strategy. First, a *temporal concealment*: the cut between the interior of the room and the exterior of the building also functions as an ellipse when it brackets a fundamental part of the event (the one in which Otto takes Archie by force and moves him out of the window to threaten him and get his apologies). The 'absence of space-time continuity'—the term Arnheim would use to explain what makes this editing technique possible—allows this temporal concealment. Second, a *spatial concealment*: the actual position of the character is hidden by the narrow framing that shows only the face in the foreground, without any reference to the surrounding environment. The figure occupies most of the visual field and therefore eclipses the background. According to Arnheim (1957), '[t]he effect of surprise is achieved by making use of the fact that the spectator will be looking at the situation from a certain definite position' (136) determined by the position of the camera.

In addition, rotation is abrupt and sudden (as in *Cape Fear*), so much so that it cannot be attributed to the movement of a character or associated with his point of view. The rotating motion of the camera is explicitly an 'artefactual' movement, outside the diegesis. The intent is indeed to make this artificiality explicit, in the logic of the gag. This 'revealing' function of the rotating movement is made effective by the progressive enlargement of the field, which reveals the spatial context and the relationship between the figures and the background, thus removing the ambiguity that resulted from the sampling of a limited part of the surrounding environment (the wall of the building), which did not offer any reliable point of reference.

Here, therefore, the rotation is a fleeting playful moment offered to the spectator in a film that is generally over the top (a comedy with deliberately excessive acting style). Like the dialogue between the two characters, the sequence ends with an agreement, namely with physical laws finally re-established in the representation of the fictional environment: Otto head up, Archie upside down. Overall, this is a violation of a classic editing rule: the sequence of establishing shot/close-ups/re-establishing shot is truncated in the first part, so that the spectator does not immediately realize the general situation and interprets things in a way that will ultimately be overturned. Spatial and temporal concealment therefore corresponds to a dilation of the process through which the spectator comes to a full understanding of the scene. This is an aspect that characterizes the film experience in general terms: since there are no clues that tell the spectator what the camera orientation is in respect to the profilmic scene (if, for example, the character is right-side up or upside down in the environment in which he moves), virtually any position is possible. The ambiguity arises from the lack of a disambiguation element, an anchorage, a visual or cognitive reference that would allow us to accurately determine the character's position with respect to the environment. Potentially, any shot that isolates the *figure* from any element of its *background* is an image that, while maintaining the usual axioms aligning the representation with ordinary experience, may depict a subject that is actually oriented upside down. The case of the *plongée* shot is emblematic: once the camera position aligns with that of the subject, the orientation of the latter with respect to the force of gravity becomes ambiguous. As Arnheim noted, '[t]he screen is vertical, although since the camera was turned downward it actually represents a horizontal surface' (33). According to Arnheim, the only way that a correct interpretation can be guaranteed is through a contextualization of a visual character: 'This effect can be avoided only by showing enough of the surroundings in the picture to give the spectator his bearings' (33). By transforming this 'differentiating factor' into a 'formative mean', the film finds formal solutions that, by playing on temporal and spatial concealment, ambiguity, and the dilation of the process of correct interpretation, produce an expressive effect.

Bat's-eye-shot

It must be added that the ambiguity of the upside-down motif and consequent expression of the 'cinematic gesture' can also cover cases where there is a camera movement that is not clearly recognizable as such. Although other examples could be taken into consideration, I want to explore one final case from *The Dark Knight* (Nolan 2008). In a crucial scene, a classic shot/reverse-shot dynamic is used in a very particular way. Batman has been captured by the Joker and is balanced on a ledge of a Gotham skyscraper. He manages to free himself from his rival's clutches and throw him into the void. The Joker's fall is shown with a bird's-eye shot (Batman's point of view). As we know, Batman's morality forbids him from killing: instead, he launches one of his cables and hooks the Joker. A low-angle shot immediately follows the high-angle shot: Batman starts to pull his opponent up. The Joker is hanging by his feet, upside down. Initially, Batman is upright, the Joker is upside down, and both are represented as such. Almost immediately, the Joker starts to rotate slowly anticlockwise, until he reaches an upright position. The film has normalized the orientation axes by returning them to the usual upright perception, according to the orientation of the seated spectator. In this way, he can experience the dialogue in the 'conventional' manner. This allows us to grasp the psychological and communicative intent of the representation: as with Cady, the Joker's face is even more effective *downside up* than upside down in expressing his antagonistic, inverted morality, his madness.

But we have to look deeper. This rotation is hiding something curious. Unlike in *The Great Dictator*, in *The Dark Knight* there is no simple editing cut that perceptually normalizes the axes of orientation, nor is the rotation intended to show off the nature of cinematic language or obtain a comic or surprise effect. When we watch the sequence, it *seems* first that the shot is static and that the Joker rotates. The viewer is inclined to think that, once he has hooked him with his cable, Batman is also straightening his rival up. The shot size (close-up) is calculated to temporarily deceive the spectator. It takes a while for the spectator to see that the Joker's long hair, his coat-tail, his pocket watch—just like in *The Great Dictator*!—are hanging *upwards*, contrary to the law of gravity. Therefore, this is not a diegetic movement on the part of the Joker but an artefactual 'move' of the film itself—a camera rolling. It is not an internal transformation, but rather an external normalization whose subtle workings are, at least temporarily, concealed.

This effect is possible thanks to the conflict between visual and tactile perceptions. As Arnheim states,

> there is relativity of movement in film. Since there are no bodily sensations to indicate whether the camera was at rest or in motion, and if in motion at what speed or in what direction, the camera's position is, for want of other evidence, presumed to be fixed. Hence if something moves in the picture this motion is at first seen as a movement of the thing itself and not as the result of a movement of the camera gliding past a stationary object (31-32).

When the spectator cannot count on any 'evidence', or in cases in which evidence is not immediately available, he tends to perceive the character's orientation as a function of his own, head upwards, ordinarily. It must be added, however, that the deliberate lack of clues that leads to the orientation's unrecognizability also depends on cognitive factors connected to the narrative, the 'subject matter'. As Arnheim writes:

> In everyday life we always know whether we are looking straight ahead or up or down; we know whether our body is at rest or in motion, and in what kind of motion. But [...] the spectator cannot tell from what angle a film shot has been taken. Hence, unless the subject matter tells him otherwise, he assumes that the camera was at rest and that it was shooting straight. If a moving object appears in the shot, the spectator's first assumption will be that the object is really in motion and not simply that the camera is running past a stationary object (32).

This deliberate deception is achieved through a very precise formal strategy aimed at delaying the viewer's correct interpretation of the situation. Most importantly, the speed of the rotational movement here is *slow*. In contrast with the rapid and abrupt rotation of the camera in *Cape Fear* and *A Fish Called Wanda*, in *The Dark Knight* the camera moves slowly and silently, softly, and stealthily. The aim is to disguise its artefactual nature and to pass the movement off, at least for a moment, as diegetic. The film has the deliberate intention of *dissimulating* its artefactual nature through an anthropomorphic simulation of the ways in which the character's body moves.

Downside-up

Let us summarize our analysis of the cinematic use of upside-down images and the 'normalization' that the cinema performs on behalf of the spectator.

Both *Royal Wedding* and *2001: A Space Odyssey* use static shots and non-gravitational rotational movements of characters to disorient the spectator's bodily orientation. This is justified emotionally in the first case, diegetically in the second. In both *A Fish Called Wanda* and *The Great Dictator*, the means used to obtain the comic effect is montage (and not rotation). Whereas in the latter film the montage consists of a spatial edit, in the former it also involves a temporal cut (the rotation/enlargement reveals the real situation and creates the surprise). Both *Cape Fear* and *A Fish Called Wanda*, as well as *Alice in Wonderland*, use rapid rotational camera movements presented as explicitly artefactual that cannot be misinterpreted in any way. In the first case, the character is upside down and presented as such—the camera rotation is used not for surprise but rather to present Cady's upside-down morality to dramatic effect. In the second case, the character is upside down but is initially presented 'mendaciously' as upright though the contextualization of a close-up. The combination of rapid camera rotation and extension of the visual field reveals the real situation, creating a surprise effect. When the 'overturning' gesture is not concealed through the editing (as in *The Great Dictator*) and is explicitly performed, as in the case of a rapid camera rotation, the orientation system is suddenly perturbed—a perturbation experienced as disorientation by the spectator.

Editing, shot size, point of view, and camera movement are specific means though which cinema (de)regulates the relation between the spectator's and the character's bodily orientations. That the frame is still and oriented head-up/feet-down lends stability and balance, even if the character is moving contrary to the law of gravity (*Royal Wedding*) or in a zero-gravity or artificial-gravity environment (as in the first part of the sequence in *2001: A Space Odyssey*). The editing may complicate the situation, as it offers upside-down images and leaves it up to the spectator to interpret whether they are upright or upside down (*The Great Dictator*). When this 'filmic gesture' is not hidden in the editing cut but is instead explicitly depicted, as in the case of rapid rotation (*A Fish Called Wanda* and *Cape Fear*), the orientation system changes suddenly and causes a different emotional effect.

All these cases can be viewed as representations of the various stages of Stratton's experiment, described by Merleau-Ponty in *Phenomenology of Perception*. As we have seen, in *The Great Dictator*, the editing *uprights an upside-down* image. The cinema has materialized the perceptual work performed by the embodied human mind. The film does the work on behalf of the spectator: it normalizes the perceptual relational orientation system, often by *'upside-downing' an already upside-down* body or face. Phenomenologically, something in the appearance of this upright image has changed after the upside-downing; restored normality is not quite the same as normality—it is a *downside-up* image. The *downside-up* process consists of a sort of objectification of the deep meaning of images. Through the 'overturned overturn', the character's inner state is effectively communicated, and the moral and symbolic meanings of his physical position are fully articulated, thus engaging the spectator on various levels. The same happens in *A Fish Called Wanda*, where the spectator sees an upside-down body turned upright and experiences comic surprise. But the fact that Archie is *initially* represented as upright even though he is actually upside down supports the Merleau-Pontian idea that the space is constructed in relational rather than in imposed, absolute terms.

In *The Dark Knight*, once the spectator realizes the initial 'deception', he comprehends the psychological and communicative aim of the representation: as for Max Cady in *Cape Fear*, in order to express the character's *inverted* morality, the Joker's *downside-up* image is more effective than the merely upside-down one.[1]

In all these occurrences, the result of the 'double inversion' corresponds to a 'normalization' of the disturbed balance, although it produces an image that inevitably differs from the initial one. As in the first moment in the *Alice in Wonderland* sequence, this *downside-up* image corresponds to the moment when the subject of Stratton's experiment is adapted to the inverted visual orientation. Nevertheless, what is lacking in the film experience, in contrast to Stratton's experiments, is not only the actual physical activity of the spectator (which may help him to better coordinate the sensation of his own body in the environment) but also the time for that inverted world to become a 'normal' (double inverted) one. Every upside-down image lasts no more than a few seconds on the screen. Narrative cinema offers a *representation* of the downside-up image and the process of double inversion, but it does not provide an *experience* of that process.

The cases I have considered are, in fact, exceptions, since mainstream narrative films generally obey the internal or fictional physical laws, and that of gravity in particular. Upside-down images are used sparingly, since a film needs to make itself generally intelligible to its spectators, who would not enjoy continuously having to make the effort to restore the usual patterns of perception, or deliberately thinking and inferring how the upside-down image would be when upright. It is true that we initially enjoy seeing the world inverted. The use of upside-downing aims to take the sense of dizziness that the character is experiencing and to recreate it in the spectator. Even so, it cannot last for more than a few seconds. Upside-downing is, in fact, limited in quantity and duration, since prolonged exposure to such a perceptual reversal would convey a proprioceptive disorientation to the spectator that may impair his pleasure in the film experience. If a film uses upside-down images too often or for too long, or if it does not hide the artifice behind them, its linguistic and artefactual nature becomes explicit, with a consequent dilution of illusionary power. This is avoided in (both

1 On the making of this sequence, director of photography Wally Pfister stated: 'We went back and forth trying to decide whether to leave him upside down in the frame for the whole scene or rotate the camera and have him right-side up and we did not make our decision until that day. Chris [Nolan] felt that, as long as we showed the camera rotation, and let the audience 'in,' that the scene would play better with the Joker's face upright. The end result is, of course, this eerie right-side-up image that defies gravity', qtd. in Tapley 2009.

classic and postmodern) mainstream cinema, which, in order to be coherent and to offer a canonical and intelligible experience, can only *represent* this process. Upside-downing inevitably leads to a dilution of illusionary power, leaving the spectator both conscious of the artefactual nature of cinema and self-conscious of his sensorimotor, activity.

The Dark Knight seems to offer something peculiar. Whereas in *A Fish Called Wanda* and *Cape Fear* the camera rotation is rapid and explicitly artefactual, in Nolan's film the slow and rotational camera movement temporarily conceals its artefactual nature and defers the moment when viewers will understand what is actually happening. Its approach sheds light on one aspect of the development of styles in cinematic representation, eloquent signs of a more general relationship between the subject and the world. This example suggests that, in order to face disorientation caused by the *disembodying* phase (the upside-down), and to restore a comprehensible and recognizable relationship with the world, the film assumes bodily form and provides a *reembodying* phase (the *downside-up*) in which it *dissimulates* its artificiality and *simulates* human bodily qualitative features (i.e. slowness). As the Joker says, '[t]his is what happens when an unstoppable force meets an immovable object'.

Bibliography

Arnheim, Rudolf. 1957. *Film as Art*. Berkeley: University of California Press.

Dolezal, Hubert. 1982. *Living in a World Transformed*. New York: Academic Press.

Harris, Charles S. 1965. 'Perceptual Adaptation to Inverted, Reversed, and Displaced Vision'. *Psychological Review*. 72 (6): 419-444.

Held, Richard, & Sanford J. Freedman. 1962. 'Plasticity in Human Sensorimotor Control'. *Science*. 142 (3591): 455-462.

Kohler, Ivo. 1961. 'Experiments with Goggles'. *Scientific American*. 206 (5): 62-86. DOI:10.1038/scientificamerican0562-62.

Kohler, Ivo. 1964. 'The Formation and Transformation of the Perceptual World'. *Psychological Issues* 3 (4, Monogr. 12): 1-173. DOI:10.1016/0042-6989(64)90016-1.

Linden, David E.J., Ulrich Kallenbach, Armin Heinecke, Wolf Singer, & Rainer Goebel. 1999. 'The Myth of Upright Vision. A Psychophysical and Functional Imaging Study of Adaptation to Inverting Spectacles'. *Perception*. 28 (4): 469-481. DOI:10.1068/p2820.

Merleau-Ponty, Maurice. 2002. *Phenomenology of Perception*. New York: Humanities Press/London: Routledge & Kegan Paul.

Michelson, Annette. 1969. 'Bodies in Space: Film as "Carnal Knowledge"'. *Artforum VII.* (6): 53-64.

Richter, Hans O., S. Magnusson, Kazuyuki Imamura, Mats Fredrikson, Masaaki Okura, & Yasuyoshi Watanabe. 2002. 'Long-Term Adaptation to Prism-Induced Inversion of the Retinal Images'. *Experimental Brain Research.* 144 (4): 445-457. DOI:10.1007/s00221-002-1097-6.

Rock, Irvin. 1966. *The Nature of Perceptual Adaptation.* New York: Basic Books.

Smith, Karl U., & William K. Smith. 1962. *Perception and Motion. An Analysis of Space-structured Behavior.* Philadelphia: Saunders.

Stratton, George M. 1896. 'Some Preliminary Experiments on Vision without Inversion of the Retinal Image'. *Psychological Review.* 3 (6): 611-617. DOI:10.1037/h0072918.

Stratton, George M. 1897a. 'Upright Vision and the Retinal Image'. *Psychological Review.* 4 (2): 182-187. DOI:10.1037/h0064110.

Stratton, George M. 1897b. 'Vision Without Inversion of the Retinal Image'. *Psychological Review.* 4 (5): 463-481. DOI:10.1037/h0071173.

Tapley, Kristpoher. 2009. 'The Top 10 Shots of 2008'. February 25. http://maibaap123.blogspot.com/2011/02/top-10-shots-of-2008-kristopher-tapley.html.

Taylor, James G. 1962. *The Behavioral basis of Perception.* New Haven: Yale University Press.

Welch, Robert B. 1978. *Perceptual Modification: Adapting to Altered Sensory Environments.* New York: Academic Press.

Wertheimer, Max. 1961. 'Experimental Studies on the Seeing of Motion'. In *Classics in Psychology.* Edited by Thorne Shipley, 1032-1089. New York: Philosophical Library.

Yoshimura, Hirokazu. 2002. 'Re-acquisition of Upright Vision While Wearing Visually Left-Right Reversing Goggles'. *Japanese Psychological Research.* 44 (4): 228-233. DOI:10.1111/1468-5884.t01-1-00024.

VI Drift

Ungraspable environments

Abstract
The directionality and intentionality inherent in the previous tensive motifs break down in the case of the movement of characters in environments without gravity. The chapter 'Drift. Ungraspable environments' adopts an ecological approach to visual perception based on James Gibson's concept of affordance and analyses a series of cinematic 'space walks' (with particular reference to Alfonso Cuarón's *Gravity*). The weakening of the human capacity to intentionally grasp objects and to have a stable sense of one's own body in space, which is characteristic of the space-exploration genre, shows that the 'sense of the void' experienced on a psychophysical level also affects the spectator in symbolic terms.

Keywords: Space-exploration films, Affordance, Proprioception, James J. Gibson, Canonical neurons, *Gravity*

'I'm scared'.
—Hal 9000, *2001: A Space Odyssey* (Kubrick 1968)

'Why should I not think of the moon as something like an earth, and therefore something like a dwelling place of living beings?'
—Edmund Husserl, *Foundational Investigations of the Phenomenological Origin of the Spatiality of Nature*, 1934 (1981)

Four spacewalks

Frank and Dave never imagined that HAL could read lips. The two astronauts of *2001: A Space Odyssey* (Kubrick 1968) lock themselves in one of the auxiliary capsules used for extra-vehicular operations and discuss

D'Aloia, A., *Neurofilmology of the Moving Image. Gravity and Vertigo in Contemporary Cinema.* Taylor & Francis Group 2021
DOI: 10.5117/9789463725255_CH06

the possibility of excluding the onboard computer from the *Discovery One* support management system. However, at the earliest opportunity, HAL takes his revenge. Frank is outside the spaceship for a second check on the component reported as broken. HAL waits for the astronaut to leave the capsule and uses its mechanical arms to strike the man, throwing him away into the emptiness of space and causing the oxygen supply tube to detach. In the dark background of the sidereal space and in the most absolute silence, Frank rapidly rotates around his barycentre; he shakes his arms convulsively and desperately seeks, in vain, to grasp and reconnect the tube.

In *2010: The Year We Make Contact* (Hyams 1984) engineer Walter Curnow performs his first spacewalk: he must reactivate the *Discovery*, which David switched off at the end of *2001: A Space Odyssey*, just after HAL's killing of Frank. Anxiety is clearly visible on the man's face, behind the large visor of the helmet: his eyes are wide open, his facial muscles are tensed, he is breathless and fear has immobilized his body. Will he be able to complete the job?

In *Mission to Mars* (De Palma 2000) an accident forces the astronauts to abandon the spacecraft and to approach the Red Planet with the aid of an orbiting support module. Commander Woody Blake realizes that the only way to intercept the module is to launch himself towards it using the residual fuel of the rockets in his suit while pulling a cable with which his colleagues will then be able to reach the module. Woody jumps towards the module and manages to hook the cable to a handle on its surface, but because of the excessive speed reached during the approach path he is unable to brake. His hands frantically look for something to grasp onto, without success. Woody floats in space beyond the module, still moving too fast to be reached and rescued.

In the opening sequence of *Gravity* (Cuarón 2013) a rain of debris collides with the shuttle *Explorer* while Dr. Stone and Matt Kovalsky are outside for a repair mission. The shuttle begins to rotate dramatically, the debris hits the mechanical arm and casts Dr. Stone adrift. The astronaut rotates around and moves into the void of outer space, her breath intensifying as her oxygen runs out. Her long and perilous trip back to Earth begins...

On the narrative level, all of these scenes represent crucial moments in the development of the respective films. Despite the stylistic differences and the use of varying cinematic techniques, these four spacewalks (one from each of the last four decades) have several traits in common: the astronauts wear their space suits and are engaged in delicate extra-vehicular operations in an environment in which they cannot fully control their movements and actions. The representation of a narratively and sensorially dramatic event insists on strongly bodily elements, such as lack of oxygen, difficulty in grasping objects, and weakening body coordination. In each case, the filmic involvement strategy plays on the *limitation* of the characters' capacity to move and act, their inability to control the situation and determine the course of events, their failure and their being at constant risk of death.

In this chapter I argue that space-exploration films, particularly in their spacewalk sequences, are able to convey to the absence of gravity to the spectator more effectively than 'gravitational genres', and they do this by communicating the absence or at least the reduction of intentionality in the acts performed by the astronauts. Compared with the motifs described in the previous chapters, the 'drift' in zero-gravitational space is characterized precisely by being set in a space constitutionally devoid of the force that usually provides the character's movements and actions with intentionality. As I shall discuss, although this condition may not be considered the exclusive prerogative of space-exploration cinema, it indicates the exemplarity of this genre, in which embodied cognition is radically called into question. Although perception and cognition are embodied by their very nature, in non-gravitational fictional worlds a sense of disembodiment is in fact a specific characteristic of the spectator's experience. It therefore calls into play complex *reembodying* strategies, as a detailed analysis of some film's body 'gestures' from the opening scene of *Gravity* throughout the chapter will show.

Desensitization

One of the conditions that most affects the reduction of intentionality perceived by the spectator is a literal form of incorporation. As long as the astronaut is inside the spacecraft, he or she can rely on a 'hospitable' environment, as it is supplied with oxygen, heated, and sometimes provided with artificial gravity. Often a fault compromises such hospitality and renders the spaceship 'a trap from which there is little hope of escape', forcing the astronaut into 'a coffin-like confinement' (Sobchack 1987, 70). But the extreme and hostile conditions of the extra-vehicular environment (too cold and devoid of oxygen) force the astronaut to protect his body and secure his biological functions by wearing a space suit. The suit in fact creates a vital micro-environment that completely envelops the body. The suit is not merely a piece of clothing, but also a kind of protective surface, a hermetic packaging for the insides of a captive body. It is something that is neither inside the body nor completely outside; it is, at the same time, the first—close to the skin—level of a foreign environment, and a separation 'film' that allows for the exploration of the hostile environment. The suit is a labile threshold that both creates a separation and guarantees contact, and its protective character therefore renders it *restrictive.* Above all, it is a cumbersome jacket that makes both bodily movements and manipulative actions (such as touching and grasping) difficult. The restriction of motion has three results: speed reduction, the impossibility of giving directions, and the limitation of the range of movement. The fundamental issue is in fact the astronaut's *control* of his bodily movement with respect to his *intentions.* A further important aspect is that such incorporation involves a denial or at least a weakening of the body's *sensitivity.* By entirely covering the astronaut's body, the suit is in fact a tool of *desensitization*, which reduces or even forbids any surface contact with the outside and attenuates the intensity of tactile sensations. In this chapter I will discuss the effect of such desensitization on the spectator's proprioception (the sense of one's body), equilibrioception (the sense of balance), and haptic perception (the sense of touch).

The function of the spacesuit conceived as such seems to reflect the similarly mediated nature of the film experience in at least three respects. First, the suit is a *medium* in the double sense of the term: it allows exploratory experience that would otherwise be impossible, but at the same time it does not undo the distance between the subject and the world. Secondly, as a surface covering the body and thus reducing the intensity of the stimuli perceived by the character, it reflects the spectator's automatic tendency, by virtue of the neurophysiological processes of simulation, to reproduce an observed action *less intensely.* Neuroscience describes this lessening of intensity as a specific aspect of the activation of neural circuits in the observer's brain. Third, the spacesuit seems to reflect that peculiar 'contact-at-a-distance' that, as we have seen in Chapter II's discussion of empathy and simulation, characterizes the film spectator's modes of involvement. In sum, the spacesuit, as a thin threshold of mediation, is a kind of transparent and elastic membrane that brings the spectator into the character while still keeping them separate. This offers a good way to conceive of the *sensitive experience of insensitivity* characteristic of space-exploration film spectatorship.

Ungraspability

As the four spacewalks show, the astronaut's engagement in a risky extra-vehicular operation often does not yield a satisfactory result. The insistence on ineffective grasp is an obvious symptom of a general lack of tactile sensitivity and prehensile capacity. Due to its large and padded gloves, the space suit prevents the astronaut's hands from grasping objects and appreciating the sensitive qualities of touched surfaces. Despite the contact being made, the hands do not feel and do not grasp. What happens if the spectator observes a tactile action desensitized by the alteration of the character's skin or a tactile gesture that does not function despite its intentionality? This 'ungraspability' is by no means an exclusive feature of space-exploration films. The inaccessibility of objects or the reduction of tactile sensibility can also manifest in gravitationally bounded worlds, especially in scenes in which the characters are engaged in actions where the grasping and holding of objects or points of support are crucial elements for the success of the performed action (usually rescue scenes). However, the lack of gravity and the conditioning imposed by the spacesuit (in particular the gloves), with the consequent reduction in the ability to control the movement and the effectiveness of prudent actions, makes the deficit clearer.

In this sense, my hypothesis is that the characters' actions and movements in non-gravitational environments are perceived as instances of 'frustrated intentionality'—that is, as characterized by precarious and unstable intentionality—precisely because the expressive power of an intentional prehensive action is reduced. On the one hand, it is true that in an immersive experience such as that provided by spacewalk sequences in space-exploration films, the spectator has the bodily impression of experiencing the bodily perception of the character. This hypothesis is supported by psychological and neurophysiological research on *body ownership* and self-consciousness, in particular in regard to the 'rubber hand illusion', a perceptual process by which a fake hand is perceived as being part of one's own body. In the rubber hand experiment, one real hand of a subject (hidden to her sight) and a synthetic hand are simultaneously brushed. The viewing of the fake limb is sufficient to produce a feeling of ownership of it in the subject (cf. Botvinick & Cohen 1998). Psychologist James Gibson (2015) already emphasized the correlation between visual impressions and somatic sensations in providing body self-perception in the 1970s, but the relatively recent neurophysiological implementation of the rubber hand paradigm allowed for the overcoming of the dominant role of vision and revelation of the cross-modal and multisensory nature of body ownership (cf. Ehrsson, Holmes & Passingham 2005), supported by the neural activity in the premotor cortex. In this sense, it can be hypothesized that, in particularly immersive conditions, the spectator experiences the tactile perception of the characters through their hands as if they were his own rubber hands.

In the film experience, in fact, the 'mirroring' of the character's actions also puts in play the perception of the spectator's own body. On the other hand, the neurologically implemented rubber hand paradigm does not resolve the paradox of the perception of reduced or 'frustrated' intentionality typical of manipulative actions in space-exploration films, in which the issue at stake is the sensing of a desensitized stimulus. In order to consider the spectator's experience of reduced intentionality, I will rely further on James Gibson's research and its neural correlates with the aim to delineate an ecological approach to the film experience alternative to that proposed in cognitive film studies (Anderson 1996).

One of the fundamental assumptions of the ecological approach to perception proposed by Gibson is the concept of *affordance* (Gibson 1977; 2015, 119-135). Affordances are described as physical properties of an object or an environment that suggest and allow an individual (animal or human) to perform an action or a set of possible actions. Closely related to the shape of our bodies and our ability to perform actions, affordances 'define the environment as situations of meaning and circumstances for action' (Gallagher & Zahavi 2007, 138). Following the definition of *demand character* of an object introduced by Gestalt psychologist Kurt Koffka (1935),[1] Gibson (2015) says that '[e]ach thing says what it is' (129); everything is inherently equipped with an 'invitation character'[2] for a certain behaviour and the achievement of an end.[3]

As far as we are concerned in this chapter, it is significant that Gibson's affordance theory is based upon a reflection on the nature of Earth's surface and its main properties, namely horizontality, flatness, rigidity, and extension:

> If a terrestrial surface is nearly horizontal (instead of slanted), nearly flat (instead of convex or concave), and sufficiently extended (relative to the size of the animal) and if its substance is rigid (relative to the weight of the animal), then the surface *affords support*. It is a surface of support, and we call it a substratum, ground, or floor. It is stand-on-able,

1 The exact quote is as follows: 'To primitive man each thing says what it is and what he ought to do with it: a fruit says, "Eat me;" water says, "Drink me;" thunder says, "Fear me," and woman says, "Love me"' (7).

2 The expression 'invitation character' refers instead to the translation of the term *Aufforderungscharakter*, as proposed by another Gestalt psychologist, Kurt Lewin (1926).

3 Gibson states, however, that '[t]he affordance of something does *not change* as the need of the observer changes' (130), whereas the concepts of 'demand character' and 'invitation character' predicted value of this variability.

> permitting an upright posture for quadrupeds and bipeds. It is therefore walk-on-able and run-over-able. It is not sink-into-able like a surface of water or a swamp, that is, not for heavy terrestrial animals. Support for water bugs is different (119).

These properties, therefore, represent the affordances of support, which 'permit equilibrium and the maintaining of a posture with respect to gravity, this being a force perpendicular to the surface' (123). Balance and posture are also 'prerequisite to other behaviours, such as locomotion and manipulation' (123). In sum, for Gibson, '[t]he ground is quite literally the *basis* of the behaviour of land animals' (123).

In addition, Gibson states that the Earth to which he refers is not compatible with a Copernican conception and evokes a return to the old belief that the Earth was flat (obviously only within the logic of affordance), namely with respect to the idea that the properties of the environment are 'commensurate' to the size of the living species that inhabit it: 'This is not, of course, the earth of Copernicus; it is the earth at the scale of the human animal, and on that scale it is flat, not round' (123). The ante-Copernican astronomy and anti-Newtonian physics proposed almost provocatively by Gibson have a radical phenomenological motivation: the environment is not equivalent to the physical environment and space is not geometric space; it is instead the 'living space of the environment' (110). As Gibson states, '[t]he doctrine that we could not perceive the world around us unless we already had the concept of space is nonsense. It is quite the other way around: We could not conceive of empty space unless we could see the ground under our feet and the sky above. Space is a myth, a ghost, a fiction for geometers' (xv). We could say then that the Earth possesses certain affordances, and in particular that of offering a *support* or a *ground,* but only when the individual is within the Earth's atmosphere. It is evident that the Earth has different properties when the individual in question is instead an astronaut outside the atmosphere. As we shall see, given the particular dual psychophysical condition of the film spectator—who is both a terrestrial person in the physical space of the cinema *and* has the impression of being immersed in a non-gravitational space—the Earth *continues* and at the same time *does not continue* to offer itself as ground. Accordingly, the same affordances of support and ground are at the same time valid and invalid (or significantly reduced).

This all conceives of affordance with respect to surfaces. But Gibson also identifies affordances of objects, referring specifically to activities of 'manipulation'. The shape and size of objects configure the affordances for their grasping. 'Locomotor approach often terminates in reaching and grasping. *Reaching* is an elongation of the arm-shape and a minification of the five-pronged handshape until contact occurs. If the object is hand-size, it is graspable; if too large or too small, it is not' (224). It follows that the 'invitation character' of objects, such as a hammer, a knife, a ball, a rope, or a pencil, may be, respectively, striking, cutting, hurling, wrapping around, and drawing on surfaces (124-127). Likewise, an outstretched hand says 'shake me', and so—to use a number of typical aerospace objects—a button says 'push me', a lever says 'use me', and so on. Any difficulties on the part of the astronaut to accomplish the affordance of objects is experienced by the spectator as a 'failed' affordance.

Prehensile neurons

Recent neurocognitive research has provided empirical evidence to support the psychological phenomena described so far. I have previously referred to two particular classes of neurons identified in the premotor cortex of primates (including humans). The bimodal or visuomotor neurons, i.e. those equipped with visual *and* other functional properties, fire both when an individual performs an action and when she simply observes an object or someone else performing the action. As neurophysiologists Garbarini and Adenzato (2004) claim in an article on the relationship between the concept of affordances and the functioning of visuomotor neurons, 'the central point of Gibson's theory was his explicit rejection of the dichotomy between *action* and *perception*. [...] Gibson's pioneering efforts and his ecological perspective certainly represent a fundamental foundation for the paradigm of *embodied cognition*' (101). As Gibson (2015) points out, '[w] e are told that vision depends on the eye, which is connected to the brain. I shall suggest that natural vision depends on the eyes in the head on a body supported by the ground, the brain being only the central organ of a complete visual system' (xiii).

A class of neuron called 'canonical neurons' is crucial to understanding this point. These brain cells have been detected in the monkey and human ventral premotor cortex and discharge during motor act execution and in response to the presentation, in the peripersonal space, of three-dimensional objects according to their shape, size, and spatial orientation (Murata et al. 1997; Rizzolatti, Fogassi & Gallese 1999; Murata et al. 2000; Raos et al. 2006). In the case of manual grasping, for example, canonical neurons do not encode the prehensile action, but rather the object's affordance, allowing an immediate and automatic selection of the inherent properties that allow the subject to interact with the object. In neurophenomenological terms, canonical neurons encode intentional acts, or movements coordinated by a precise goal (Rizzolatti et al. 1996). In other words—to relate these neural mechanisms to Gibson's proposal—objects have 'tactile' characteristics that are immediately 'grasped' by the subject. The new element lies in the fact that such 'internal grasping' occurs at the neural level, whether the subject is performing an action or she is observing someone else performing that action, precisely because of the selective response of these neurons to visual stimuli, or even imagining that action. Empirical studies tell us that the observation of tactile sensations of another subject activates the same neural circuits involved during the experience of being touched oneself (Keysers et al. 2004; Blakemore et al. 2005; Ebisch et al. 2008; Ebisch et al. 2011; Gallese & Ebisch 2013). This dual mode of activation of the same somatosensory areas of the brain suggests that our ability to experience or directly understand the tactile experience of others is mediated by embodied simulation.

It is important to clarify that the activity of canonical neurons is only possible in association with that of another class of bimodal neurons, the so-called 'mirror neurons', which are located in the same brain area and respond both during the execution of an action and when an action executed by other individuals is observed. When someone observes the action of another subject, her neural system evokes a mirrored response, as if she were carrying out that action herself (cf. *infra*, Ch. 1). Equally important is that these neurons fire only when the action is 'transitive' and goal-oriented, for example, when the hands interact with an object, but not when gesturing. Neuroscientists have even proposed a classification of mirror neurons based on the various types of transitive manual movements, namely grasping, holding, manipulating, and releasing (Rizzolatti & Fadiga 1998).

The 'combined' activation of canonical and mirror neurons thus seems to support the hypothesis that affordances emerge when the spectator watches a film character performing an intentional and transitive act, as if the spectator were performing that action. Moreover, neuroscience supports the hypothesis that the reduction or invalidation of gravity and the consequent reduction of a character's sensitivity due to movement difficulties and bodily encapsulation in the spacesuit—especially hands in gloves—generate interference in the spectator's perception of affordances. In *Mission to Mars* the affordance of grasping is explicitly suggested by the representation, with a camera movement forward in the direction of the module (Woody's POV shot). The shot of Woody's hands preparing to grab the handle and that of the faces of his colleagues (which show anxiety and worry) are clearly directed towards the goal and clarify the intentions of the character.[4] However, although the affordance is valid, the gloves and the uncontrolled speed prevent the character from realizing his intention and grabbing the pole on the module. The same happens in the (very similar) climax scene of *The Martian* (Scott 2015), when Mark Watney is rescued by Melissa Lewis: as the two astronauts make physical contact, the hold of their two hands is lost due to the speed of their bodies and the metal ash on their gloves.

At this point, in light of the link between affordances and visuomotor neurons, it can be argued that when the observed subject's gripping act fails in its intent (the motor component of the process is 'defective'), canonical neurons are still activated in order to 'grab' that object (the visual component of the process is normally performed). If the character's action is intentional, if it is goal-directed, such an action and the intentions involved in it are simulated as a function of the affordances offered by the object, even when there is a significant reduction in the prehensile capacity of the character and the observed action does not accomplish its intentions.

On the one hand, the spectator, if effectively guided by the formal modes of representation, can grasp objects that the character's hands cannot grasp by virtue of the activation of visuomotor neurons that encode the implicit intention of the action, and can feel a tactile stimulus that cannot be felt by the character thanks to a synaptic perceptual dynamic that captures tactile sensations based on visual stimuli. Therefore, thanks to simulation and its haptic nature, the filmic mediation does not preclude graspability and tactility (cf. Blakemore et al. 2005; Banissy & Ward 2007). On the other hand, the spectator nonetheless experiences action failure and insensitivity, an experience of ungraspability and intangibility. Faced with a hand that touches but does not feel due to a barrier that reduces sensitivity, the spectator perceives a *desensitization,* the absence of a tactile consistency, and then she tends, as noted, to 'complete' the task not fully performed by the character on the basis on physiological mechanisms and automatic processes. In sum, a peculiar mode of perceptual experience exists: the spectator empathetically experiences what the character cannot or is not able to feel, as well as his or her weakened and desensitized feelings.

4 On the activity of the canonical neurons compared to camera movements and the management of point of view, cf. Gallese & Guerra 2012; 2019.

Ungrounding

More than once I have used the term 'suspension' to indicate not only the spectator's state of cognitive and emotional *suspense* (i.e. the sense of excitement or anxiety elicited by the uncertainty of the events that may occur in the film), but also the literal bodily condition of being suspended in space. By re-creating micro-gravity cinematographically, Alfonso Cuarón and Emmanuel Lubezki designed *Gravity* to immerse the spectator in a psychophysical state analogous to that of the character: a state of vulnerability, fatality, and irreversible expulsion into space. This strategy of engagement emphasizes archetypical situations and solutions characteristic of space-exploration film style, the most obvious being Kubrick's *2001: A Space Odyssey*, but another antecedent for its use of rotational figures and the disruption of horizontal/vertical axis of orientation is Michael Snow's experimental film *La Région Central* (Thompson 2013a). '*Gravity* and *2001*', writes Scott Richmond (2016) in his proprioceptive analysis of the two films, 'are both centrally concerned with the perception of space as an embodied phenomenon and the modulation of this embodied perception of space as a fundamental aesthetic affordance of the cinema' (4). *Gravity*, however, marks a caesura, a 'point of no return' in the history of the genre. The suspense is literally and bodily experienced (thanks also to the skilful use of 3D); all formal solutions are fully functional in transmitting the character's psychophysical state to the spectator, who experiences both disorientation and suspension with immediacy: 'the awareness of proprioception *Gravity* brings does not take the form of a cognitive apprehension of embodied, lower-level perceptual processes. Rather, proprioception becomes thematic by means of embodied affect. I don't *think* my disorientation [...] I *feel* it' (135).

This experience depends on the fact that outside the atmosphere the notion of suspension, as well as any other mode of relationship between body and space (for example, the notion of up and down), acquires a value that is free from the orientation suggested or even imposed by gravity. As we have seen in the previous chapter, one piece of evidence for the interference between the gravitational perceptual frame and the non-gravitational one is the use of the motif of the upside-down figure, in which the inverted representation of the body (disanchoring of the character from the 'ground' of the fictional world) aims to suspend the spectator (creating the impression of disanchoring from the empirical ground of the cinema). In this sense, the relativity of point of view provided by the mediation of the camera is a valid potential disorientation factor even in gravitational environments. But in spite of the fact that they are not exclusive to space-exploration cinema, disorientation or 'eradication' from the ground are, in this genre, more intimately linked to the devaluation of the intrinsic forces that govern the fictional world and extend their validity—and therefore also their *invalidity*—beyond the threshold of the screen. The question then is the interference that arises between the natural disposition of human beings to be subject to gravity and the abrupt cancellation of this physiological constrain. This 'liberation' from the orientation principle results in a character's disorientation, almost a 'loss' which, under certain particularly immersive film experience conditions, also affects the spectator, her sense of the position and equilibrium, due to perturbation of both proprioception (i.e. the function of muscle receptors, joints and tendons to provide information about the body's position in space) and her vestibular system (i.e. the sense of balance and awareness of spatial orientation).

To better understand this dynamic, let us start again from a concrete case. In *2010: The Year We Make Contact*, Curnow is hesitant and awkward in his movements even before passing through the spaceship door and advancing into the void separating him from the surface of Jupiter. As soon as he is out of the spaceship, he remains motionless in an awkward posture: his arms spread out from the torso as if trying to keep his balance and at the same time protect himself from falling into the void, although this is not a possible event, at least not in the same physical way that it would occur in a gravitational environment. The character in fact experiences a conflict between the ordinary gravitational mode of bodily experience and an extraordinary non-gravitational mode. Whereas in a gravitational environment the character could be compared to an acrobat suspended on a wire in mid-air, here the astronaut has to literally *walk on the void*, to perform an unknown action he has never carried out before. His acrophobia is augmented by a fear connected to its own *inexperience*: the fear of the void, or the fear of the unknown. The question obviously lies in understanding how the spectator experiences such a situation, given that it is still taking place in the gravitational environment of the cinema, in which visual perception and proprioception may be used (for creative purposes) in reciprocal contrast.

In order to delve into the interference between visual sensations and tactile sensations I will turn again to James Gibson. In his book, the psychologist discusses the results of the 'visual cliff' experiment conducted by Eleanor Gibson and Richard Walk (1960). In the experiment, aimed at investigating the perception of depth in humans (especially children) and animals, a sheet of heavy Plexiglass, similar to a table in its dimensions, height from the floor, and shape, was horizontally positioned. The subjects of the experiment were placed on the Plexiglass sheet in two different conditions. In the case in which a high-contrast checkered fabric was pressed up against the underside of the glass to make it appear solid, the children or animals tested walked or crawled normally. If instead the fabric was placed on the ground, subjects stopped, crouched, or showed signs of agitation and fear once they had moved onto the glass area. The behaviour of individuals, then, was different depending on the presence or absence of 'optical information', although the tactile information provided by the contact of the feet or limbs on the glass sheet was the same in both cases. As Gibson (2015) notes,

> The optical information in this experiment, I believe, is contradictory to the haptic information. One sees oneself as being up in the air, but one feels oneself in contact with a surface of support and, of course, one feels the normal pull of gravity in the vestibular organ (149).

The disoriented and scared behaviour of the subjects depended, according to Gibson, on the emergence of erroneous and inappropriate affordances, due precisely to the transparency of the glass plate and to the contradiction between the visual and tactile sensations it generated. 'The brink of a cliff affords falling off; it is in fact dangerous and it looks dangerous to us' (133) whereas a transparent and thus visually unperceived surface of support that extends over the edge, 'no longer affords falling and in fact is not dangerous, but it may still *look* dangerous' (133). The support surface, in other words, was traded for 'air' in terms of optical specification and such '[a]ir downward affords falling and is dangerous' (133), while in fact the subject *does not* feel as though they are falling. By virtue of this contradiction, '[t]he mistaken perceptions led to inappropriate actions' (133). The reaction that led the subjects to stop and even to feel fear and adopt 'precautionary' behaviour was due to the fact that '[t]he optical information in this experiment [...] is contradictory to the haptic information' (133). Consequently, Gibson notes that 'the sight of a cliff is *not* a case of perceiving the third dimension. One perceives the affordance of its edge. A cliff is a feature of the terrain, a highly significant, special kind of dihedral angle in ecological geometry, a falling-off place' (133). According to this perspective, the edge of a cliff is a 'jump' not commensurate with the dimensions of humans (or animals).

Now, to return to the *2010: The Year We Make Contact* example, although Curnow's situation is not literally similar to the visual cliff experiment, the latter offers insights that allow us to describe the spectator's situation when watching the scene. Leaning into the void from the edge of the spaceship over the distant surface of Jupiter, Curnow reacts like a scared child on the Plexiglass sheet, deprived of the expected tactile information, which contrasts with optical information. For a subject used to moving in a gravitational environment, absence of gravity creates the illusion of 'walking on the void', because the sequence offers the 'inappropriate' affordance of support.

On the one hand, Curnow's psychophysical suspension and disorientation is expressed through a formal style that communicates a psychophysical suspense to the spectator. This condition depends on the film's ability to extend the absence of fictional gravity into the spectator's real space; to join the darkness of the theatre to the sidereal space of representation; to establish a common area of experience in which one has the impression of losing, at least temporarily, the feeling of being still rooted to the ground, located on a supporting surface, and subject to real-world gravity. In the indefinite darkness of the cinema the spectator feels almost like an astronaut, engaged in a risky spacewalk into deep and infinite outer space. In this sense, the condition of the astronaut is not only a metaphor for that of the spectator, whose physical and mental condition during the experience of watching a space-exploration film can double that of the character, whose bodily orientation is disanchored from a precise reference to the *ground*. In the absence of a reference point in both the fictional and the empirical worlds, the spectator not only imagines being suspended in the same space as the character, but also experiences a condition of *disanchoring* by virtue of a simulation process that embodies the absence of sensitivity; an undocked and potentially confusing situation characterized by a vague sense of *intangibility*.

On the other hand, the spectator nevertheless has proprioceptive information about the position and posture of her own body and can, for example, ascertain the presence of the support offered by the real-world ground by moving her feet. In increasing the spectator's proprioceptive awareness, this fact explicitly provides tactile contact information that conflicts with visual information. The spectator continues to be suspended in outer space, while simultaneously feeling supported by a surface. We may even think of the screen as a transparent extension of the ground, as in the visual cliff experiment. The spectator experiences a 'loss' resulting from the optical contrast between suspension and tactile support, and in this sense behaves like Curnow, adopting a gravitational behaviour in respect to a non-gravitational—and therefore new and unknown—psychophysical situation. Like the astronaut, the spectator is somehow in constant search of a foothold, a reference, an anchor that compensates for the desensitization caused by the suspension in the void—a *reembodying* of sensitivity.

The most important aspect of the analysis of this sequence is that, although there are no diegetic reasons to use an orthogonal orientation of the spectator with respect to the astronaut and of the astronaut with respect to Jupiter (and therefore, by virtue of an eyeline match, the spectator with respect to the orientation of astronaut to planet), the articulation of the shots suggests a perception in accordance with the usual gravitational pattern. Similarly, even though the spectator may think that the fear felt by the character is caused by his inexperience as an astronaut and his terror of the void, the way emotions and internal states are represented here conveys a sense of vertigo, or the fear of *falling*. As soon as Curnow walks through the door and exits into the space *above* Jupiter, in fact, his state of agitation does not appear as a vague fear of the void, but rather as a precise fear of the altitude, despite the fact that the very notion of altitude does not make sense in an environment without gravity, nor we can say in absolute terms he is *above* the planet. The articulation of the points of view shows this strategy precisely: a close-up shows Curnow's face as he tries not to look *down*; a subjective shot shows his legs and, *below* him, Jupiter's surface.

Imbalance

I have repeatedly referred to the sense of balance as a crucial element in the simulation of a film character's suspension in zero-gravity environments. Gibson himself stressed the importance of the role of the vestibular system in providing information about the individual's position in space and determining their sense of balance. It will thus be of interest to look more deeply into how filmic experience can also be described by resorting to this perceptual mode.

The vestibular apparatus consists of an organ located deep in the inner ear. The information gathered from the vestibule arrives in the brain, where it is used by the balance system to ensure the proper alignment of the individual's posture and to perceive vertical acceleration (experienced, for example, in an elevator), horizontal acceleration (experienced in a car), and the rotational movements of the head and body (the so-called angular accelerations) (cf. Goldberg et al. 2012; Purvers et al. 2010, 315-335).

The vestibular system is multimodal in the sense that it integrates and interprets the vestibular information not only with that provided by the direct perceptual channels of sight and hearing, but also with that provided by other peripheral receptors, in particular the skin and proprioceptive ones (especially if coming from the foot, that is, the only fixed reference in an erect posture). The vestibular system can be considered a sort of a 'sixth sense' which attests to the importance of the physiological, automatic, and pre-reflective nature of perceptual experience. At a neural level, even if we are seated in front of a cinema screen and our organism does not receive direct stimuli (such as linear or rotational acceleration) from the film environment, structures in the inner ear vestibule (i.e. the utricle and saccule) detect the position of our head in respect to the gravitational axis of our empirical environment. That is to say that, even in absence of stimuli, the vestibular sense works to detect spatial orientation relative to gravity (cf. Angelaki & Cullen 2008, 126).

As noted by Luis Rocha Antunes (2016) in a recent book on the role of multisensory perception and kinaesthetic engagement in film experience, '[a]lthough we are in a seated position, the vestibular shapes our perceptual experience of a film at all times. Much of the perceptual information that we commonly believe to be purely visual is actually also vestibular' (49). 'The mere act of sight, that is, experience with a body-centred frame of reference, is a vestibular experience' (51). It should be added that the relevance of the effect of the tensive motifs on the spectator's vestibular system emerges, once again, by negation, i.e. as a function of induced pseudo-pathological perceptual conditions, as the result of a sort of 'sabotage' accomplished by the film itself when it refutes or invalidates the physical laws that regulate the relationship between the body and the environment. 'Deceptive' affordances, for example, interfere with or even prevent the vestibular system from functioning properly, with the result of providing the spectator a sense of *imbalance*. Vestibular information conflicting with that drawn from visual perception can cause discomfort and lead to inappropriate behaviour, just as in the case of the visual cliff. When the vestibular system is compromised and not operate normally due to disease, oculomotor disorders of balance and posture arise. Vertigo is in fact the erroneous feeling that the surrounding environment is moving with respect to one's own body ('objective vertigo') or the body in respect to the environment ('subjective vertigo'), which makes it impossible for the subject to stand.

Now, the film spectator is generally seated and vertigo is thus attenuated, because the information derived from proprioception is less effective. However, as we have seen, by virtue of physiological and neurophysiological mechanisms, the film experience intensifies the impression of suspension. Although the spectator simulates the bodily states of another subject—i.e. the character—and does not experience her own, the film's premeditated 'tampering' with the vestibular sense generates a weakening or even a reversal of intentionality, understood as the orientation of the action and the movement towards an object or a goal. In the spacewalks, this apparent *unintentionality* is mainly carried out through a subtraction of sensory stimuli that contribute to determining the sense of balance through the vestibular apparatus. *Gravity*, for example, is an action film in which action is progressively frustrated: the story centres on difficult-to-achieve tasks, on the lack (and the loss) of points of reference, and on the continuous risk of suffocation. The spectator empathetically experiences the character's difficulty in moving or breathing. As Rocha Antunes (2016) argues, '[t]he affective and visceral impact of *Gravity* arises [...] from the sensory context of the film's world, from the senses themselves, including the vestibular and proprioceptive energies of the spacecraft descending at full speed through outer space to Earth' (18). As Richmond (2016) writes, 'the absence of onscreen weight and the dissolution of any vertical or horizontal axes engender a more constant, if subtle, rupture between my vision and my vestibular sense' (134).

Adrift

In the sequence of *2001: A Space Odyssey* mentioned at the beginning of this chapter, HAL causes Dr. Frank Poole's death. Frank's colleague, Dave Bowman, follows the operations from Discovery and witnesses the events. David can see Frank's body through the cockpit window as it moves from left to right in the frame. The astronaut moves away from the ship into the void, rotating in an uncoordinated fashion. At this point, a long shot shows Frank's body rotating, while he frantically tries to reconnect the oxygen tube to his helmet. The astronaut's body is kept at the centre of the frame. After a cut to Dave's reaction, Frank's body enters the shot from below; he is dead from asphyxiation and drifts in the void. Both the module and Frank's body continue to rotate by inertia, the first at double the speed of the second, and recede into the background until almost swallowed by the darkness. A completely reversed shot then shows Frank's body coming from the background towards the camera before exiting the visual field in the upper part of the screen. In this sequence we find at least two strategies of representation of the 'drift' combined. The first is *rotation*: Frank's body rotates seamlessly around its own barycentre, as though in a sort of continuous reversal. The second is the *translation* towards the background or, in two-dimensional terms, a *reduction* of scale: the body appears smaller and smaller the more distant in depth.[5]

The most interesting aspect of this sequence is our inability to precisely determine the camera angle. While the presence of another body allows us to establish a reciprocal orientation between the visible bodies, such a relationship is not intelligible in absolute terms, i.e. with respect to the ground. As Rudolf Arnheim (1957) points out,

> One of the factors that determine the difference between looking at a motion picture and looking at reality is the absence of the sense of balance and other kinesthetic experiences. In everyday life we always know whether we are looking straight ahead or up or down; we know whether our body is at rest or in motion, and in what kind of motion. But [...] the spectator cannot tell from what angle a film shot has been taken (102).

In this sense, given that the spectator receives ambiguous information because of the conflict between visual and proprioceptive cues, her perceptual and interpretative faculties are exposed to a relative and ambiguous orientation. The consistency of the character's position with respect to the edges of the screen and the fact that it does not therefore move into the fictional space in depth makes the shot seem flat. The orientation of the visual field attribution depends, gestaltically, on the activity of the spectator's perception. A likely perceptual interpretation obeys the law of *continuity of direction*, by virtue of which the direction of movement in a shot is perceived as the same as the movement represented in the previous one, regardless of its actual direction with respect to the edges of the frame. Consistent with the scene in which Frank's body moves from left to right through the window of the cockpit, the spectator tends to perceive Frank's body at the centre of the frame as if he is moving left to right.

However, since the spectator may think that Frank is also moving from one point in space to another because he has been violently pushed by HAL, the prevailing perceptual interpretation will be to establish a frontal and flat perspective on the represented body. Given this basic condition, there is

5 This solution can be found, for example, in *Outland* (Hyams 1981), where one of the astronauts dies due to an extreme increase in the pressure inside the spacesuit (his face literally swells and explodes). His body 'falls' into space spinning in a spiral and away into the background. At the beginning of *Interstellar*'s (Nolan 2014) 'tesseract' scene, the astronaut's 'fall' is rendered through both body rotation and point-of-view shots of the characters watching downwards (his legs and feet are visible), i.e. a solution that suggests the descendant movement based on the orientation of the camera angle in respect to the character's body.

an element that gives the spectator the impression that Frank's movement takes place towards *the bottom* and is therefore a 'fall', according to the force of gravity. The stars, visible in the background, 'move' upwards (although along a semi-circular axis which increases the sense of Frank's agitation while attempting to reconnect the oxygen tube). Given that there are no other bodies included in the frame, and that the distances between Frank and the edges of the shot remain unchanged, the upward 'flow' of the stars provides the spectator a visual reference and causes the astronaut's movement to be perceived as a descent. In other words, thanks to the presence of the stars, the spectator has the impression that Frank is not only rotating around his own barycentre, but that he is also moving from one point in space to another. At the same time, therefore, the spectator also has the impression that the shot is not static, but rather that the camera falls down with Frank, accompanying his movement in space.

However, the mutual position and mobility or immobility of bodies in the representational space does not necessarily provide clear indications about the direction of movement. The direction in fact can only be seen as such if there is a further absolute reference point, namely the ground. In the absence of these conditions, the spectator finds it hard to differentiate between a frontal and a vertical shot angle. In other words, since in the non-gravitational space up and down and or left and right cannot be determined in absolute terms, the spectator has the impression that the frame may be oriented either frontally or vertically. The camera angle is thus ambiguous and reversible. The film can even play with this ambiguity, as in an optical illusion, to shift the interpretation from one angle to another.

Postures

Some physiological and neurophysiological experiments offer interesting elements of reflection on how the observer perceives orientation. An experiment conducted by Lackner and Graybiel, for example, investigated the relationship between the posture of a subject placed within a spaceship that fluctuates parabolically (in order to create a micro-gravitational environment) and the subject's perception of the orientation of both her own body and that of the spaceship (cf. Lackner & Graybiel 1979; Lackner & Graybiel 1983; cf. also Lackner 1988; 1992. For a discussion of these experiment, cf. Morris 2004, 133 ff.). The experiment could be varied by changing three factors: the head position and gaze direction (towards the body/forward/away from the body), the orientation of the face (ceilingward/

floorward), the head orientation (to the fore/aft). The most interesting result was found in the case of the combination of gaze towards the body and face floorward: with subject's head aft, the aircraft is felt as having tail down; with head to the fore, the aircraft is felt as nose down. This shows that, in the particular condition of suspension obtained by micro-gravitation, the perceived orientation does not depend on the subject's posture, nor the visible architecture of the environment (the spaceship space), nor even the direction of the gaze, so that the same results are obtained even when the subject keeps her eyes closed. There is also a uniform correlation between the sensed body orientation and the perceived orientation of the spaceship: it is an *internally relative* guidance system. In other words, the orientation is not determined objectively in absolute terms, nor in a purely subjective manner (given also the quantitative significance of the results): 'orientation perception is not rooted in an a priori intuition or a fixed, immediate principle; the principle is twofold and mediated by movement' (Morris 2004): 'Orientation has a *sense*, is phenomenal [...] and depends on movement that crosses a postured body with the world' (136).

A reflection on the results of this experiment is relevant if the film experience is conceived not simply as a relationship between a spectator seated and invariably oriented orthogonally with respect to a screen placed in front of her. The case of the character's body movements in non-gravitational environments tells us something more: Frank's rotation without references is exposed to the reversibility or ambiguity of the determined point of view because the form of representation makes the spectator lose her usual sense of posture inside the cinema, conceived as a sort of spaceship, a *vehicle* in flight above the Earth.

In 1940, in his provisional yet seminal proposal of an 'Overthrow of the Copernican theory in usual interpretation of a world view', Edmund Husserl (1981) already traced the basis for such an exploration. According to the German philosopher, '[m]otion occurs on or in the earth, away from it or off it. In conformity with this original idea, the earth does not move and does not rest; only in relation to it are motion and rest given as having their sense of motion and rest' (233). Earth so conceived is the 'total-body: the vehicle of all bodies' (223), 'the genesis of our idea of the world' (222) the originary body in respect of which it is possible to consider movement. But as the earth is considered as a body among many others in the universe, 'in the open plurality of surrounding bodies' (224) motion and rest become relative notions. The same relativity can be found in the film experience, where the relationship between the spectator's body and the earth is *always* mediated by a 'vehicle' that becomes a new basis-body: as when travelling on a car or a train, the body is at rest on a moving basis-body (cf. 224), and the relativity of cinematic postures may allow the phenomenon of *vection*—i.e. the illusion of self-motion caused by visual and/or acoustic information that belong to the vestibular sense—to arise, since in the film experience we paradoxically move at rest.[6]

As Annette Michelson (1969) argues in her analysis of Kubrick's *2001: A Space Odyssey*, the capability of the film to *revolutionize* the orientation system of both the representation and the spectator's experience is not a mere formal solution, but rather an 'evolutive epistemology'. Suspension is both a physical condition experienced by the spectator and a reflexive act of apperception:

> Viewing becomes [...] the discovery, through the acknowledgment of disorientation, of what it is to see, to learn, to know, and of what it is to be, seeing. Once the theatre seat has been transformed into a vessel, opening out onto and through the curve of a helmet to that of the screen as into the curvature of space, one rediscovers, through the shock of recognition, one's own body living in *its* space. One feels suspended, the mind not quite able to 'touch ground' (58).

As is evident, for Michelson this 'feeling' implies reflexivity: 'one becomes conscious of the modes of consciousness'; the film 'solicits, in its overwhelming immediacy, the *relocation of the terrain upon which things happen*', a terrain that is in between the screen and the spectator: 'It is the area defined and constantly traversed by our active restructuring and reconstitution, through an experience of 'outer' space, of the 'inner' space of the body' (59).

As suggested in the analysis of the upside-down motif in the previous chapter, orientation is not given in itself, but is the result of a negotiation between subjectivity and objectivity as a function of the fact that the subject, to use Merleau-Ponty's terms, 'inhabits the world', she is rooted, embodied. In non-gravitational space this is even more true and obvious: when one floats weightless, various objective reference points can be equally regarded as 'up-down' or 'down-up' and therefore orientation is neither in the world nor in the body, but in the movement that 'crosses' the two, precisely in an

6 The first reports on vection, or the sensation of illusory self-motion in the absence of physical movement through space, date back to the late 19th century (cf. Mach 1875; Wood 1895). Vection is still at the center of psycho-physiological research (cf. Palmisano et al. 2015), also for its relationship with 'motion-sickness' (cf. Keshavarz, Riecke & Hettinger 2015) and its relevance in the study of virtual environments (cf. Hettinger et al. 2014).

intermediate space between subjectivity and objectivity. The epistemological *revolution* that Michelson describes leads to the dissolution of the body/mind dualism:

> So, too, the voyage of the astronauts ultimately restores us, through the heightened and complex immediacy of this film, to the space in which we dwell. This navigation of a vessel as instrument of exploration, of the human organism as adventurer, dissolves the opposition of body and mind, *bringing home* to us the manner in which 'objective spatiality' is but the envelope of that 'primordial spatiality,' the level on which the body itself effects the synthesis which is a fusion of meaning as experienced, tending toward equilibrium (60).

Celestial motions

The combination of translation and rotation that characterizes Frank's motion in *2001: A Space Odyssey* can also be found in the opening long-take of *Gravity*, mentioned at the beginning of the chapter. Cuáron and Lubetzki, however, use innovative technological and formal solutions to create the film aesthetic. The sequence consists in fact of a series of 'elastic shots', as Lubezki himself calls them.[7] During their extra-vehicular operations, while Stone is attached to a mechanical arm, Kovalsky is free from any physical connection to the shuttle yet equipped with jetpacks that allow him to direct his movements in space. When a rain of debris collides with the spacecraft, the shuttle begins to rotate dramatically, and the debris hits the mechanical arm, causing it to detach from the *Explorer* and thus casting Stone adrift. Shortly thereafter, encouraged via radio by Kovalsky, Stone manages to break away from the mechanical arm but continues to rotate adrift. The rotation of the shuttle transfers to the mechanical arm after its detachment, and the rotation of the arm transfers to Stone after her detachment. Stone's movement therefore combines translation into the depth of space (a linear displacement) and *rotation* around her own barycentre (a spiral-like, recursive, and 'reflexive' movement). In the complex system of outer space, in which bodies are in constant and reciprocally influenced motion, the

7 The shooting of *Gravity* took place in an *LED light box*, in which actors hung from wires to perform choreography while being suitably lit in relation to a light source (emulating the sun); pre- and post-production computer adjustments allowed for the perfectly simulated extra-atmospheric setting to be inserted. On shooting techniques in *Gravity*, cf. Adams 2013.

character and the spectator establish a relationship akin to that between the character and the camera. Debris colliding with the shuttle causes it to spin, along with both the mechanical arm and Stone, who is attached to it. At this point the frame is mostly static, showing the entire structure rotating along the horizontal axis of the screen. Three-dimensionality is emphasized as the character, located at the tip of the arm, passes in front of the camera, departs from it, and continues to spin.

When debris hits the arm and causes it to detach from the shuttle, the arm (and Stone along with it) wildly rotates away from the shuttle. The frontal point of view makes this motion imperceptible, as it is directed towards the camera: the profilmic movement is thus 'neutralized' as the camera recedes. This time, rotation is perpendicular to the screen. After a few 'flips', Stone passes close to the camera, which now has slowed its backtracking. Exactly at this moment a crucial move is performed: through the combination of rolling and tracking, the camera *attaches* to the character's movement and now *embodies* both her translational motion in space as well as her rotation around herself.[8] Given that Stone continues to move deeply into space, translation and rotation combine. Yet this double move is not perceivable, because the attachment has 'stabilized' the character at the centre of the frame. As in the *2001: A Space Odyssey* example, by keeping the image fixed the film allows the spectator to see the character's face reflected on the helmet's visor, along with her tension and emotions. The only object that 'moves' on-screen is the background: the Earth's surface appears and disappears cyclically behind the character.

The camera moves slightly from Stone's face to her gloved hands as she attempts to release the clip that anchors her to the mechanical arm. She succeeds but continues to rotate adrift. To portray the abrupt change of speed due to the detachment from the mechanical arm, the camera suddenly ceases both translation and rotation movements. Now kept at the centre of the frame, with a fixed point of view, the character becomes smaller as she moves away into the background and is swallowed by the void.

The next shot mirrors the previous one: the camera is placed opposite the character, farther into space; Stone reappears at the centre of the image and approaches the camera; the motion of the camera resumes as she passes in front of it. Here the camera performs a new 'gesture', i.e. a whip pan to the left that follows the character's movement. Immediately thereafter, the camera activates again as it attaches to the character in order to 'follow' her translation in space (while she continues to rotate). Subsequently, the

8 The same word ('attaches') is used by Thompson 2013b.

camera attaches to Stone's rotation: once more, a 'double attachment' of the camera—following the character and rolling with her—is performed. The Earth's surface flows back behind the character and is reflected on the helmet's visor (which is, unsurprisingly, spherical like a planet).

In this complex combination of 'gestures' performed by the film's body (a series of virtual camera movements), the strategy of *attachment* emerges not only as a film technique but also a strategy of mediation of the disorientation generated by the uncontrolled movement of the characters. In non-gravitational fictional environments, the relation between *what* movements represent and *how* movements are represented acquires strategic importance. In performing this 'attachment', the film adopts a 'gravitational aesthetic', with the effect of 'fixing' the movement and therefore reducing the sense of disorientation and imbalance. Paradoxically, attachment implies 'hiding' the character's movements. Yet, it is precisely because of such obliteration that the film engages the spectator at both the motor and the emotional level. Once 'fixed' on Stone's face at the centre of the frame, the spectator's attention focuses on the character's expressions and her psychophysical anxiety. The more the camera emulates the character's movements, the more emotional involvement replaces motor alignment.

Respiratory failures

What about sound? The acoustic dimension of the film certainly has an impact on the determination of the spectator's sense of balance and orientation with respect to the characters' postures and movements. Sound too is in fact a multisensory phenomenon and not exclusively auditory. Auditory perception involves the physiological layer of perceptual experience: the somatosensory quality of sound waves, which are received by both the auditory and the haptic system, alters the body temperature and induces galvanic responses of the skin, thereby providing bodily spatial information.[9] In the spacewalks I analysed, auditory stimuli are programmatically reduced or even removed from the soundtrack of the film. In *2001: A Space Odyssey*, Frank's body drifts in absolute silence. The absence of auditory stimulation has the effect of 'displacing' the vestibular system, giving the spectator a feeling of physical and psychic instability.

9 The study of interaction between auditory stimuli and galvanic adaptation is not a recent line of research, cf. for example Coombs 1938. On the interplay of physical, biological, and psychological processes underlying hearing, cf. Schnupp, Nelken & King 2011.

Perceptually, a sound source cannot be precisely visually detected. Moreover, sound has the ability to surround and immerse the listener. In the cases analysed, the spectator hears the amplified astronaut's breath distinctly and thus has the impression of being inside his helmet (the screen would correspond to the visor). It is as if the entire cinema had turned into a spacesuit and the audience shared the astronaut's breathing space, a space that is not entirely outside the body, but rather precisely both internal and external, a connecting space. Given the intensification of the character's physiological reactions, by virtue of the basic simulation mechanisms the spectator's breath tends to intensify and to synchronize with that of the astronaut. To the extent that the spectator has the impression of being subject to the same stress, as if she were suffocating in the helmet, she experiences in the first person the same breathlessness suffered by the astronaut. As Gibson (2015) writes, '[a]ir affords breathing, more exactly, respiration' (122), and when the mimetic impression of breathlessness contrasts with this affordance (which exists in the normally oxygenated space of the cinema), the spectator experiences the same duality I described with respect to ungraspability and disanchoring.

A literal embodiment, again, provided by the spacesuit and in particular the helmet, functions as a 'compensation'. The helmet encapsulates the astronaut's head, and such encapsulation allows an intensification of biological functions, especially of breathing. In *2001: A Space Odyssey*'s 'Mission Jupiter' chapter, in which the astronauts wear suits and helmets for their spacewalks, while shot sizes vary from the long shot to the extreme close-up and the bodies are presented both upright and upside down, sound remains focused on the deep and steady breathing of characters, heard as a background hiss. Similarly, in *2010: The Year We Make Contact*, although the film is far from having the meditative charge of Kubrick's masterpiece, Curnow's fear and anxiety during his first spacewalk are expressed mainly by focusing on his heavy breathing. A similar acoustic strategy is used, for example, in *Interstellar* (Nolan 2014) just before the 'tesseract' scene, in which Joseph Cooper 'falls' into a four-dimensional space resembling an infinite stream of bookshelves, capable of peering into his daughter Murphy's bedroom at all points in time. Cooper's passage into the black hole, which precedes this scene, is rendered through a subjectification of sound: the spectator can hear his intensified breath. In these particular cases, the 'point-of-listening' is embodied in the astronauts' breathing, a solution that effectively communicates a state of physiological tension and suspense and that suggests, through its materiality, the uncertainty, delicacy, and potential danger of the situation.

The perceptual salience of the character's heavy breathing and the uncomfortable feeling perceived by the spectator also has a narrative function, constantly reminding the latter that oxygen is a scarce resource in extra-atmospheric environments. Most space-exploration films use this strategy as a recurring narrative trope. In many films, the problem that the astronauts face is a progressive exhaustion of the oxygen reserve due to the passage of time or to an accident that causes a gradual depressurization of the spaceship. Invariably, at several points of the narrative, a 'countdown' to death by suffocation intensifies suspense.[10] Most interesting as far as my argument is concerned is that, in opposition to the indefinite and silent outer space, spacewalk scenes offer a confined and personal space, within which acoustic stimuli are *subjectified*.

This further 'gesture' performed by *Gravity* film's body masterfully combines visual and auditory subjectification. The camera doubly attaches to Stone's drifting and slowly approaches her face, showing the character's tension and stress. The 'point-of-listening is placed inside the helmet and gives acoustic salience to her difficulty breathing. This is underlined both visually by the continuous steaming up of the visor, and verbally as Stone gasps— 'I can't breathe...'. As the camera focuses on Stone's face, her breathing stops and she is in apnoea, aware of her possible imminent death. While the slow approaching movement continues, the point of view *passes through* the transparent visor and penetrates inside the helmet. The exact moment of penetration is depicted acoustically through a change in soundscape, from an external environment to an internal environment (similar to the effect produced by pressure change after immersion in water). The crucial element is that the visual threshold of the visor is passed through without any interruption, without any material break (i.e. without an editing cut). Now inside the helmet, the camera's point of view turns until it aligns with the direction in which the character is looking. For a few seconds, aligned to Stone's point of view, the spectator can see data and indicators on the visor, clearly displaying the level of oxygen supply falling below 10%. As Lubezki (Adams 2013) said in an interview,

10 Examples of this intensification can be found in the first and in the final parts of *Mission to Mars*, characterized respectively by the reduction of pressure and the discovery of the presence of oxygen inside the mysterious Martian head. In *Red Planet* (Hoffman 2000) the same progressive reduction of oxygen on board the spacecraft, the risk of asphyxiation for astronauts, and the discovery of oxygen on Mars can also be found.

> When you feel things are happening in real time and there's that immediacy with the actors, and the camera is doing all of these elastic shots that are very objective shots that then become subjective shots, and you see what Sandra [Bullock]'s going through, you see it through her eyes, and then you also see objectively from the audience's point of view, I think all that creates an energy, a tension, and a feeling of being immersed that otherwise you cannot achieve.

Stone finally finds a point of orientation and responds to Kovalsky's pressing demands to provide a visual reference that might be useful for her localization and rescue. At this point, the camera takes the reverse path: it departs from the optical alignment, shows the character's profile, leaves the helmet (with the corresponding pitch change), and moves slowly away. Stone tries to communicate her condition to Houston, albeit without any reply. The sequence ends with a final 'detachment' of the camera from alignment with the character's movement: a static shot depicts Stone spinning towards the void.

Gravitational aesthetics

To recount the preceding analyses, the strategy of space-exploration filmic involvement tends to disembody the spectator by triggering a sense of detachment and despair equal to that experienced by the character. The continuous capsizing, breathlessness, fogging of vision, etc. intensify the character's psychophysical experience while conveying it to the spectator. As a result, the spectator feels like an astronaut immersed in the sidereal darkness of the cinema, at least temporarily facing a dramatic series of physical difficulties. Yet, while the film makes the body's reference system ambiguous and tends to disembody the spectator, it also adopts representational solutions typical of gravitational environments, i.e. it reembodies the spectator's perception. As we have seen in the previous chapter, in the overturning motif the tendency to represent reversed bodies and faces with frontal shots and 'head-up' orientation, or even to 'normalize' the inverted image, is clear evidence of the use of a 'usual orientation', to prevent perceptual and cognitive interference from breaking the narrative and emotional continuity. Although free to use the upside-down motif, since the latter is diegetically justified and therefore functional to a realistic orientation of bodies in space, space-exploration films resort to gravitational stylistic solutions and establish a mutual orientation between the spectator and the fictional world in order to ensure clear legibility. Thus, even the sense of void and imbalance in zero-gravity environments are communicated to the spectator through a *gravitational aesthetics*. If, as Michelson concludes, the spectator meets the challenge of the disruption of ordinary coordinates and readjusts the coordinates of perception and cognition, the film facilitates this process of equilibrium restoration.

To conclude, the aspect that the motif of the drift adds to the overturning is that it often carries out reembodiment by putting characters that move in non-gravitational environments into a psychophysical condition similar to the one they would experience in gravitational environments. We could say then that, if it is true that the character and the spectator can experience a gravitational vertigo even in a non-gravitational space, it is also true that a filmic experience of a 'non-gravitational fall' is possible. The drift as a particular form of the human body's movement in space is characterized by the fact that, given the lack of gravity, the movement is not goal-oriented; it is not intentional. Phenomenologically, what is missing is the intentional force that pushes the body to the fulfilment of the action (in the gravitational space, such fulfilment would correspond to the impact with the ground). Even in this case, the film adopts formal solutions that communicate the experience of a fall even if the astronaut's body is not falling at all.

This strategy also involves the emotional dimension of experience. When the spectator relates closely to the drifting astronauts' emotion, a series of 'perceptual disturbance' factors emerge, producing affective *disembodying intensification*. As we have seen, the hostile conditions of the external environment and the consequent need to wear a spacesuit influence the mode of representation of emotions. The astronaut's head is confined within the helmet and therefore her face is framed within the visor, which acts as a sort of second screen. Inside the helmet, breathing intensifies and expresses anxiety and fear. These emotions acquire a pivotal role thanks to their acoustic salience. In *Gravity*, a slow (and therefore almost unnoticed) approach to the character's face, until the camera penetrates the helmet without being obstructed by the obstacle of the visor, is used in order to compensate the respiratory intensification. The approach and penetration corresponds to an embodying process, culminating in optical-cognitive alignment: the point-of-view shot. Even in this case, the process of subjectification, through which reembodiment of perception is maximally achieved, paradoxically results in the 'concealment' of the character's face (which is the surface for communicating her emotions). However, at the end, the camera movement *re-objectifies* the point-of-view.

Point of no return

The neuro-ecological approach I have adopted in this chapter demonstrates that every film experience offers a potential conflict between the optical (disembodied) and the tactile (embodied) framework, and that film uses this interference to generate a sense of suspension and suspense in the spectator due to a lack of tangibility.

First, the representation focuses on a lack of hand-prehension efficacy. Because of the spacesuit gloves and the absence of gravity, the character's tactile sensoriality and control of movement are reduced. When a hand-prehension action performed by an astronaut during a risky operation fails, the object is perceived as ungraspable, *intangible*. The spectator experiences the sense of ungraspability of a nevertheless graspable object; she feels the desensitization. However, the mediated nature of the film experience and the combination of perceptual dynamics (synesthesia) and psychological processes (affordance) serve to 'invert' desensitization in a special kind of sensoriality that is specific to the film experience. This special form of sensoriality is rooted in the neurophysiological mechanisms that automatically activate in the spectator's brain. Visuomotor neurons, in fact, play a role in spectators' impression of grasping objects or touching surfaces even when they are *not* grasped or touched by the character. Through visuomotor neurons, when a subject observes a graspable object, she does in fact grasp that object. Similarly, the spectator accomplishes the character's intention, finalizing the grasping action on behalf of the character.

The visuomotor activation works to complete the character's incomplete action. In fact, visuomotor neurons codify the objects' intrinsic properties, allowing the spectator to interact with them (affordance related to canonical-neuron activation) through an embodied simulation of the character's actions and intentions (affordance related to mirror-neuron activation). Moreover, when a tactile action is executed by the character, visuomotor neuron activation provides a special kind of 'com-prehensive' experience that connects the visual information of the image and the tactile impression of touching the fictional object. By virtue of synesthetic perception, when a subject observes another subject touching, say, a rough surface, she senses its roughness—even if the character's skin is covered by a mediation surface, such as gloves. Bridging the visual and the motor system at a neurological level, visuomotor neurons can be seen as the neural substratum of synesthetic perception.

Second, the same dynamic is valid regarding the whole-bodily sensoriality, as the spectator simulates the character's state of suspension and detachment from the ground due to lack of gravity and weightlessness. This 'unsensoriality' of the character extends its influence to the spectators since external perception also affects her sense of space and her relationship with the outside world. As the application of the visual cliff experiment to filmic spacewalks demonstrates, the spectator experiences a contradiction between the affordance of falling and that of support. Since the relativity of filmic orientation both liberates and disrupts the usual framework of movement, when this contradiction arises, the spectator initially experiences disorientation and receives the impression of having lost contact with the ground. Although the spectator derives pleasure from the destabilizing effect of being upside down, she soon needs to be reoriented and tends to establish a new system of reference based on her own body. Proprioception thus acquires a crucial role in re-grounding the spectator's body in respect to that of the astronaut, even offering a re-attachment to his or her motion and emotion. Narrative film often negotiates the conflict between loss of position and proprioceptive sensibility on behalf of the spectator, embodying in its stylistic and formal solutions the spectator's natural tendency towards psychophysical equilibrium. The gravitational reembodying strategy has the aim and the effect of restoring intentionality and tangibility to situations in which the lack of gravity causes a lack of *orientation towards* a goal (which is, very often, to survive in hostile environments such as deep space).

This strategy of detachment and re-attachment, or desensitization and re-sensitization through intensification of haptic perception, in addition to visuomotor neural activation and proprioception, expresses the lack of tangibility and its recovery on different levels of experience. On a basic physiological level, a 'sensorimotor void' is expressed via ungraspability and weightlessness, both mirrored and compensated for by the spectator's natural tendency to implicitly simulate the character's actions and postures. Also, at a cognitive level, a state of suspense is conveyed through the lack of 'com-prehensibility' and the detachment from the ground. This 'cognitive intangibility' manifests itself in the difficulty of interpreting the ineffective and uncontrolled gestures of the film characters and their movements in space. The implicit understanding of the character's intentions is functional to an explicit and narrative comprehension of the film. Suspense is almost a sort of *suspicion* related to story development—i.e., a feeling of danger, or, the imminence of an irreparable tragedy.

The psychological implications of canonical neurons and other neural activity suggest a more figurative meaning of 'grasping'. The act of comprehending a manipulative action can be related to the general act of understanding the deep meaning of the action and, more generally, the meaning of the film. Finally, the spectator is invited to face inefficacy and unbalancedness as a 'sense of void' that can also be understood, philosophically, as an 'existential loss'. In this sense, the ground has to be conceived of as a point of both material and symbolic reference and orientation that is lost and needs to be restored. Spatial emptiness and the body's detachment from the ground can be perceived by aware spectators as a form of remoteness from human nature itself—that is, the lack of a *grasp* on the world in which we are temporarily *grounded*.

My analysis of *Gravity* (and of the other space-exploration films) untangles the multiple meanings and forms of film embodiment. First, in terms of mere representation, space-exploration films propose a *literal* embodiment, that is, a filmic integration of the character's body and its physiological functions into material 'cases' such as the spacecraft, the spacesuit, and the helmet. These pressurized and oxygen-supplied containers can be conceived as the *media* of experience, as they mark a distance from, and at the same time allow the character to act within a hostile environment.

At a more abstract level, well-described by phenomenological film theories, the disembodying-reembodying dynamic reflects a process of strategic compensation for dizziness and suspense through the adoption of a bodily based formal articulation: the spectator takes on the film's 'attitudes', 'movements', and 'reactions', reflecting and embodying them, even when this entails a peculiar corporeality, not ontologically comparable to yet 'compatible' with that of the spectator.

In addition to 'anthropomorphic' embodiment, the correspondence between the spectator's corporeality and the film's physicality indicates an almost organic form of embodiment. The analysis of *Gravity* relates the pleasure inherent in immersion (as the voluntary escape from ordinary and secure perceptual parameters) and the rational need to re-emerge from immersion. As in any mainstream narrative film, a reembodiment is needed to balance the imbalance, to alleviate dizziness, to lighten the traumatic load, to recalibrate the excess of energy. This is akin to a biologically activated homeostatic process in the spectator: seeking a foothold when feeling as though falling, closing one's eyes to avoid seeing violence, tilting one's head to align with angled faces, etc. The film embodies the same reactions through its own particular 'body', that is, translating them into concrete formal proposals of *découpage* (which is negated in the long take), point of view (between objectivity and subjectivity), 'attached' camera movements, etc.

Finally, embodiment can be understood symbolically and philosophically: the intensified involvement in space-exploration films explicitly or implicitly refers to an incumbent and essential danger: the drift into the abyss with no chance of return or rescue. In *Gravity*, physical danger and existential drift are mutually embodied. Like most of the films set in space, *Gravity* is about emptiness in its literal and metaphorical senses; it reflects the very nature of space, the precarious balance between the infinite and the indefinite, between the inconceivable and problematic spatiality, and the limits of human possibilities. More generally, space-exploration films successfully provide the spectator a meaningful experience at all levels of embodiment, relating the feeling of emptiness to the profound meaning of the void.

Bibliography

Adams, Bryan. 2013. 'One of the Greatest Cinematographers Ever: *Gravity*'s Emmanuel Lubezki', *The Credits*. October 4. https://www.mpaa.org/2013/10/one-of-the-greatest-cinematographers-ever-gravitys-emmanuel-lubezki.

Angelaki, Dora E., & Kathleen E. Cullen. 2008. 'Vestibular System: The Many Facets of a Multimodal Sense'. *The Annual Review of Neuroscience*. 31: 125-150.

Arnheim, Rudolf. 1957. *Film as Art*. Berkeley: University of California Press.

Banissy, Michael J., & Jamie Ward. 2007. 'Mirror-Touch Synesthesia is Linked with Empathy'. *Nature Neuroscience*. 10 (7): 815-816. DOI:10.1038/nn1926.

Blakemore, Sarah-J., Davina Bristow, Geoffrey Bird, Chris Frith, & Jamie Ward. 2005. 'Somatosensory Activations During the Observation of a Case of Touch and Vision-Touch Synaesthesia'. *Brain*. 128 (7): 1571-1583. DOI:10.1093/brain/awh500.

Botvinick, Matthew, & Jonathan Cohen. 1998. 'Rubber Hands "Feel" Touch that Eyes See'. *Nature*. 391 (6669): 756. DOI:10.1038/35784.

Ebisch, Sjoerd J.H., Francesca Ferri, Anatolia Salone, Mauro Gianni Perrucci, Luigi D'Amico, Filippo Maria Ferro, Gian Luca Romani, & Vittorio Gallese. 2011. 'Differential Involvement of Somatosensory and Interoceptive Cortices during the Observation of Affective Touch'. *Journal of Cognitive Neuroscience*. 23 (7): 1808-1822. DOI:10.1162/jocn.2010.21551.

Ebisch, Sjoerd J.H., Mauro G. Perrucci, Antonio Ferretti, Cosimo Del Gratta, Gian Luca Romani, & Vittorio Gallese. 2008. 'The Sense of Touch: Embodied Simulation in a Visuotactile Mirroring Mechanism for Observed Animate or Inanimate Touch'. *Journal of Cognitive Neuroscience*. 20 (9): 1611-1623. DOI:10.1162/jocn.2008.20111.

Ehrsson, H. Henrik, Nicholas P. Holmes, & Richard E. Passingham. 2005. 'Touching a Rubber Hand: Feeling of Body Ownership is Associated with

Activity in Multisensory Brain Areas'. *J. Neurosci.* 25 (45): 10564-10573. DOI:10.1523/JNEUROSCI.0800-05.2005.

Gallagher, Shaun, & Dan Zahavi. 2007. *The Phenomenological Mind: An Introduction to Philosophy of Mind and Cognitive Science.* London: Routledge.

Gallese, Vittorio, & Sjoerd Ebisch. 2013. 'Embodied Simulation and Touch. The Sense of Touch in Social Cognition'. *Phenomenology & Mind.* 4: 269-291. DOI:10.13128/Phe_Mi-19602.

Garbarini, Francesca, & Mauro Adenzato. 2004. 'At the Root of Embodied Cognition: Cognitive Science Meets Neurophysiology'. *Brain and Cognition.* 56 (1): 100-106. DOI:10.1016/j.bandc.2004.06.003.

Gibson, Eleanor J., & Richard D. Walk. 1960. 'The "Visual Cliff"'. *Scientific American.* 202 (4): 64-71.

Gibson, James J. 1977. 'The Theory of affordances'. In *Perceiving, Acting, and Knowing: Toward an Ecological Psychology.* Edited by Robert Shaw & John Bransford, 127-143. Hillsdale, NJ: Erlbaum.

Gibson, James J. 2015. *The Ecological Approach to Visual Perception. Classic Edition.* New York/London: Taylor & Francis.

Goldberg, Jay M., Victor J. Wilson, Dora E. Angelaki, Kathleen E. Cullen, & Kikuro Fukushima. 2012. *The Vestibular System: A Sixth Sense.* Oxford/New York: Oxford University Press.

Husserl, Edmund. 1981. 'Foundational Investigations of the Phenomenological Origin of the Spatiality of Nature'. Translated by Fred Kersten. In Edmund Husserl, *Shorter Works.* Edited by Peter McCormick & Frederick Elliston, 222-233. Notre Dame, IN: University of Notre Dame Press.

Keysers, Christian, Bruno Wicker, Valeria Gazzola, Jean-Luc Anton, Leonardo Fogassi, & Vittorio Gallese. 2004. 'A Touching Sight: SII / PV Activation during the Observation and Experience of Touch'. *Neuron.* 42 (2): 1-20. DOI:10.1016/s0896-6273(04)00156-4.

Koffka, Kurt. 1935. *Principles of Gestalt Psychology.* New York: Harcourt Brace.

Lackner, James R. 1988. 'Some Proprioceptive Influences on the Perceptual Representation of Body Shape and Orientation'. *Brain.* 111 (2): 281-297. DOI:10.1093/brain/111.2.281.

Lackner, James R. 1992. 'Spatial Orientation in Weightless Environments'. *Perception.* 21 (6): 803-812. DOI:10.1068/p210803.

Lackner, James R., & Ashton Graybiel. 1979. 'Parabolic Flight: Loss of Sense of Orientation'. *Science.* 206 (4422): 1105-1508. DOI:10.1126/science.493998.

Lackner, James R., & Ashton Graybiel. 1983. 'Perceived Orientation in Free-Fall Depends on Visual, Postural, and Architectural Factors'. *Aviation Space and Environmental Medicine.* 54 (1): 47-51.

Lewin, Kurt. 1926. 'Vorsatz, Wille und Bedürfnis, mit über die Vorbemerkungen psychischen Kräfte und Energien und die Struktur der Seele'. *Psychologische Forschung*. 7 (4): 294-385.

Michelson, Annette. 1969. 'Bodies in Space: Film as "Carnal Knowledge"'. *Artforum VII*. (6): 53-64.

Morris, David. 2004. *The Sense of Space*. Albany: SUNY.

Murata, Akira, Luciano Fadiga, Leonardo Fogassi, Vittorio Gallese, Vassilis Raos, & Giacomo Rizzolatti. 1997. 'Object Representation in the Ventral Premotor Cortex (Area F5) of the Monkey'. *Journal of Neurophysiology*. 78: 2226-2230. DOI:10.1152/jn.1997.78.4.2226.

Murata, Akira, Vittorio Gallese, Giuseppe Luppino, Masakazu Kaseda, & Hideo Sakata. 2000. 'Selectivity for the Shape, Size and Orientation of Objects in the Hand-Manipulation-Related Neurons in the Anterior Intraparietal (AIP) Area of the Macaque'. *Journal of Neurophysiology*. 83: 2580-2601. DOI:10.1152/jn.2000.83.5.2580.

Purves, Dale, George J. Augustine, David Fitzpatrick, William C. Hall, Anthony-Samuel LaMantia, James O. McNamara, & S. Mark Williams, eds. 2010. *Neuroscience* (5th ed.). Sunderland: Sinauer Associates.

Raos, Vassilis, Maria Alessandra Umiltà, Akira Murata, Leonardo Fogassi, & Vittorio Gallese. 2006. 'Functional Properties of Grasping-Related Neurons in the Ventral Premotor Area F5 of the Macaque Monkey'. *Journal of Neurophysiology*. 95: 709-729. DOI:10.1152/jn.00463.2005.

Richmond, Scott C. 2016. *Cinema's Bodily Illusions. Flying, Floating and Hallucinating*. Minneapolis/London: University of Minnesota Press.

Rizzolatti, Giacomo, & Luciano Fadiga. 1998. 'Grasping Objects and Grasping Action Meanings: the Dual Role of Monkey Rostroventral Premotor Cortex (Area F5)'. *Novartis Found Symp*. 218: 81-95; discussion 95-103. DOI:10.1002/9780470515563.ch6.

Rizzolatti, Giacomo, Luciano Fadiga, Vittorio Gallese, & Leonardo Fogassi. 1996. 'Premotor Cortex and the Recognition of Motor Actions'. *Brain Research: Cognitive Brain Research*. 3: 131-141. DOI:10.1016/0926-6410(95)00038-0.

Rizzolatti, Giacomo, Luciano Fogassi, & Vittorio Gallese. 1999, 'Cortical Mechanisms Subserving Object Grasping. A New View on the Cortical Motor Functions'. In *The Cognitive Neurosciences*. Edited by Michael S. Gazzaniga, 539-552. Cambridge, MA: The MIT Press.

Rocha Antunes, Luis. 2016. *The Multisensory Film Experience: A Cognitive Model of Experiential Film Aesthetics*. Chicago/Bristol: Intellect.

Schnupp, Jan, Israel Nelken, & Andrew J. King. 2011. *Auditory Neuroscience Making Sense of Sound*. Cambridge, MA: The MIT Press.

Sobchack, Vivian. 1987. *Screening Space: The American Science Fiction Film*. New York: Ungar Press.

Thompson, Kristin. 2013a. '*Gravity*, Part 1: Two Characters Adrift in an Experimental Film'. *Observations on Film Art*, November 7. http://www.davidbordwell.net/blog/2013/11/07/gravity-part-1-two-characters-adrift-in-an-experimental-film.
Thompson, Kristin. 2013b. '*Gravity*, Part 2: Thinking inside the Box'. *Observations on Film Art*, November 12. http://www.davidbordwell.net/blog/2013/11/12/gravity-part-2-thinking-inside-the-box.

VII Flight

Towards an Ecofilmology

Abstract

As a conclusion, the chapter 'Flight. Towards an Ecofilmology' offers a synoptic view of the characteristics of the five tensive motifs, carrying out a general anatomy of the strategies used to generate cinematic tension with particular reference to their narrative role in the light of the embodied simulation hypothesis. The fundamental aspect highlighted is the link between the different ways in which the tensive motifs embody *intentionality* and the dynamic of *disembodying-reembodying* involved. Accordingly, the motifs can be understood as a means of negotiation between the desire for vertigo and excess and the necessity of bringing overstimulation back beneath the threshold that assures the legibility and reception of the film, in perceptual as well as moral, social, and commercial terms.

Keywords: Gravity, Contemporary film experience, Intentionality, Embodiment, Ecofilmology

As the nineteenth century dies it bequeaths us two new machines. Both of them are born on almost the same date, at almost the same place, then simultaneously launch themselves upon the world and spread across continents. They pass from the hands of the pioneers into those of operators, crossing a 'supersonic barrier'. The first machine realizes at last the most insane dream man has pursued since he looked at the sky: to break away from the earth. Until then, only the creatures of his imagination, of his desire-the angels-had wings. This need to fly, which arises, well before Icarus, at the same time as the first mythologies, seems to all appearances the most infantile and mad. It is also said about dreamers that they do not have their feet on the ground.

—Edgar Morin, 'The Cinema, the Airplane', in *The Cinema, or The Imaginary Man*, 1956 (2005, 5)

D'Aloia, A., *Neurofilmology of the Moving Image. Gravity and Vertigo in Contemporary Cinema.* Taylor & Francis Group 2021
DOI: 10.5117/9789463725255_CH07

Vertiginous feelings

We have walked alongside an acrobat on a high wire suspended in mid-air, fallen at breakneck speed towards a fatal impact with the ground, and performed somersaults and upside-down flips that have taken us into outer space, into the shoes of an astronaut drifting in the void. It has been a journey without pause, a progressive abandonment of firm certainties and a drawing closer to the unfathomable. At the end of this journey, we saw ourselves reflected in the characters that cinema uses to engage us, above all through *its* corporeality, through a series of aerial motifs that vertiginously put our sense of gravity in tension. Like *Inception*'s dreamers, after our exploration into the psychic depths of filmic, we can now awake and make some general reflections on the 'anatomy' of the tensive motifs. Cobb's totem, however, will keep spinning...

The fundamental argument this book is that one of the main characteristics of contemporary narrative cinema is its tendency to intensify bodily perception and to offer a corresponding mitigation of the shocking effects that such an exacerbation produces through formal solutions that embody the spectator's natural psychophysical response. Cinema's capacity to offer a sensational experience, prior to or separate from narrative and escapism from the worries of reality, has proven an attractive topic throughout the entire history of film theory. Many pioneers were fascinated by the 'elemental and primitive emotion' elicited by the performance 'of the juggler and the acrobat' on the screen (Freeburg 1918, 18); or by the 'strong sensations' and the 'magnified feelings' (Epstein 1988, 240) offered by a means that, like a merry-go-round, enables a prismatic perspective and a centrifuge of vertiginous feelings (cf. 237), a 'seismic shock' that transforms everything in 'movement, imbalance, crisis' (235). As Epstein wrote in the early 1920s, '[w]aiting for the moment when 1000 meters of intrigue converge in a muscular denouement satisfies me more than the rest of the film' (235). The cinema is a dual experience that, on the one hand, 'can induce the feeling of *vertigo*' and 'places us on the very edge of the *abyss*' (Balázs 2010, 66), but on the other allows us to enjoy 'the *risk-free danger* of the filmed sensation' (65). The coexistence of exposition and protection offered by the cinema remains in the tension between the thrill of losing gravity and the need to restore equilibrium that we found at the very heart of the tensive motifs' psychophysical dynamic. As we have seen in the chapters of this book, the primordial sensational vocation of moving images has progressively evolved into a more complex and controversial tension between an enthusiasm for vertigo and the contentious aspects of sensorial modulation.

The tensive motifs resemble and relaunch this originary tendency, yet they should be distinguished from what Sergei Eisenstein (1988) called 'attractions'. In his 1923-1924 essays on the 'montage of attractions', the Soviet filmmaker and theorist maintains that the cinema—just like theatre—must 'attack' the spectators and manipulate their physical state in order to affect them emotionally and intellectually. As he writes,

> An attraction [...] is any aggressive moment in theatre, i.e. any element of it that subjects the audience to emotional or psychological influence, verified by experience and mathematically calculated to produce specific emotional shocks in the spectator in their proper order within the whole. These shocks provide the only opportunity of perceiving the ideological aspect of what is being shown, the final ideological conclusion (34).

For Eisenstein, attractions thus provide an opportunity for the spectators to perceive the ideological aspect of the film and induce them to combine emotional elicitation with intellectual reflexivity. In particular, the way in which this is achieved is a '*fictive* collaboration with what is being shown (through motor imitation of the action by those perceiving it and through psychological "empathy")' (40). As Eisenstein elaborated in his later writings on 'expressive movement', the actor is capable of transferring emotion to the public as a result of an attraction effect that has been previously 'calculated' by the director. This emotion is conveyed by precise facial and bodily expressions according to the 'biomechanical' acting process adopted from Constructivist theatre and the circus, as theorized by Vsevolod Meyerhold. The viewer automatically and 'reflexively repeats in weakened form the entire system of an actor's movements: as a result of the produced movements, the spectator's incipient muscular tensions are released in the desired emotion' (Eisenstein & Tretyakov 1979, 37).

The connection between motor imitation, automatic reflexes, emotions, and cognition—also derived from William James' (1884) link between psychological and physiological states—provides a first conceptualization of embodiment and of empathy in the film experience. As I have extensively discussed in the chapter on the motif of acrobatics, however, empathy is a highly complex and variegated concept, the multiple meanings of which must be carefully distinguished and examined. Whereas the meaning of motor imitation and empathy to which Eisenstein (1988) refers derives from Lipps' neoromantic doctrine of *Einfühlung* (cf. 40), he seems to embrace a notion of empathy that capsizes its self-projective nature into an 'other-injection' process led by the actor's expression. As Eisenstein (1993) wrote in 1929, '[t]he actor was and is the most direct object of imitation. We never know precisely *what* is going on inside another person. We see his expression. We mimic it. We empathise. And we draw the conclusion that he must feel the same way as we feel at that moment. The actor shows us how to feel' (68).

In this book, I have proposed an alternative interpretation of empathy and an application to the film experience based on Stein's phenomenology and have shown that it is compatible with contemporary accounts of film perception based on the analogy between canonical narratives and the architecture of the embodied brain. The tensive motifs are immediate forms of experience that, however, do not involve a 'confusive identification' between spectator and character on the basis of an 'inner imitation' of observed movements, nor do they activate the spectator's reflexivity retrospectively. The tensive motifs are forms of embodied cognition that do not entail any logical or temporal separation between the bodily *reflexes* and intellectual *reflexivity*. Experiencing a tensive motif cannot be reduced to a passive reception of stimuli that are re-elaborated in the aftermath in order to reflect on ideological implications; such an experience is, rather, a creative and interactive act in which *sense* emerges through the *senses*. Furthermore, the application of Stein's model to the film experience resolves some of the conflicts between the corporeal nature of the filmic intersubjective relationship and the permanence of the cognitive aspects of this experience.

It bears noting that Eisenstein derived the idea of 'attractions' from the fairground and the circus. As he clarifies,

> The attraction has nothing in common with the stunt. The stunt, or more accurately, the trick [...] is a finished achievement of a particular kind of mastery (acrobatics, for the most part) and it is only one kind of attraction that is suitable for presentation (or, as they say in the circus, 'sale'). In so far as the trick is absolute and complete *within itself*, it means the direct opposite of the attraction, which is based exclusively on something relative, the reactions of the audience (34-35).

Although I have included tightrope acrobatics among the tensive motifs (primarily because this is a recurring figure in the debate on *Einfühlung*) the latter, however, are not at all complete *within themselves*, nor do they really resemble a circus act. In fact, and most important, the tensive motifs do not aim at eliciting the spectators' *reaction*, but rather at *enacting* them. They do not only subject the spectators to a shock release and expect that they respond mechanically to the stimuli, but furthermore involve them in a special form of *action* based on embodied simulation of the character's actions, emotions, and intentions that are embedded in the film's physical and narrative environment.

Despite this *distinguo*, Eisenstein can undoubtedly be considered a full-fledged precursor of a 'neurophysiology of cinema' that studies a spectacle's capacity to create emotions that the spectators reproduces internally, albeit in a weaker form, as a result of an automatic and infectious repetition bypassing cognition, thus experiencing the observed emotions in their own body. As Maria Belodubrovskaya (2018) notes in an exploration of the affinities between Eisenstein's attractions, mirror neurons, and contemporary action cinema, he 'apparently intuited the existence of a mechanism of involuntary, nonevaluative emotional engagement—a system akin to the mirror system' (9; cf. also Tikka 2008).

The relevance of the constitutively embodied nature of the film experience was implied in the emphasis that French Filmology in the 1940s and 1950s gave to the film spectator's physiological responses. Gilbert Cohen-Séat (1946), in particular, highlighted film's ability to offer 'a turmoil of shock-like emotions' that elicits more or less unconscious 'responses and organic movements'. Such a 'physiological tempest' produces a 'mental vertigo' (92). Not by coincidence did Siegfried Kracauer (1960) combine Cohen-Séat's *vertige mental*, Henri Wallon's (1947; 1953) idea of weakened consciousness as characteristic of the film experience, and Epstein's aforementioned notion of cinema as a drug that satisfies the spectator's non-rational needs. Kracauer noted that 'film images affect primarily the spectator's sense, engaging him physiologically before he is in a position to respond intellectually' (Kracauer 1960, 158). Seeing the moving image has 'a "resonant effect," provoking in the spectator such kinesthetic responses as muscular reflexes, motor impulses, or the like' (158). The specific audio-visual and technical means of the cinema, for Kracauer, affect the 'spectator's physiological make-up' since they 'involve not so much his power of reasoning as his visceral faculties' (159).

As I have shown in the analysis of the tensive motifs, the fascination of Filmology for the precognitive aspects of the film experience and its interest in adopting experimental methods to study the spectator's participation empirically should be today updated and revitalized in a new and comprehensive theoretical framework. Combining the theoretical significance of the results of laboratory experiments with philosophical, psychological, and aesthetical reflections, the approach that I call Neurofilmology (cf. *infra*, Ch. I) helps to overcome the separation between first-person and third-person methods, between the description of the experience and the explanation of its causes, which remains evident today in the resistance of the large part of cognitive film studies against the relevance of embodiment and critical neuroscience in the study of the film experience.

Vanishing bodies

As the brief and partial review of the previous paragraphs have shown, classical film theories described cinema as an experience capable of providing fascination though the playful, the acrobatic, the spectacle, and of manipulating the spectator to obtain a desired and controlled response. However, rather than being 'attractive', the tensive motifs can often be even *repulsive* in the first place (that is, in what I called the *disembodying* phase), as the spectator's physiological response to excessive speed, dizziness, violence, etc. tends to reject the trauma they imply. The completing *reembodying* phase demonstrates that the nature and function of the tensive motifs are much more subtle than the pure fascination for the moving image and are much more articulated than mechanical and *non-self-reflexive reflexes* to conditioning stimuli.

After the euphoria for the first stylized and 'caricaturedly' expressive bodies of the cinema and their material significance (cf. Elsaesser 1990; Dahlquist et al. 2018), the advent of sound and of narrative montage changed both film acting and viewing. *Talkies* led to a significant reduction of the actor's mimicry, gestures, and bodily performance, and early cinema soon emancipated itself through narrative forms built on the so-called 'continuity system', which aimed at placing the spectator at a vantage point from which, as an invisible witness, he can fully enjoy and understand the plot (Murch 2001; Bordwell & Thompson 2006; Smith 2012). The apparently natural spatiotemporal causality, paradoxically reached through strong linguistic manipulation and the strategic employment of the natural inattentional gap in the spectator's perceptual activity, led to a sort of disappearance of the physical body. Absorbed into identification with both the character and the film, both the spectator's and the film's body dissolve into abstract entities. As Maria Poulaki (2019) summarizes, this

> Mise en abyme creates an out-of-body experience of observation since, by duplicating the frames and structures of gaze within the scene, it reflexively refers to the structure of looking at the screen as well as the cinematic configuration and the positioning of the viewers' body within it, looking at, in and through the screen (305).

The rise and the implementation of semiotics and psychoanalysis in film studies in the 1970s and 1980s paved the way for the postulation of a radically disembodied spectator. The concrete and sentient body was replaced by an abstract enunciational figure constructed by the text. As Christian Metz (1982) writes,

> Spectator-fish, taking in everything with their eyes, nothing with their bodies: the institution of the cinema requires a silent, motionless spectator, a vacant spectator, constantly in a sub-motor and hyper-perceptive state, a spectator at once alienated and happy, acrobatically hooked up to himself by the invisible thread of sight, a spectator who only catches up with himself at the last minute, by a paradoxical identification with his own self, a self filtered out into pure vision (97).

The primacy of vision over (and the denial of) bodily perception lies at the core of Metz's application of the Lacanian theory of identification (and Émile Benveniste's (1971) theory of enunciation) to the film experience. Rather than carrying out a 'secondary' identification with the film characters, the spectator preliminarily and 'primarily' identifies with an '(invisible) seeing agency of the film itself as discourse, as the agency which puts forward the story and shows it to us' (Metz 1982, 97). An invisible viewing subject and an invisible seeing agent (the film), reciprocally invisible, are the two poles of a completely disembodied act of film attendance. In this sense, the paradigm of identification/projection with the film and with the characters is perhaps the most controversial stage of a history of corporeality in the filmic experience. The notion of empathy that I discussed critically in Chapter II provides a more adequate, albeit equally problematic, theoretical ground for the description of the film experience starting from its corporeality.

The body as a sweetened temple of the soul as has been proposed by Hollywood was challenged by a critique of the linguistic, artificial, and ideological nature of the film. In different phases of the history of film—the avant-gardes, the *vagues* of modern cinema and experimental cinema—in opposition to the continuity system, defamiliarization and estrangement conceived a spectator external to the narrative, with an emphasis on cognitive 'short circuits', critical awareness, and ideological denunciation, with the result of constituting a subject who, struggling to mirror himself in the subjectivity of the characters, loses her own and reflects on her loss. The diversion of attention from the narrative to the modes of its representation and the self-reflexivity of the medium, however, did not correspond to a re-emergence of the spectator's body, which instead continued to be hidden in the discontinuity of *inconclusive* stories, or even neglected.

In an in-depth analysis of *Psycho* (Hitchcock 1960), Linda Williams (2000) argues that postmodern cinema is the 'new cinema of attractions', using a label that early-cinema scholar Tom Gunning (1986) coined in the wake of Eisenstein to delineate 'a cinema that displays its visibility, willing to rupture a self-enclosed fictional world for a chance to solicit the attention of the spectator' (64; cf. also Strauven 2006). For Gunning (1989),

> Rather than being an involvement with narrative action or empathy with character psychology, the cinema of attractions solicits a highly conscious awareness of the film image engaging the viewer's curiosity. The spectator does not get lost in a fictional world and its drama, but remains aware of the act of looking, the excitement of curiosity and its fulfilment. Through a variety of formal means, the images of the cinema of attractions rush forward to meet their viewers. [...] This cinema addresses and holds the spectator, emphasising the act of display. In fulfilling this curiosity, it delivers a generally brief dose of scopic pleasure (36).

According to Williams (2000), *Psycho* 'offers an intensification of certain forms of visuality, and certain appeals to the senses' (355) that anticipate postmodern cinema. Williams explains that early and postmodern cinema share the same characteristics: 'While narrative is not abandoned in ever more sensationalized cinema, it often takes second seat to a succession of visual and auditory 'attractions'' (356). Of course, they are not exactly the same attractions. While early cinema was part of fairs in which the beholders were invited to choose sights and shows, in postmodern cinema what can be defined as attraction is the 'experience of being caught up in the literal sensations of falling, flying, careening in the roller coaster' (356). Just like a contemporary amusement park, blockbuster films, such as *Jurassic Park* (Spielberg 1993) or *Titanic* (Cameron 1997), 'simulate the bodily thrills and visceral pleasures of attractions that not only beckon to us but take us on a continuous ride punctuated by shocks and moments of speed-up and slow-down' (356). In her comparison of the roller-coaster experience and film viewing, Williams uses the term 'roller-coaster sensibility' to indicate the 'pleasurable destabilization' grounded in the anticipation of the shock (such as terror in *Psycho*).

Upon a deeper look, however, two apparently opposite kinds of spectatorship coexist in postmodern cinema. Sensory over-excitation and immersion in a discontinuum of stimulations suggests a new spectacular vein of cinema, one in which the pleasure of visible bodies prevails over narrative causality and comprehension. We are, of course, in front of bodies quite different from those of early cinema. The introduction of innovative techniques and technologies and the digitalization of production and post-production processes allows for the dematerialization of the actors' physical bodies. Thanks to the chroma key, motion capture, and CGI, in many blockbuster films the characters' bodies may be decontextualized from the real environment or even created artificially. Anthropocentrism has been replaced by anthropomorphization, so much so that the permanence of the actor's flesh in a virtual or hybrid environment ends up making the inadequacy of the postmodern body even more evident. The latter is increasingly emptied of its humanity and vitality and appears as divided, reflected, shattered, altered, alien and alienated, monstrous, mutilated, mutant, contaminated, cybernetic, and virtual. The pitfalls of the progress of cinematographic techniques dangerously pushed film theory towards the deterministic logic according to which corporeality is annihilated by those same technologies that allowfor the representation of its dissolution. It almost seems that it is the 'machinations' of cinema that destroy the sense of corporeality and identity.

Nonetheless, the disappearance of the actor's physical body has been countered by a growing intensification of styles and formal means of representation and, consequently, of the bodily nature of spectatorship. More than ever before, visual effects allow both superheroes and 'common' characters to be shown while they fly, fall, run away, jump, fight, and burn credibly and realistically. Hence, without the negation of the body we would not have bodily intensification. In this sense, and in the framework of an embodied and enactive approach to the filmic experience adopted here, the study of the tensive motifs will bring out an extended notion of bodily involvement and participation. In a situation as apparently disembodied as that of sitting in front of a screen, the distance between the spectator's body and the character's body is reduced thanks to sensorimotor activation deriving from a close contact of *intentions*. This is the main reason why, as I will argue, empathy (or dis-empathy) is a notion more useful than identification (either in Metz's or Carroll's meaning) to discuss and describe the spectator's involvement in the character's and the film's internal and external movements and motions.

Rather than opposing mind and body, surface and depth, unity and fragmentation, continuity and discontinuity, and consciousness and unconsciousness, it makes more sense to involve both these dimensions as reciprocally implicated. The new spectator should be considered as a subject who is in constant and dynamic relationship with characters as both bodies in motion and as narrative vehicles, as well as with the camera's movements and film 'language', not only as a way to access to the film world visually or as an entity to identify with (as psychoanalytical semiotics maintained), but as a pseudo-subjectivity with which they can empathetically relate. Undoubtedly, the potential conflict between sensation and comprehension has heightened, but considering the emphasis of 2000s cinema on sensorial stimulation as an exclusive characteristic at the expense of cognitive activity is misleading. A more balanced discourse on the complex relationship between film style, intensification of perception, and narrative forms in a historical and aesthetic era in which the originary cinema's predilection for the body has re-emerged should invoke a theoretical approach capable of dealing with the richness and complexity of the contemporary times.

As has been discussed throughout the previous chapters, although the five tensive motifs are moments of sensorimotor intensification, their multilevel psycho-psychological nature and structure provide them with a strategic role in the development of the narrative and thus in its comprehension by part of the spectator. As Poulaki (2019) argues, it is not only immersion, transparency, naturalness, and continuity that create or sustain embodiment; distancing, self-reflexivity, and defamiliarization also offer embodied sensations and states:

> Moments of distancing can enrich the immersive experience of narrative; [...] Rather than a separation of the mind from the otherwise embodied narrative experience [...] or an intellectual flight in the lyrical ethers of saturated associations [...], distancing is embodied and feeds back into the embodied experience of narrative, a double gesture so characteristic of the aesthetic experience of cinema (308).

In a similar vein, the disembodying-reembodying dynamic that characterizes the tensive motifs corresponds to the coexistence of discontinuity and continuity—two seemingly opposite models of spectatorship—within the same aesthetic *topos*. In one phase, an acceleration puts the bodily nature of perception in tension, to the extent of misaligning the spectator's body and the character's body (often with the complicity of the film's body); in the other phase, a deceleration allows perception to slow down and restore the conditions of intelligibility and experienceability.

Embodied stories

Williams' emphasis on the attractionist nature of postmodern cinema, however, overestimates the visceral and kinetic power of the cinema and underestimates the role of cognitive activity in processing the narrative and preparing the anticipation that then results in bodily shocks. It may seem obvious that contemporary narrative cinema cannot be explained through a radical and exclusive attention to the virulent impact of bodily shocks. The contemporary film experience is a combination of sensorial, emotional, and rational activity in which the tension between narrative comprehension and bodily stimulation should not be seen as conflictual but rather as cooperative.

First, it must be noted that the intensification of film style does not necessarily imply a disruption of the narrative. For David Bordwell (2006), since the New Hollywood studio-era classic continuity has been replaced by *intensified continuity*: rapid editing, bipolar extremes of lens lengths, reliance on close shots, and wide-ranging camera movements are the four strategies of camerawork and editing that are characteristic of a new standard style that aims at keeping the viewer's attention constantly high (121-138). However, intensified continuity is not at all a form of discontinuity, but rather the amplification of the continuity system:

> Far from rejecting traditional continuity in the name of fragmentation and incoherence, the new style amounts to an intensification of established techniques. Intensified continuity is traditional continuity amped up, raised to a higher pitch of emphasis. It is the dominant style of American mass-audience films today (120).

For Geoff King, the spectacular qualities of cinema have also become increasingly important to Hollywood in recent decades because of the universality of action across cultural and language boundaries. However, in popular film production spectacularity does not automatically imply the disruption of narrative. As King (2000) underlines, '[n]arrative is far from being eclipsed, even in the most spectacular and effects-oriented of today's blockbuster attractions'; '[n]arrative and spectacle can work together in a variety of changing relationships'; '[s]pectacle is often just as much a core aspect of Hollywood cinema as coherent narrative and should not necessarily be seen as a disruptive intrusion from some place outside' (3-4). By recognising a multiple logics at work in Hollywood cinema, King confirms that the contemporary spectator seeks two kinds of pleasure: that of spectacular excess, and that of narrative coherence.

Moreover, the predilection for the surface and the kinetic effect that contemporary cinema has inherited from postmodern cinema does not necessarily imply that the narrative will not be engaging. As Bordwell noted, contemporary directors are interested in creating more intricate fictional worlds through complex audio-visual design and the combination of materials and techniques that, in spite of everything, preserve the pleasure of viewing (cf. Bordwell 2006). This path is pursued through the construction of increasingly twisted and exasperated narratives, no longer, as in Modern cinema, for the purpose of denouncing the artificial and ideological nature of film, but rather to flaunt its self-awareness and its ability to make the spectators think, asking of demanding cognitive effort aimed at reconstructing the plot from non-chronological and non-consequential narrative and continuously restructuring their cognitive maps (on complex storytelling in contemporary cinema, cf. Buckland 2009b; Kiss & Willemsen 2017; Hven 2017; Grishakova & Poulaki 2019). The category of 'puzzle film' is particularly indicative of the tendency to provide not only bodily shocks but also 'narrative shocks' that displace the spectator expectations (as in the case of *Psycho*). One might therefore say that today cinema is as least as much 'sensationalist' (spectacular, visceral, corporeal) as it is 'conceptualist' (reflective, cerebral, enigmatic) and that these two options are not at all mutually exclusive. At the basis of both of these tendencies seems to lie the same strategy of intensification, and this requires a model of analysis capable of including both high-level and low-level processes as part of the same circuit.

As Steven Shaviro (1993) notes, the cinematic apparatus enables a form of embodied experience that is characterized by a continuity between physiological and emotional responses (255). This continuity is closely connected to cinema's modes of presence—to the spectator's impression of being immersed in the diegetic world and experiencing the film in sensorimotor terms, similarly to the way he would experience real life. In this sense, Shaviro (2008) argues, the cognitive is not opposed to the visceral and the corporeal in the film experience. Indeed, somatic and semantic forces reciprocally feed off of one another. The potential conflict between the somatic and the semantic, between the irrational and the rational, or between the need to feel the thrill of vertigo and the necessity of recalibrating the excess, intensifies, but the two terms do not necessarily cancel each other out.

The point, however, is not to determine the level of relevancy to be attributed to the body to detriment of cognitive processes, but rather to analyse the *modes* in which bodily elicitation and cognitive activity are combined into one *embodied* perception (that is, the coupling of body and mind) as a new way to conceive the experience of narrative films. Two analyses of the same sequence of *Psycho* may elucidate the shift from the bodily vs. cognitive opposition to embodiment. When Norman Bates pushes Marion's car into the swamp after her murder, its slow sinking stops momentarily, suggesting the possibility that Norman's plan may fail. This would seem to satisfy the moral tendency of the spectator to hope that the criminal is discovered and punished for his guilt. But as Torben Grodal (1997) notes in his study on the cognitive labelling of emotions as a narrative strategy, this is not the response of the spectator, who 'worries during the short halt in the sinking and experiences a feeling of relief when the car starts to sink again' and disappears into the swamp. Grodal ascribed this perverse response as a matter of identification, expressed in mere quantitative terms:

> The viewer has cognitively identified himself with the young man over a longer period of time, and has, during this period, been 'forced' to 'actualize' the emotions which are presupposed in order to give coherence and meaning to his acts. If the viewer had other points of identification, for instance a sympathetic detective or a concerned friend or relative, that character could anchor the empathy of the viewer and thereby reduce the empathic elements in the cognitive identification with the young man. But the first part of the film has only provided Norman Bates and the young woman as points of identification and empathy. When she dies, a vacuum is created which the young man partially fills; and when the film later presents new points of identification, the sister and the lover of the murdered woman, this 'unnatural sympathy' with the young man fades away (95).

In more recent study, Steffen Hven discusses exactly the same sequence and asks the same question but attempts a different explanation, intead resorting to the notion of 'pre-hodological space' proposed by Gilles Deleuze in *Cinema II: The Time-Image*. Gestalt psychologist Kurt Lewin's (1936) used the expression 'hodological space' to refer to the most effortless but not necessarily the shortest path, defined psychologically and not topologically, to reach a given region in space. Quoting Gilbert Simondon (1964), Deleuze (1989) conceptualized pre-hodological space as a space with 'overlapping of perspectives, which does not allow the grasping of a given object because there are no dimensions in relation to which the unique set would be ordered' (129). While hodological space holds the sensorimotor schema together as the field of forces, oppositions, and tensions are resolved according to their goals, in pre-hodological space higher cognitive process are not yet formed. As Hven (2017) writes, this sequence

> arouses a primordial bodily sensation that is in dissonance with our higher-level cognitive response to the scene. If spectators become consciously aware of this dissonance, the eerie sensation may intensify further once we feel relieved to see the car being swallowed by the nothingness of the swamp. How are we to explain this phenomenon? [...] Before our bodily responses are formed in accordance with the action we are about to perform and to the sensory-motor linkages that enfold this action in line with our beliefs, judgements, and morality [...] we inhabit a 'pre-hodological' space (133).

The spectator thus follows and accompanies the character's anxiety and the car's sinking and expects or even desires this to be fulfilled without relating it to the implied criminal intentions. This occurs *before* any moral judgment of the character's goals, and not because the spectator has *not yet* identified with him (as Grodal argued). Hven's argument allows for a reconceptualization of the notion of *fabula* (or, more generally, of narrative comprehension) by challenging various assumptions of the cognitive-formalist model: the search for an unambiguous, chronological, coherent, and inferentially deduced storyline that excludes from narrative comprehension the immediate, bodily, sensuous, visceral, and affective dimensions of the cinematic experience (cf. 112). The 'embodied fabula', as he calls it, 'proposes an intimate linkage of action, cognition and perception [...] in contrast with the classical cognitive position, which assumes that these belong to clearly separate domain' (117).

This perspective is in line with an enactive account of the human experience, which rejects a vertical distinction and, at the neural level, a modular stratification of perception, cognition, and action. The narrative value of the tensive motifs lies in the embodied understanding of the cinematic events on the basis on the spectator's tendency to action, which implies a unity of perceptual and mental acts. In this sense, the revision of the notion of empathy as a process in which, beginning at the neural level, motor and emotional processes are bound together and provide an immediate grasping of the narrative situation, will offer an effective model to describe the spectator's response to contemporary cinema. Rather than a mere representation of events, watching a film is the *enactment* of a performance in which the spectator internally reproduces the character's psychophysical condition and, in doing so, empathetically experiences the *sense* of such a condition. Rather than being functional to a narrative *comprehension* of the events, the tensive motifs are narrative *prehension*, a grasping of the meaning on the basis of a bodily simulation of the character's actions and intentions through the mediation of the film's embodied actions and intentions. The *spectator-as-organism* is as a living subject that *emerges* from the relationship with the environment in which he is *immersed*, whether it be hospitable or hostile.

As the analysis of the tensive motifs has shown, the spectator's response in fact depends on the energetic forces that put the relationship between the character and the fictional environment in tension and that extend such a tension beyond the screen to the relationship between the spectator and the experiential environment (which includes the former). *Enaction* is thus the form of such an *interactive* and intersubjective response that fills the gap between the mere watching of bodies moving on the screen and experiencing their *intentions* empathically. This tension, in fact, affects not only the visual level of perception but also manifests itself as a sensation of vertigo, a perceivable effect of an 'attractive' force, as though the film were able to draw the spectator inside the screen before he is able to project himself into it. In this dynamic that involves 'filmic forces' and the spectator's tendency to 'enactivate' them, the bodily nature of the experience acquires a fundamental role. These factors seem to integrate and build upon the originary intuition of psychologist Hugo Münsterberg (2002) that the film functions on the basis of human structures of perception, attention, memory, and imagination (for example, a close-up corresponds to the spectators' need for a closer and more detailed view). The approach I adopt in this book, however, aims at overcoming this notion of 'disincarnated embodiment' of human cognitive needs in favour of a conception of the film experience as *constitutively* embodied.

Narractions

I can now better describe the tensive motifs' anatomy and function. While they appear with different motivations, objectives, and concrete modalities in accordance with the fictional pact made with the spectator, their use transcends genres and the overall style of the film: intensification is not only used, as might be simplistically assumed, in action and horror films, nor only in either classical or postmodern cinema, nor can it by excluded a priori from dramatic and comedy films. Instead, it is a tendency that manifests itself across all genres and progressively throughout all eras of film history. Although intensification is a prominent characteristic of contemporary action films, in which the advancements in technology and in visual effects have a direct impact on the spectacularity of the film, tensive motifs can also be found in other genres. In this sense, the motifs also diverge from the associations proposed by Linda Williams (1991) between genre (i.e. pornography, horror, or melodrama) and the kind of the pleasurable response of the spectator (arousal, screams, and tears, respectively) elicited on the basis of a mimicry of the film characters.

The function of the tensive motifs consists in achieving the spectator's engagement through the controlled management of sensory energy throughout the narrative arc. Internal and external tensions are dosed out over the relatively prolonged duration of a single film's narration. The motifs are in fact often strategically placed at key points in the narration (prologue, epilogue, climax, etc.) in order to create moments of energy condensation that then echo across the whole film and modulate the energy that has been collected up to that point.

Furthermore, the tensive motifs act along a stratification of experiential levels. The appearance of a tensive motif during the course of the narration first generates a basal state of activation, a raising of the 'threshold of physical attention' through a stimulation that produces automatic and instinctive physiological reactions. At this basic level, the motifs begin to 'move' latent forces in the common space of experience constituted by the intersection between the character's space of action and the spectator's space of reception. The spectator's empathetic orientation towards the film and the film's expressive movement towards the spectator give rise to a circuit in which neurophysiological mechanisms, perceptual dynamics, cognitive and affective processes, and symbolic interiorization reciprocally interact.

It is true that the film experience is based on a perceptual activity in which optic and acoustic stimuli are the main factors contributing to the representation of movement, the guidance of attention, and the instantiation and maintenance of affective relationships with the characters. Differing from the classical approaches of the cognitive sciences, enactivism posits that perception and comprehension have a motor and practical basis. As neuroscientific evidence suggests, the mere act of watching someone else performing intentional actions directly engages the observer through an embodied form of simulation, one that should be conceived as integrative and not necessarily substitutive of the standard simulation by which we 'read' the other's mind by postulating a theory about her inner state. The embodied simulation hypothesis supports the idea that the spectator carries out a series of simulative acts that allow her to make a foreign experience her own, and to grasp the character's intentions and emotion even prior to their axiological and ethical evaluation. Moreover, embodied simulation compensates for a lack of literal interactivity and of actual physical co-presence. In that liminal area that is formed between the imaginary world of the film and the physical reality in which the spectator nonetheless remains, the latter not only watches the fictional world, but also participates in it as a subject of corporeal stimulation and engagement built on a somatosensory basis.

It follows that the tensive motifs can be conceived as sorts of interferences within canonical narrative continuity. Rather than interrupting the narrative and the attentional flow, they are topical moments in which continuity intensifies but is not disrupted. In this sense, rather than opposing the regime of continuity to that of discontinuity, the *intensified continuity* typical of contemporary cinema would be better defined as a *modulated continuity*, given the constant interplay of peaks and drops of energy that stress but do not destroy continuity.

The cinema of tensions

The most innovative theoretical concept that emerges from the analysis of the five tensive motifs concerns the correlation of tension and intensification with *intentionality*, understood essentially, albeit with partial reformulation, in the phenomenological sense of the term (cf. Brentano 1874; Husserl 1900-1901). Albeit with substantial disagreement about whether or not intentionality is at the basis of the distinction between psychic and physical phenomena, in general this describes consciousness' typical characteristic of 'pointing at something', of being *aimed* or *directed*, of focusing *on* something, and of perceiving, feeling, understanding, and judging something. What is intentional is thus the *orientation* of consciousness towards an object (which is defined as an 'intentional object') (cf. Gallagher & Zahavi 2007, 107-128).

As we have seen in the chapter on the motifs of the fall, emotions play a crucial role in the motivation-action dynamic and in the process of homeostasis and are, in fact, considered to be *action tendencies* in cognitive psychology (Frijda 1986; 1987). As Grodal (2009) underlines in regard to the role of embodied simulation in his PECMA flow, '[m]irror neurons in the premotor cortex may play a major role in prompting action tendencies in viewers that mirror the actions and intentions of the characters' (150), and '[t]he tension may be transformed into relaxation when the goals are implemented' (150).

It bears noting here that etymologically the word 'tension' indicates a state of nervous excitement, one that is accompanied by emotional instability, a stretching that may precede a rupture. Tension thus describes a state, whether emotional (tension as anxiety, apprehension, being on guard) or motor, that leads to the self-perception of one's own body: after all, the fibrous connections between the muscles and the skeleton that allow the human being to obtain information about the position of the body (proprioception) are called *tendons*. Tension, however, is also at the root of essentially cognitive terms: 'in-tend', in the sense of understanding or interpreting, or even as a teleological term in the sense of 'having intention to', demanding, and/or wanting. In a figurative sense, to intend indicates 'tending (towards something)' and thus 'striving, turning oneself towards, forcing oneself towards, seeking or being ready to do anything in order to reach' a goal. The noun 'intention' in fact derives from the Greek *éntasis* (effort, exertion) and thus refers to an 'effort to understand'. In the same way, the term 'intense', which derives from the Latin *intĕntu(m)*, past participle of *intĕndere*, connects intensification to the same semantic area as tension and intentionality.

Beyond etymological and philosophical discourses on the exact nature of intentionality, and in particular on the 'persistence' of consciousness in precognitive acts, the proposition that implicitly subtends the interpretation of the functions of tensive motifs of air is that these themselves incorporate an intentionality, each managing the specific 'tensive object' towards which the motif *tends* according to specific strategies, and thus *orienting* the spectator's consciousness towards a 'something', an end, understood not so much in terms of the materiality of the character's physical movement in the fictional environment but rather as the ideal 'end point' of the movement intended by the motifs or experienced by the spectator by way of an empathetic act. This form of *embodied intentionality* implies that sort of corporeal pre-reflexive knowledge that Merleau-Ponty (2002) calls 'motor intentionality' (127) and from which Sobchack (2004) implicitly borrow her ideas of 'carnal knowledge', but furthermore adds the idea that not only the spectator's live body but also the character's and the film's lived bodies are involved in a composite intentional act.

I am aware of the risks of this argument. If intentionality describes consciousness' typical characteristic of 'pointing at something', it cannot exist without a consciousness, which makes its application to the film experience seem more problematic given that film represents an 'intersection of consciousnesses'. In a film, we first find the quasi-consciousness of the character, or rather an entity who acts within the world of the film according to an intentional dynamic that is planned out in advance but that is perceived by the spectator as having its own intentionality, possessing mental states and, therefore, thus emotional ones as well. Then there is the pseudo-consciousness of the film, or rather that particular form of corporeality that moves, directs, orients itself, and as a body, manifests its own intentionality. Both of these *sui generis* forms of 'preconstituted consciousness' are perceived as 'present' by the only consciousness that one can really count as such, namely that of the spectator. The spectator is in fact the subject of the intentional act intrinsic to the tensive motifs, and it is for the spectator that these motifs are projected, despite this act being mediated by the pseudo-consciousness of the film and the quasi-consciousness of the character.

Tension, *intensification*, and *intentionality* thus form a semantic complex that describes the reciprocal interaction between the energy radiated by the film's corporeality, the dynamic forces modulated by that energy, and the empathic act through which the spectator intends his own consciousness, more or less deliberately and reflexively, towards an intentional object that is more or less near, reachable, and stable. I will now recap the main assumptions of the analysis of the tensive motifs by emphasizing how the position of the intentional object and the path to reach it varies in each of the motifs, as well as the modality through which the *disembodying-reembodying* dynamic takes place.

Walking on the wire

In the tensive motif of acrobatics, the spectator is literally held by a thread. The action is tensive because the latter is continuously exposed to the risk of tragic failure, or rather the appearance of a consequent motif, namely the fall. This risk is perceived in the condition of precarious equilibrium and expressed through formal techniques that directly convey a sense of vertigo to the spectator, or that implicitly *warn* him of the danger of an imminent fall. The 'tensive object' thus finds itself in a perpetual state of undecidability, in continuous oscillation, suspended between two possible outcomes whose likelihood changes from moment to moment, without either seeming about to happen in the immediate future.

The formal style of the representation is strategically constructed to convey a sense of vertigo to the spectator, understood as a sense of the instability and undecidability of the tensive object towards which the motif is directed. This vertigo is not simply the result of the interaction between the empirical force of gravity, to which the spectator is subject, and the force of gravity that works upon the characters within the fictional environment; rather, it is the result of its incorporation into the formal elements of the film (such as oscillatory camera movements, whip pans, extreme close-ups). The surface-level corporeal expressivity of the character (facial muscles, posture, skin, hand movements) conveys the human incapacity to act in dangerous and literally 'unstable' situations. This gives rise to a disturbance of sensation and perception, which produces a feeling of instability and vertigo.

This vertigo and excess of tension, however, are unfailingly accompanied by a series of restabilizing principles that function on a perceptual level (the insertion, from time to time, of a re-establishing shot that allows the spectator to recontextualize the relationship between the character and the environment in several phases) and on a cognitive level (the insistence on a character's face in order to achieve a strong emotional bond and highlight salient points in the narrative). The spectator is invited to form a stable relationship with the acrobat, one characterized by a form of empathy that functions on different levels and that, while offering contact and a close meeting, continues to preserve distance, as anticipated by classical Filmology.

Falling down

In the fall, the individual inevitably loses her contest with gravity and with her own physical powers and finds herself in a system in which the tensive object has suddenly changed its position: she is suddenly moved away from the action and brought 'down to earth', to the ideal site of impact, the point towards which movement is directed and unstoppably tends. The tensive object even seems to generate an attraction that is strengthened by the body's distance from the ground. When taking place before the fall, acrobatics represents a potential fall and functions both as preparation for a fall and as a 'loading' of energy; during the actual fall, the accumulated energy seems to suddenly discharge over the course of an increasingly rapid and inalterable trajectory. The tensive object almost seems to go towards the falling body, with the effect of increasing the sense of speed and anticipating the moment of contact.

For this reason, cinema employs strategies that reduce intentionality in order to reconstitute homeostatic equilibrium, carrying out a biological regulation of the organism in response to the 'energetic excursion' that has been caused by major modifications to the 'sensorial temperature'. Mainly, this happens above all through the dilation of the temporal dimension of the representation of the fall. This is achieved first through the use of *slow motion*, which lightens the movement, diffusing its energetic charge and emphasizing its emotional and symbolic valence. Slow motion distances the movement from the point of impact, delaying it without cancelling out its certainty, and sometimes dispersing a large amount of the energy during the fall in order to make the impact less visceral. Second, this can be accomplished through a temporal dilation and spatial expansion, a pulling back and re-distancing. A descending movement is generally shown from several visual perspectives (but also, in narrative terms, from a multiplicity of sympathetic and emotional alignments) in such a way that it does not conclude too quickly. One of the most frequent variations of this strategy is an alternating dynamic between the subjective and the objective. Empathetically participating in a filmic fall does not only mean aligning oneself perceptually with the character who is falling. Furthermore, we hardly ever witness and experience a fall completely through the falling character's subjectivity: first we need to see the altitude from which he is falling, the facial expression and posture his body takes on during the fall, what path he will take, whether there is someone watching and, if so, with what psychological attitude they are watching. In short, these techniques carry out an objectivization that allows for participation in the fall in a more complete way. These strategies of temporal and spatial expansion affect a repeated distancing from the tensive object of the motif, despite the inevitable fate towards which it precipitously tends.

Hitting the ground

In the motif of the impact, the tensive object takes on a momentary and localized form which is nevertheless highly intensified, given that the energy progressively dissipated during the 'slowing down' of the fall gives way, in the final instants, to a dramatic recharging that ends with a veritable explosion. As in an explosion, the effect is traumatic, and the released energy continues to echo in the surrounding environment for some time afterwards.

To make the trauma more 'digestible', cinema hides the impact or represents it in a strategic way. This is less applicable in cases in which the physical laws of the fictional space do not correspond to those of the real world: superheroes fall to learn how to fly, and their bones never break; comic bodies invite us simply to laugh at their misfortune, robots and cyborgs can at most draw closer to humans through their experience of an inner suffering, but will certainly not be bruised by a fall; the avatar-like bodies of digital cinema and virtual words do not have to worry about flesh and blood but rather about 'code' and the 'matrix'; characters on intergalactic missions can simply teleport themselves to safety at the last moment before the impact. What are more interesting are cases in which the film maintains the physical laws of the real world. Here, a full-fledged censorship of impact takes place, a hiding which can occur through the total blackening (or whitening) of the visual field at the end of a fall, or at least its last stages, which reflects the character's subjectivity.

These strategies embody the physiological and psychological reactions of the spectators, who either *fail* to see or do not *want* to see what they perceive as an event that is overly violent on a physical, psychological, or even philosophical level, such as the events of 9/11. Significantly, this perceptual censorship does not succeed in allowing the subject to escape the effects of the trauma, since on a neural and mental level even movements or trajectories of events that are occluded one or more times are 'completed'. Faced with a sight that is too difficult to look at—so much that the spectator tends to look away from the screen or instinctively activates defensive reactions—cinema seems to carry out the task in the spectator's place, incorporating these reactions into its own 'bodily language'.

Turning upside-down

Phenomenology teaches that the way in which human beings perceive and think about the world is shaped by what the biological body allows or excludes as a function of its basic posture (erect) and motor capacity. The tensive motif of overturning suggests that in each film experience there are two systems of orientation at work, whether in cooperation or mutual conflict, but in any case independent of one another: the potentially disembodied expressive system of the screen and the perceptual system embodied in the spectator. Cinema does not have to respect the 'gravitational' orientation of characters, even when the laws of gravity apply to the fictional environment. The film, taken as the mediating principle of the relationship between the character and the spectator, can continue to respect the laws of physics while at the same time upsetting the system of orientation through which the spectator experiences this relationship, troubling his perceptions and her sense of balance. Through the encounter between the *non-gravitational* system on the screen and the *gravitational* system in front of the screen, cinema has the ability to offer an experience that is always subject to the progressive or momentary invalidation of the law of gravity.

This *relativity* of orientation leads to the expressive use of techniques that overturn the tensive object, placing it in an ambiguous position, upside down and for this reason seemingly unrecognizable. Before an overturned image, in particular one of a face, the spectator's natural tendency to compensate for the disorientation by 'repositioning' the elements in the field according to 'ordinary' axes of orientation (for example, tilting the head to the side before the image of an upside-down face, or imagining the uprighted image) emerges. On the other hand, the spectator can always abandon himself to the disorientation, adapting the fictional pact with the film to a new cognitive and perceptual regime, or see the overturning as an aestheticized form of representation, taking pleasure in it. This second option, however, is only momentary, and is inevitably followed by the necessity of uprighting. To avoid a situation in which the effort at reconfiguration and interpretation damages narrative continuity and affective homeostasis, the image has to normalize itself, thus carrying out the uprighting in the place of the spectator. This normalization can be carried out through a clear break in the editing or a rotation of the camera; in the case of the latter, this sometimes occurs in such a way that the 'move' performed by the film-body goes unnoticed or is attributed to the movement of the characters. In any case, despite being the inversion of an inversion, this 'unoverturning' leads not to the restoration of the original state but rather to a new condition of orientation.

Drifting in the void

Emancipation from the usual axes of orientation becomes a stylistically justified option due to the very nature of the fictional world when the spacewalks of astronauts are depicted. With the force of gravity absent from the fictional world, the intentional structure of movement is substantially weakened. Movement is deprived of its directionality due to the weakening or impossibility of the character completely controlling his body's posture or the direction of his movements, as well as a clear reduction in the efficacy of actions involving manipulating objects, grasping, and the sense of touch. Such ungrounding and ungraspability are symptoms of the *non-intentionality* that characterizes the motif of the drift, or rather of the suspension of the character's ability to *apprehend* or *comprehend* both the objects of his actions and his own intentions. In the drift, the tensive object remains in a way unreachable because it is too vague, suspended in an atmosphere lacking the tensive force of gravity. This particular environment is functional to the creation of ambiguous and unstable affordances, in which the gap between optical information and tactile information is deliberately used to create a sense of suspension.

It is possible that under certain conditions the 'empty' space that separates the spectator from the screen is, so to speak, invaded by the 'void' that is depicted in the fictional environment, instantiating a spatial and psychological continuity that gives the spectator the sense of floating in the cosmos: he feels the desensitization of the character's perceptual and motor faculties. Just at the moment when this happens, however, the spectator becomes a kind of 'celestial body', a cluster of matter that has mass and thus exercises its own force of gravity. In this way, the drift ends up reaffirming the spectator's 'empirical' physical condition, which is that of a body situated in an environment that is subject to the force of gravity and anchored to the ground, in respect to which he orients himself. Ungrounding and suspension force the spectator to find a new centre of orientation, namely her own body. Her proprioceptive faculties re-emerge from their attenuated state and 'tacit presence', and impose themselves as the principle of reorientation.

In this case as well, however, we find the usage of filmic strategies of re-incorporation that aim to restore *grasp* and *support* to the spectator's experience, substituting for or working in tandem with physiological mechanisms and cognitive processes. The film negotiates the conflict between the loss of position and proprioceptive re-emergence, adopting a 'gravitational aesthetic' even to represent gestures, postures, movements, and emotions that take place in a non-gravitational context. This happens when the vertigo experienced by the character is conveyed to the spectator not as a non-gravitational fear of the void, but as a gravitational fear of heights, or when a drifting movement is represented through the stylistic devices used to depict a fall. The film thus restores and embodies the force of gravity in its own representational style, even in cases in which this force does not exist in the depicted environment.

Elemental imagination

Re-distancing in order to deal with the vertiginous stimulation of acrobatics; dilation, slowing, and emotional filling to compensate for the dramatic acceleration of the fall; hiding, substitution, redirection of attention, and cushioning to attenuate the violent traumatic charge of the impact; the inversion of the inversion to remedy the destabilization and ambiguity of the overturning; the adoption of a gravitational aesthetic in order to deal with the ungrounding and ungraspability of the drift. While on a more figurative level each of these motifs corresponds to an intentional act that can be phenomenologically attributed to the spectator's consciousness, in each the tensive object takes on an extreme position, different depending on the case, following various paths that share the common characteristic of a certain inability to reach the object. Beneath these forms of 'threatened intentionality' lies a strategy of disembodying of the spectator's constitutive *embodiedness* through the intensification of sensory stimuli, giving way to the activation of 'defensive' physiological mechanisms or cognitive processes of compensation, only to then incorporate these mechanisms and processes into the body of the film itself, thus fully restoring the intentional character of movement. The tensive motifs are moments in which the lived body is in some sense 'thrown off' by overly dizzying, fast, disorienting, or destabilizing movements. It is as though the intention of the motifs ran at a pace too fast for the spectator's consciousness to match, and thus a temporal delay or a spatial gap between that intention and the spectator's consciousness is created. This disturbance, however, is counterbalanced by a complementary process, carried out by the film itself, that restores the temporarily lost equilibrium. Subject to the disembodying-reembodying dynamic, we oscillate between immersion into the narrative and the awareness of our own body, which re-emerges from its 'transparency' due to the hyperstimulation of somatosensory perception and serves as a point of reference in a disorienting environment permeated by uncontrollable forces. And finally, the film's body comes to our aid, helping to reorient perception and comprehension.

Many aspects of this *enactive ecology* should be discussed further in the light of the neurofilmological paradigm (hence, the neologism 'ecofilmology' that I introduced in this final chapter's title). As though reflecting Gaston Bachelard's use of elemental analysis to describe the processes of the literary imagination and its poetics (on the element of air, cf. Bachelard 1988), the motifs of air suggest the existence of others within the field of cinema: water, earth, and fire. This line of research in film studies remains to be developed over time, but has already been contributed to by important interventions that rediscover the philosophical value of the elements in the contemporary imagination (cf. Macauley 2010). From the very first page of his *The Marvelous Clouds*, John Durham Peters (2015) claims that 'a philosophy of media needs a philosophy of nature' and 'offers a philosophy of elemental media—the elements that lie at the taken-for-granted base of our habits and habitat' (1). Media 'are vessels and environments, containers of possibility that anchor our existence and make what we are doing possible' (2). Responding to such a need, this book has offered a journey through filmic *aerial* forms that allow us to experience significant aspects of our relationship with the Self, the Other, and the World. I hope this can be the first step in a wider exploration of our *elemental* imagination through the cinema and other somatosensory media.

Bibliography

Bachelard, Gaston. 1988. *Air and Dreams: An Essay on the Imagination of Movement.* Translated by Edith Farrell & Frederick Farrell. Dallas: Dallas Institute of Humanities and Culture.

Balázs, Béla. 2010. *Early Film Theory: The Visible Man.* Edited by Erica Carter, translated by Rodney Livingstone. New York: Berghahn Books.

Belodubrovskaya, Maria. 2018. 'The Cine-Fist Eisenstein's Attractions, Mirror Neurons, and Contemporary Action Cinema'. *Projections.* 12 (1): 1-18. DOI:10:3167/proj.2018.120102.

Benveniste, Émile. 1971. *Problems in General Linguistics.* Translated by Mary E. Meek. Coral Gables: University of Miami Press.

Bordwell, David, & Kristin Thompson. 2006. *Film Art: An Introduction.* New York: McGraw-Hill.

Bordwell, David. 2006. *The Way Hollywood Tells It: Story and Style in Modern Movies.* Berkeley: University of California Press.

Brentano, Franz C. 1874. *Psychologie vom empirischen Standpunkt.* Leipzig: Duncker & Humblot.

Buckland, Warren, ed. 2009b. *Puzzle Films: Complex Storytelling in Contemporary Cinema.* Wiley-Blackwell, Malden.

Cohen-Séat, Gilbert. 1946. *Essai sur les principes d'une philosophie du cinéma, I. Introduction générale – Notions fondamentales et vocabulaire de filmologie.* Paris: PUF.

Dahlquist, Marina, Doron Galili, Jan Olsson, & Valentine Robert. 2018. *Corporeality in Early Cinema: Viscera, Skin, and Physical Form.* Bloomington: Indiana University Press.

Deleuze, Gilles. 1989. *Cinema 2: The Time Image.* Translated by H. Tomlinson and R. Galeta. Minneapolis: University of Minnesota Press.

Durham Peters, John. 2015. *The Marvelous Clouds. Toward a Philosophy of Elemental Media.* Chicago: Chicago University Press.

Eisenstein, Sergei M. 1988, *Selected Works*. Volume I: *Writings, 1922-34*. Edited and translated by Richard Taylor. London: British Film Institute.

Eisenstein, Sergei. 1993. 'Imitation as Mastery'. In *Eisenstein Rediscovered*. Edited by Ian Christie & Richard Taylor, 66-71. London/New York: Routledge.

Eisenstein, Sergei. 1993. 'Imitation as Mastery'. In *Eisenstein Rediscovered*. Edited by Ian Christie & Richard Taylor, 66-71. London/New York: Routledge.

Elsaesser, Thomas. 1990. *Early Cinema: Space Frame Narrative*. London: British Film Institute.

Epstein, Jean. 1988. 'Magnification'. Translated by Stuart Liebman. In *French Film Theory and Criticism, 1907-1939, Volume 1*. Edited by Richard Abel, 235-240. Princeton: Princeton University Press.

Freeburg, Victor O. 1918. *The Art of Photoplay Making*. New York: MacMillan.

Frijda, Nico H. 1986. *The Emotions*. Cambridge: Cambridge University Press.

Frijda, Nico H. 1987. 'Emotion, Cognitive Structure, and Action Tendency'. *Cognition & Emotion*. 1 (2): 115-143. DOI:10.1080/02699938708408043.

Gallagher, Shaun, & Dan Zahavi. 2007. *The Phenomenological Mind: An Introduction to Philosophy of Mind and Cognitive Science*. London: Routledge.

Grishakova, Marina, & Maria Poulaki, eds. 2019. *Narrative Complexity Cognition, Embodiment, Evolution*. Lincoln: University of Nebraska Press.

Grodal, Torben. 1997. *Moving Pictures: A New Theory of Film Genres, Feelings, and Cognition*. Oxford: Clarendon Press.

Grodal, Torben. 2009. *Embodied Visions: Evolution, Emotion, Culture, and Film*. New York: Oxford University Press.

Gunning, Tom. 1986. 'The Cinema of Attraction[s]: Early Film, Its Spectator and the Avant-Garde'. *Wide Angle*. 8 (3): 63-70.

Gunning, Tom. 1989. 'An Aesthetic of Astonishment: Early Cinema and the (In) Credulous Spectator'. *Art & Text*. 34: 31-45.

Husserl, Edmund. 1900-1901. *Logische Untersuchungen*. The Hague: Nijhoff.

Hven, Steffen. 2017. *Cinema and Narrative Complexity: Embodying the Fabula*. Amsterdam: Amsterdam University Press.

James, William. 1884. 'What is an Emotion?'. *Mind*. 9 (34): 188-205.

King, Geoff. 2000. *Spectacular Narratives: Hollywood in the Age of the Blockbuster*. London: I.B. Tauris.

Kiss, Miklós, & Steven Willemsen. 2017. *Impossible Puzzles: A Cognitive Approach to Contemporary Complex Cinema*. Edinburgh: Edinburgh University Press.

Kracauer, Siegrefied. 1960. *Theory of Film: The Redemption of Physical Reality*. New York: Oxford University Press.

Lewin, Kurt. 1936. *Principles of Topological Psychology*. Translated by Fritz and Grace Heider. New York: McGraw-Hill.

Macauley, David. 2010. *Elemental Philosophy: Earth, Air, Fire, and Water as Environmental Ideas*. Albany: SUNY Press.

Merleau-Ponty, Maurice. 2002. *Phenomenology of Perception*. New York: Humanities Press/London: Routledge & Kegan Paul.

Metz Christian. 1982. *The Imaginary Signifier: Psychoanalysis and the Cinema*. Bloomington/Indianapolis: Indiana University Press.

Morin, Edgar. 2005. *The Cinema, or The Imaginary Man*. Translated by Lorraine Mortimer. Minneapolis/London: University of Minnesota Press.

Münsterberg, Hugo. 2002. *Hugo Münsterberg on Film:* The Photoplay: A Psychological Study *and Other Writings*. Edited by Allan Langdale. New York/London: Routledge.

Murch, Walter. 2001. *In the Blink of an Eye: A Perspective on Film Editing* (2nd ed.). Los Angeles: Silman-James Press.

Poulaki, Maria. 2019. 'Between Distancing and Immersion: The Body in Complex Narrative'. In Grishakova & Poulaki, eds., 291-313.

Shaviro, Steven. 1993. *The Cinematic Body*. Minneapolis: University of Minnesota Press.

Shaviro, Steven. 2008. 'The Cinematic Body Redux'. *Parallax*. 14 (1): 48-54. DOI:10.1080/13534640701781370.

Simondon, Gilbert. 1964. *L'individu et sa genèse physico-biologique*. Paris: Presses Universitaires de France.

Smith, Tim. 2012. 'The Attentional Theory of Cinematic Continuity'. *Projections*. 6 (1): 1-27. DOI:10.3167/proj.2012.060102.

Sobchack, Vivian. 2004. *Carnal Thoughts: Embodiment and Moving Image Culture*. Berkeley: University of California Press.

Strauven, Wanda, ed. 2006. *The Cinema of Attractions Reloaded*. Amsterdam: Amsterdam University Press.

Tikka, Pia. 2008. *Enactive Cinema: Simulatorium Eisensteinense*. Helsinki: University of Art and Design.

Wallon, Henri. 1947. 'De quelques problèmes psycho-physiologiques que pose le cinéma'. *Revue internationale de filmologie*. 1 (1): 15-18.

Wallon, Henri. 1953. 'L'acte perceptif et le cinéma'. *Revue internationale de filmologie*. 4 (13): 97-110.

Williams, Linda. 1991. 'Film Bodies: Gender, Genre, and Excess'. *Film Quarterly*. 44 (4): 2-13.

Williams, Linda. 2000. 'Discipline and Fun: Psycho and Postmodern Cinema'. In *Reinventing film studies*. Edited by Linda Williams & Christine Gledhill, 351-378. London: Arnold.

Bibliography

Adams, Bryan. 2013. 'One of the Greatest Cinematographers Ever: *Gravity*'s Emmanuel Lubezki', *The Credits*. October 4. https://www.mpaa.org/2013/10/one-of-the-greatest-cinematographers-ever-gravitys-emmanuel-lubezki.

Agosta, Lou. 2004. *A Rumor of Empathy: Rewriting Empathy in the Context of Philosophy*. New York: Palgrave Macmillan.

Albera, François, & Martin Lefebvre, eds. 2009. *La filmologie, de nouveau. Cinémas: revue d'études cinématographiques / Cinémas: Journal of Film Studies*. 19 (2-3). DOI:10.7202/037546ar.

Allen, Richard, & Murray Smith, eds. 1997. *Film Theory and Philosophy*. Oxford: Clarendon Press.

Amiel, Vincent, & Pascal Couté. 2003. *Formes et obsessions du inema américain contemporain*. Paris: Klincksieck.

Anderson, Joseph D. 1996. *The Reality of Illusion: An Ecological Approach to Cognitive Film Theory*. Carbondale: Southern Illinois University Press.

Anderson, Joseph D., & Barbara Fisher Anderson, eds. 2007. *Narration and Spectatorship in Moving Images*. Newcastle: Cambridge Scholars Publishing.

Angelaki, Dora E., & Kathleen E. Cullen. 2008. 'Vestibular System: The Many Facets of a Multimodal Sense'. *The Annual Review of Neuroscience*. 31: 125-150.

Apter, Michael J. 1982. *The Experience of Motivation: The Theory of Psychological Reversals*. London: Academic Press.

Arnheim, Rudolf. 1954. *Art and Visual Perception: A Psychology of the Creative Eye*. Berkeley: University of California Press.

Arnheim, Rudolf. 1957. *Film as Art*. Berkeley: University of California Press.

Arnheim, Rudolf. 1989. *Parables of Sun Light: Observations on Psychology, the Arts, and the Rest*. Berkeley: University of California Press.

Bachelard, Gaston. 1988. *Air and Dreams: An Essay on the Imagination of Movement*. Translated by Edith Farrell & Frederick Farrell. Dallas: Dallas Institute of Humanities and Culture.

Balázs, Béla. 2010. *Early Film Theory: The Visible Man*. Edited by Erica Carter, translated by Rodney Livingstone. New York: Berghahn Books.

Banissy, Michael J., & Jamie Ward. 2007. 'Mirror-Touch Synesthesia is Linked with Empathy'. *Nature Neuroscience*. 10 (7): 815-816. DOI:10.1038/nn1926.

Barker, Jennifer M. 2009. *The Tactile Eye: Touch and the Cinematic Experience*. Berkeley and Los Angeles: University of California Press.

Batson, C. Daniel. 2009. 'These Things Called Empathy: Eight Related but Distinct Phenomena'. In *The Social Neuroscience of Empathy*. Edited by Jean Decety & William Ickes, 3-15. Cambridge, MA/London: The MIT Press.

Baudrillard, Jean. 1983. *Simulations*. Translated by Paul Foss, Paul Batton & Philip Beitchman. New York: Semiotetx(e).

Baudrillard, Jean. 2002. *Power Inferno*. Paris: Galilée.

Belodubrovskaya, Maria. 2018. 'The Cine-Fist Eisenstein's Attractions, Mirror Neurons, and Contemporary Action Cinema'. *Projections*. 12 (1): 1-18. DOI:10:3167/proj.2018.120102.

Belpoliti, Marco. 2005. *Crolli*. Torino: Einaudi.

Benveniste, Émile. 1971. *Problems in General Linguistics*. Translated by Mary E. Meek. Coral Gables: University of Miami Press.

Bernard, Claude. 1949. *Introduction to the Study of Experimental Medicine*. Translated by Henry C. Greene. New York: Henry Schuman.

Blakemore, Sarah-J., Davina Bristow, Geoffrey Bird, Chris Frith, & Jamie Ward. 2005. 'Somatosensory Activations During the Observation of a Case of Touch and Vision-Touch Synaesthesia'. *Brain*. 128 (7): 1571-1583. DOI:10.1093/brain/awh500.

Boltanski, Luc. 1999. *Distant Suffering: Morality, Media and Politics*. Translated by G. Burchell. Cambridge: Cambridge University Press.

Bolter, Jay D., & Richard Grusin. 1999. *Remediation: Understanding New Media*. Cambridge, MA: The MIT Press.

Bordwell, David, & Kristin Thompson. 2006. *Film Art: An Introduction*. New York: McGraw-Hill.

Bordwell, David, & Noël Carroll, eds. 1996. *Post-Theory: Reconstructing Film Studies*. Madison: University of Wisconsin Press.

Bordwell, David. 1985. *Narration in the Fiction Film*. Madison: University of Wisconsin Press.

Bordwell, David. 1989. *Making Meaning: Inference and Rhetoric in the Interpretation of Cinema*. Cambridge, MA: Harvard University Press.

Bordwell, David. 2006. *The Way Hollywood Tells It: Story and Style in Modern Movies*. Berkeley: University of California Press.

Botvinick, Matthew, & Jonathan Cohen. 1998. 'Rubber Hands "Feel" Touch that Eyes See'. *Nature*. 391 (6669): 756. DOI:10.1038/35784.

Brain, Robert Michael. 2012. 'Self-Projection: Hugo Münsterberg on Empathy and Oscillation in Cinema Spectatorship'. *Science in Context*. 25: 329-353. DOI:10.1017/S0269889712000166.

Branigan, Edward. 1992. *Narrative Comprehension and Film*. London/New York: Routledge.

Brentano, Franz C. 1874. *Psychologie vom empirischen Standpunkt*. Leipzig: Duncker & Humblot.

Briscoe, Robert E. 2011. 'Mental Imagery and the Varieties of Amodal Perception'. *Pacific Philosophical Quarterly*. 92 (2011): 153-173. DOI:10.1111/j.1468-0114.2011.01393.x.

Bryant, Jennings, & Dolf Zillmann, eds. 1991. *Responding to the Screen: Reception and Reaction Processes*. Hillsdale, NJ: Erlbaum.

Buckland, Warren, ed. 2009b. *Puzzle Films: Complex Storytelling in Contemporary Cinema*. Wiley-Malden: Blackwell.

Buckland, Warren. 2009a. *Film Theory and Contemporary Hollywood Movies*. New York and Abingdon: Routledge.

Bukatman, Scott. 2003. *Matters of Gravity: Special Effects and Supermen in the 20th Century*. Durham: Duke University.

Burke, Luke. 1952. 'On the Tunnel Effect'. *The Quarterly Journal of Experimental Psychology*. 4 (3): 121-138. DOI:10.1080%2F17470215208416611.

Caggiano, Vittorio, Leonardo Fogassi, Giacomo Rizzolatti, Joern K. Pomper, Peter I, Martin A. Giese, & Antonino Casile. 2011. 'View-Based Encoding of Actions in Mirror Neurons of Area F5 in Macaque Premotor Cortex'. *Current Biology*. 21 (2): 144-148. DOI:10.1016/j.cub.2010.12.022.

Caillois, Roger. 2001. *Man, Play and Games*. Translated by Meyer. Barash. Urbana/Chicago: University of Illinois Press.

Calabi, Clotide. 2016. 'Amodal Completion, Perception and Visual Imagery'. *Phenomenology and Mind*. 4: 170-177. DOI:10.13128/Phe_Mi-19599.

Cannon, Walter B. 1926. 'Physiological Regulation of Normal States: Some Tentative Postulates Concerning Biological Homeostatics'. In *A Charles Richet. Ses amis, ses collègues, ses élèves*. Edited by Auguste Pettit. 91-93. Paris: Éditions Médicales.

Cannon, Walter B. 1929. 'Organization for Physiological Homeostasis'. *Physiological Reviews*. 9 (3 July): 399-431. DOI:10.1152/physrev.1929.9.3.399.

Cannon, Walter B. 1932. *The Wisdom of the Body*. New York: W.W. Norton & Company.

Carbone, Mauro. 2007. *Essere morti insieme. L'evento dell'11 settembre 2001*. Torino: Bollati Basic Books.

Carocci, Enrico. 2018. *Il inema schermo-mente. Cinema inemas e coinvolgimento emozionale*. Roma: Bulzoni.

Carroll, Noël. 1999. 'Film, Emotion, and Genre'. In Plantinga & Smith, eds., 21-47.

Carroll, Noël. 1988. *Mystifying Movies: Fads and Fallacies in Contemporary Film Theory*. New York: Columbia University Press.

Carroll, Noël. 1990. *The Philosophy of Horror, or Paradoxes of the Heart*. New York: Routledge.

Carroll, Noël. 1996. *Theorizing the Moving Image*. Cambridge: Cambridge University Press.

Casetti, Francesco. 2008. *Eye of the Century: Film, Experience, Modernity*. New York: Columbia University Press.

Casetti, Francesco. 2015. *The Lumière Galaxy: Seven Key World for the Cinema to Come*. New York: Columbia University Press.

Chalmers, David J. 1996. *The Conscious Mind: In Search of a Fundamental Theory.* New York: Oxford University Press.

Chemero, Anthony. 2009. *Radical Embodied Cognitive Science.* Cambridge, MA: The MIT Press.

Chemero, Anthony. 2016. 'Sensorimotor Empathy'. *Journal of Consciousness Studies.* 23 (5-6): 138-152.

Child, Ben. 2015. 'Zemeckis 3D high-wire biopic *The Walk* "giving audiences vertigo"'. September 30. https://www.theguardian.com/film/2015/sep/30/inema-zemeckis-3d-the-walk-audiences-vertigo.

Chion, Michel. 1994. *Audio-Vision. Sound on Screen.* Edited and translated by Claudia Gorbman. New York: Columbia University Press.

Clark, Adam, & David Chalmers. 1998. 'The Extended Mind'. *Analysis.* 58 (1): 7-19. DOI:10.1093/analys/58.1.7.

Coëgnarts, Maarten, & Peter Kravanja (2015). *Embodied Cognition and Cinema.* Leuven: Leuven University Press.

Cohen-Séat, Gilbert, & Jacques Faure. 1954. 'Retentissement du 'fait filmique' sur les rythmes bioélectriques du cerveau'. *Revue internationale de filmologie.* 16: 27-50.

Cohen-Séat, Gilbert, Henry Gastaut, & Jacque Bert. 1954. 'Modification de l'E.E.G. pendant la projection cinématographique'. *Revue internationale de filmologie.* 16: 7-26.

Cohen-Séat, Gilbert. 1946. *Essai sur les principes d'une philosophie du inema, I. Introduction inemas – Notions fondamentales et vocabulaire de filmologie.* Paris: PUF.

Coombs, Clyde H. 1938. 'Adaptation of the galvanic response to auditory stimuli'. *Journal of Experimental Psychology.* 22 (3): 244-268. DOI:10.1037/h0063313.

Coplan, Amy, & Peter Goldie, eds. 2011. *Empathy: Philosophical and Psychological Perspectives.* Oxford: Oxford University Press.

Coplan, Amy. 2004. 'Empathic Engagement with Narrative Fictions'. *The Journal of Aesthetics and Art Criticism.* 62 (2): 141-152.

Coplan, Amy. 2012. 'Empathy and Character Engagement'. In *The Routledge Companion to Philosophy and Film.* Edited by Paisley Livingston & Carl Plantinga, 97-110. London: Routledge.

Currie, Gregory, & Ian Ravenscroft. 2002. *Recreative Minds.* Oxford: Oxford University Press.

Currie, Gregory. 1995. *Image and Mind: Film, Philosophy and Cognitive Science.* Cambridge: Cambridge University Press.

Curtis, Robin, & Gertrud Koch, eds. 2008. *Einfühlung. Zu Geschichte und Greenwalt eines ästhetischen Konzepts.* München: Wilhelm Fink Verlag.

Cutting, James E., & Ayse Candan. 2015. 'Shot Durations, Shot Classes, and the Increased Pace of Popular Movies'. *Projections.* 9 (2): 40-62. DOI:10:3167/proj.2015.090204

D'Aloia, Adriano, & Ruggero Eugeni, eds. 2014. 'Neurofilmology: An Introduction'. *Cinéma&Cie. International Film Studies Journal*. 14 (22-23): 9-25.
Dahlquist, Marina, Doron Galili, Jan Olsson, & Valentine Robert. 2018. *Corporeality in Early Cinema: Viscera, Skin, and Physical Form*. Bloomington: Indiana University Press.
Damasio, Antonio R. 1994. *Descartes' Error: Emotion, Reason, and the Human Brain*. New York: Grosset/Putnam.
Damasio, Antonio R. 1999. *The Feeling of What Happens: Body and Emotion in the Making of Consciousness*. New York: Harcourt.
Damasio, Antonio R. 2003. *Looking for Spinoza: Joy, Sorrow and the Feeling Brain*. New York: Houghton Mifflin Harcourt.
Damasio, Antonio R. 2010. *Self Comes to Mind: Constructing the Conscious Brain*. New York: Pantheon.
Darwin, Charles. 1871. *The Descent of Man and Selection in Relation to Sex*. London: John Murray.
Davis, David. 2018. 'A Moderately Pessimistic Perspective on "Cooperative Naturalism"', *Projections*. 12 (2): 9-18. DOI:10:3167/proj.2018.120203.
Deleuze, Gilles. 1989. *Cinema 2: The Time Image*. Translated by H. Tomlinson and R. Galeta. Minneapolis: University of Minnesota Press.
Deleuze, Gilles. 2000. 'The Brain Is the Screen'. In *The Brain Is the Screen: Deleuze and the Philosophy of Cinema*. Edited by Gregory Flaxman, 365-373. Minneapolis: University of Minnesota Press.
di Chio, Federico. 2011. *L'illusione difficile. Cinema e serie tv nell'età della disillusione*. Milano: Bompiani.
Di Pellegrino, Giuseppe, Luciano Fadiga, Leonardo Fogassi, Vittorio Gallese, & Giacomo Rizzolatti. 1992. 'Understanding Motor Events: a Neurophysiological Study'. *Experimental Brain Research*. 91: 176-180.
Didi-Huberman, Georges. 2008. *Images in Spite of All: Four Photographs from Auschwitz*. Translated by Shane B. Lillis. Chicago/London: The University of Chicago Press.
Dolezal, Hubert. 1982. *Living in a World Transformed*. New York: Academic Press.
Durham Peters, John. 2015. *The Marvelous Clouds. Toward a Philosophy of Elemental Media*. Chicago: Chicago University Press.
Durt, Christoph, Thomas Fuchs, & Christian Tewes, eds. 2017. *Embodiment, Enaction, and Culture. Investigating the Constitution of the Shared World*. Cambridge, MA/London: The MIT Press.
Ebisch, Sjoerd J.H., Francesca Ferri, Anatolia Salone, Mauro Gianni Perrucci, Luigi D'Amico, Filippo Maria Ferro, Gian Luca Romani, & Vittorio Gallese. 2011. 'Differential Involvement of Somatosensory and Interoceptive Cortices during the Observation of Affective Touch' *Journal of Cognitive Neuroscience*. 23 (7): 1808-1822. DOI:10.1162/jocn.2010.21551.

Ebisch, Sjoerd J.H., Mauro G. Perrucci, Antonio Ferretti, Cosimo Del Gratta, Gian Luca Romani, & Vittorio Gallese. 2008. 'The *Sense* of Touch: Embodied Simulation in a Visuotactile Mirroring Mechanism for Observed Animate or Inanimate Touch'. *Journal of Cognitive Neuroscience*. 20 (9): 1611-1623. DOI:10.1162/jocn.2008.20111.

Eco, Umberto. 1994. *Six Walks in the Fictional Woods*, 75-96. Cambridge, MA: Harvard University Press.

Ehrsson, H. Henrik, Nicholas P. Holmes, & Richard E. Passingham. 2005. 'Touching a Rubber Hand: Feeling of Body Ownership is Associated with Activity in Multisensory Brain Areas'. *J. Neurosci.* 25 (45): 10564-10573. DOI:10.1523/JNEUROSCI.0800-05.2005.

Eisenstein, Sergei M. 1988. *Selected Works.* Volume I: *Writings, 1922-34*. Edited and translated by Richard Taylor. London: British Film Institute.

Eisenstein, Sergei M., & Sergei Tretyakov. 1979. 'Eisenstein's Early Work in Expressive Movement'. Translated by Alma H. Law. *Millennium Film Journal*. 3: 30-38.

Eisenstein, Sergei. 1993. 'Imitation as Mastery'. In *Eisenstein Rediscovered*. Edited by Ian Christie & Richard Taylor. 66-71. London/New York: Routledge.

Elliott, Paul. 2010. 'The Eye, the Brain, the Screen: What Neuroscience Can Teach Film Theory'. *Excursions*. 1: 1-16. DOI:10.20919/exs.1.2010.123.

Elsaesser, Thomas, & Malte Hagener. 2015. *Film Theory: An Introduction through the Senses* (2nd ed.). New York: Routledge.

Elsaesser, Thomas. 1990. *Early Cinema: Space Frame Narrative*. London: British Film Institute.

Epstein, Jean. 1981. 'The Spirit of Slow Motion'. Translated by Tom Milne. *Afterimage*. 10: 34-35.

Epstein, Jean. 1988. 'Magnification'. Translated by Stuart Liebman. In *French Film Theory and Criticism, 1907-1939, Volume 1*. Edited by Richard Abel, 235-240. Princeton: Princeton University Press.

Epstein, Jean. 2012. *Critical Essays and New Translations*. Edited by Sarah Keller & Jason N. Paul. Amsterdam: Amsterdam University Press. DOI:10.1515/9789048513840.

Ferrari, Pier Francesco, & Giacomo Rizzolatti, eds. 2015. *New Frontiers in Mirror Neurons Research*. New York: Oxford University Press.

Filion, Chrisine M., David A. Washburn, & Jonathan P. Gulledge. 1996. 'Can Monkeys (Macaca Mulatta) Represent Invisible Displacement?'. *Journal of Comparative Psychology*. 110 (4): 386-395. DOI:10.1037/0735-7036.110.4.386.

Fingerhut Joerg, & Katrin Heimann. 2017. 'Movies and the Mind: On Our Filmic Body'. In Durt, Fuchs & Tewes, eds., 353-377.

Foucault, Michel, & Ludwig Binswanger. 1993. *Dream and Existence*. Edited by Keith Hoeller. Translated by Forrest Williams & Jacob Needleman. Atlantic Highlands, NJ: Humanities Press.

Freeburg, Victor O. 1918. *The Art of Photoplay Making*. New York: MacMillan.

Freedberg, David, & Vittorio Gallese. 2007. 'Motion, Emotion and Empathy in Aesthetic Experience'. *Trends in Cognitive Sciences*. 11 (5): 197-203. DOI:10.1016/j.tics.2007.02.003.

Frijda, Nico H. 1986. *The Emotions*. Cambridge: Cambridge University Press.

Frijda, Nico H. 1987. 'Emotion, Cognitive Structure, and Action Tendency'. *Cognition & Emotion* 1 (2): 115-143. DOI:10.1080/02699938708408043.

Gallagher, Shaun, & Dan Zahavi. 2007. *The Phenomenological Mind: An Introduction to Philosophy of Mind and Cognitive Science*. London: Routledge.

Gallagher, Shaun. 1986. 'Lived Body and Environment'. *Research in Phenomenology*. 16: 139-170.

Gallese, Vittorio, & Alvin I. Goldman. 1998. 'Mirror Neurons and the Simulation Theory of Mind-Reading'. *Trends in Cognitive Sciences*. 2 (12): 493-501. DOI:10.1016/s1364-6613(98)01262-5.

Gallese, Vittorio, & Michele Guerra. 2012. 'Embodying Movies: Embodied Simulation and Film Studies'. *Cinema: Journal of Philosophy and the Moving Image* 3: 183-210. http://cjpmi.ifilnova.pt/storage/3/3_Gallese_Guerra.pdf.

Gallese, Vittorio, & Michele Guerra. 2019. *The Empathic Screen: Cinema and Neuroscience*. Translated by Frances Anderson. New York: Oxford University Press.

Gallese, Vittorio, & Sjoerd Ebisch. 2013. 'Embodied Simulation and Touch. The Sense of Touch in Social Cognition'. *Phenomenology & Mind*. 4: 269-291. DOI:10.13128/Phe_Mi-19602.

Gallese, Vittorio, Christian Keysers, & Giacomo Rizzolatti. 2004. 'A Unifying View of the Basis of Social Cognition'. *Trends in Cognitive Sciences*. 8 (9): 396-403. DOI:10.1016/j.tics.2004.07.002.

Gallese, Vittorio, Luciano Fadiga, Leonardo Fogassi, & Giacomo Rizzolatti. 1996. 'Action Recognition in the Premotor Cortex'. *Brain*. 119: 593-609. DOI:10.1093/brain/119.2.593.

Gallese, Vittorio. 2001. 'The "Shared Manifold" Hypothesis: From Mirror Neurons to Empathy'. *Journal of Consciousness Studies*. 8 (5-7): 33-50.

Gallese, Vittorio. 2003. 'The Roots of Empathy: The Shared Manifold Hypothesis and the Neural Basis of Intersubjectivity'. *Psychopatology*. 36 (4): 171-180. DOI:10.1159/000072786.

Gallese, Vittorio. 2005a. "Being Like Me": Self-Other Identity, Mirror Neurons and Empathy'. In *Perspectives on Imitation: From Cognitive Neuroscience to Social Science Volume 1*. Edited by Susan Hurley & Nick Chater, 101-118. Cambridge, MA: The MIT Press.

Gallese, Vittorio. 2005b. 'Embodied Simulation: From Neurons to Phenomenal Experience'. *Phenomenology and the Cognitive Sciences*. 4 (1): 23-48. DOI:10.1007/s11097-005-4737-z.

Gallese, Vittorio. 2007. 'Before and Below 'Theory of Mind': Embodied Simulation and the Neural Correlates of Social Cognition'. *Philosophical Transactions of the Royal Society B-Biological Sciences*. 362: 659-669. DOI:10.1098/rstb.2006.2002.

Gallese, Vittorio. 2009a. 'Mirror Neurons, Embodied Simulation, and the Neural Basis of Social Identification'. *Psychoanalytic Dialogues*. 19 (5): 519-536. DOI:10.1080/10481880903231910.

Gallese, Vittorio. 2009b. 'Motor Abstraction: A Neuroscientific Account of How Action Goals and Intentions are Mapped and Understood'. *Psychological Research*. 73 (4): 486-498. DOI:10.1007/s00426-009-0232-4.

Gallese, Vittorio. 2009c. 'Neuroscienze e fenomenologia'. In *Treccani XXI secolo*. http://www.treccani.it/enciclopedia/neuroscienze-e-fenomenologia_%28XXI-Secolo%29.

Gallese, Vittorio. 2010. 'Mirror Neurons and Art'. In *Art and the Senses*. Edited by Francesca Bacci & David Melcher, 441-449. Oxford: Oxford University Press.

Gallese, Vittorio. 2018. 'Naturalizing Aesthetic Experience. The Role of (Liberated) Embodied Simulation'. *Projections*. 12 (2): 50-59. DOI:10.3167/proj.2018.120207.

Garbarini, Francesca, & Mauro Adenzato. 2004. 'At the Root of Embodied Cognition: Cognitive Science Meets Neurophysiology'. *Brain and Cognition*. 56 (1): 100-106. DOI:10.1016/j.bandc.2004.06.003.

Gibson, Eleanor J., & Richard D. Walk. 1960. 'The "Visual Cliff"'. *Scientific American*. 202 (4): 64-71.

Gibson, James J. 1977. 'The Theory of Affordances'. In *Perceiving, Acting, and Knowing: Toward an Ecological Psychology*. Edited by Robert Shaw & John Bransford, 127-143. Hillsdale, NJ: Erlbaum.

Gibson, James J. 2015. *The Ecological Approach to Visual Perception. Classic Edition*. New York/London: Taylor & Francis.

Glynn, Alan J. 1954. 'Apparent Transparency and the Tunnel Effect'. *The Quarterly Journal of Experimental Psychology*. 6 (3): 125-139. DOI:10.1080/17470215408416658.

Goffman, Erving. 1967. *Interaction Ritual: Essays on Face to Face Behavior*. Garden City, NY: Doubleday.

Goldberg, Jay M., Victor J. Wilson, Dora E. Angelaki, Kathleen E. Cullen, & Kikuro Fukushima. 2012. *The Vestibular System: A Sixth Sense*. Oxford/New York: Oxford University Press.

Goldman, Alvin I. 2006a. 'Imagination and Simulation in Audience Responses to Fiction'. In *The Architecture of the Imagination: New Essays on Pretence, Possibility, and Fiction*. Edited by Shaun Nichols, 41-56. Oxford: Clarendon Press.

Goldman, Alvin I. 2006b. *Simulating Minds: The Philosophy, Psychology, and Neuroscience of Mindreading*. New York: Oxford University Press.

Greimas, Algirdas J. 1983. *Structural Semantics: An Attempt at a Method*. Translated by Daniele McDowell, Ronald Schleifer, & Alan Velie. Lincoln: University of Nebraska Press.

Grèzes, Julie, Jorge L. Armony, James Rowe, & Richard E. Passingham. 2003. 'Activations Related to "Mirror" and "Canonical" Neurones in the Human Brain: an fMRI Study'. *Neuroimage*. 18 (4): 928-937. DOI:10.1016/S1053-8119(03)00042-9.

Grishakova, Marina, & Maria Poulaki, eds. 2019. *Narrative Complexity Cognition, Embodiment, Evolution*. Lincoln: University of Nebraska Press.

Grodal, Torben, & Mette Kramer. 2010. 'Empathy, Film, and the Brain'. *Recherches sémiotiques / Semiotic Inquiry*. 30 (1-2-3): 19-35. DOI:10.7202/1025921ar.

Grodal, Torben. 1997. *Moving Pictures: A New Theory of Film Genres, Feelings, and Cognition*. Oxford: Clarendon Press.

Grodal, Torben. 1999. 'Emotions, Cognitions, and Narrative Patterns in Film'. In Plantinga & Smith, eds., 127-145.

Grodal, Torben. 2009. *Embodied Visions: Evolution, Emotion, Culture, and Film*. New York: Oxford University Press.

Grusin, Richard. 2004. 'Premediation'. *Criticism*. 46 (1): 17-39. https://digitalcommons.wayne.edu/criticism/vol46/iss1/3.

Grusin, Richard. 2010. *Premediation: Affect and Mediality After 9/11*. London/New York: Palgrave Macmillan.

Guerra, Michele. 2015. 'Modes of Action at the Movie, or Re-Thinking Film Style from the Embodied Perspective'. In Coëgnarts & Kravanja, eds., 139-154.

Gunning, Tom. 1986. 'The Cinema of Attraction[s]: Early Film, Its Spectator and the Avant-Garde'. *Wide Angle*. 8 (3): 63-70.

Gunning, Tom. 1989. 'An Aesthetic of Astonishment: Early Cinema and the (In) Credulous Spectator'. *Art & Text*. 34: 31-45.

Hanich, Julian. 2010. *Cinematic Emotion in Horror Films and Thrillers: The Aesthetic Paradox of Pleasurable Fear*. New York/London: Routledge.

Hari, Riitta, Nina Forss, Sari Avikainen, Erika Kirveskari, Stephan Salenius, & Giacomo Rizzolatti. 1998. 'Activation of Human Primary Motor Cortex during Action Observation: A Neuromagnetic Study'. *Proceedings of the National Academy of Sciences*. USA 95: 15061-15065.

Harris, Charles S. 1965. 'Perceptual Adaptation to Inverted, Reversed, and Displaced Vision'. *Psychological Review*. 72 (6): 419-444.

Hasson, Uri, Ohad. Landesman, Barbara Knappmeyer, Ignacio Vallines, Nava Rubin, & David J. Heeger. 2008b. 'Neurocinematics: The Neuroscience of Film'. *Projections*. 2 (1): 1-16. DOI:10:3167/proj.2008.020102.

Hasson, Uri, Ori Furman, David Clark, Yadin Dudai, & Lila Davachi. 2008a. 'Enhanced Intersubject Correlations During Movie Viewing Correlate with Successful Episodic Encoding'. *Neuron*. 57 (3): 452-462. DOI:10.1016/j.neuron.2007.12.009.

Heimann, Katrin, Maria Alessandra Umiltà, Michele Guerra, & Vittorio Gallese. 2014. 'Moving Mirrors: A High-Density EEG Study Investigating the Effect of Camera Movements on Motor Cortex Activation During Action Observation'. *Journal of Cognitive Neuroscience*. 26 (9): 2087-2101. DOI:10.1162/jocn_a_00602.

Heimann, Katrin, Sebo Uithol, Marta Calbi, Maria Alessandra Umiltà, Michele Guerra, Joerg Fingerhut, & Vittorio Gallese. 2019. 'Embodying the Camera: An EEG Study on the Effect of Camera Movements on Film Spectators' Sensorimotor Cortex Activation'. *PlusOne*. DOI:10.1371/journal.pone.0211026.

Held, Richard, & Sanford J. Freedman. 1962. 'Plasticity in Human Sensorimotor Control'. *Science*. 142 (3591): 455-462.

Hettinger, Larry J., Tarah N. Schmidt, David L. Jones, & Behrang Keshavarz. 2014. 'Illusory self-motion in virtual environments'. In *Handbook of Virtual Environments: Design, Implementation, and Applications*. Edited by Kelly S. Hale & Kay M. Stanney, 435-466. Boca Raton, FL: CRC Press.

Heuyer, Georges, & Jacque Bert. 1954. 'EEG Changes During Cinematographic Presentation; Moving Picture Activation of the EEG'. *Electroencephalogr Clin Neurophysiol*. 6 (3): 433-444. DOI:10.1016/0013-4694(54)90058-9.

Heuyer, Georges, Gilbert Cohen-Séat, Serge Lebovici, Monique Rebeillard, & M.lle Daveau. 1954. 'Note sur l'électroencéphalographie pendant la projection cinématographique chez des adolescents inadaptés'. *Revue internationale de filmologie*. 16: 51-64.

Hildebrand, Adolf von. 1893. *Das Problem der Form in der Bildenden Kunst*. Strassburg: J.H.E. Heitz.

Hoffner, Cynthia, & Joanne Cantor. 'Perceiving and Responding to Mass Media Characters'. In Bryant & Zillmann, eds., 63-101.

Hulme, Oliver, & Semir Zeki. 2007. 'The Sightless View: Neural Correlates of Occluded Objects'. *Cereb. Cortex*. 17 (5): 1197-1205.

Hume, David. 1793. *A Treatise of Human Nature*. Oxford: Clarendon Press.

Hurley, Susan. 2002. *Consciousness in Action*. Cambridge, MA: Harvard University Press.

Husserl, Edmund. 1900-1901. *Logische Untersuchungen*. The Hague: Nijhoff.

Husserl, Edmund. 1960. *Cartesian Meditations*. Translated by Dorion Cairns. The Hague: Nijhoff.

Husserl, Edmund. 1981. 'Foundational Investigations of the Phenomenological Origin of the Spatiality of Nature'. Translated by Fred Kersten. In Edmund Husserl, *Shorter Works*. Edited by Peter McCormick & Frederick Elliston, 222-233. Notre Dame, IN: University of Notre Dame Press.

Husserl, Edmund. 1989. *Ideas Pertaining to a Pure Phenomenology and to a Phenomenological Philosophy*, Second Book: *Studies in the Phenomenology of Constitution*. Translated by Richard Rojcewicz & André Schuwer. Dordrecht: Kluwer.

Hutto, Daniel D., & Erik Myin. 2013. *Radicalizing Enactivism: Basic Minds Without Content*. Cambridge, MA: The MIT Press.

Hven, Steffen. 2017. *Cinema and Narrative Complexity: Embodying the Fabula*. Amsterdam: Amsterdam University Press.

Iacoboni, Marco. 2009. *Mirroring People: The New Science of How We Connect with Others*. New York: Picador.
James, William. 1884. 'What is an Emotion?'. *Mind*. 9 (34): 188-205.
Jameson, Fredric. 1991. *Postmodernism, or, the Cultural Logic of Late Capitalism*. Durham: Duke University Press.
Johnson, Mark. 1987. *The Body in the Mind: The Bodily Basis of Meaning, Imagination, and Reason*. Chicago: University of Chicago Press.
Johnson, Mark. 2015. 'Foreword'. In Coëgnarts & Kravanja, eds., 9-13.
Johnson, Mark. 2017. *Embodied Mind, Meaning, and Reason: How Our Bodies Give Rise to Understanding*. Chicago: University of Chicago Press.
Johnson, Mark. 2018. *The Aesthetics of Meaning and Thought: The Bodily Roots of Philosophy, Science, Morality, and Art*. Chicago: University of Chicago Press.
Jullier, Laurent. 1997. *L'écran post-moderne: Un inema du recyclage et du feu d'artifice*. Paris: L'Harmattan.
Keshavarz, Behrang, Bernhard E. Riecke, Lawrence J. Hettinger, & Jennifer L. Campos. 2015. 'Vection and visually induced motion sickness: how are they related?'. *Frontiers in Psychology*. 6 (472). DOI:10.3389/fpsyg.2015.00472.
Keysers, Christian, Bruno Wicker, Valeria Gazzola, Jean-Luc Anton, Leonardo Fogassi, & Vittorio Gallese. 2004. 'A Touching Sight: SII / PV Activation during the Observation and Experience of Touch'. *Neuron*. 42 (2): 1-20. DOI:10.1016/s0896-6273(04)00156-4.
Keysers, Christian. 2011. *The Empathic Brain. How the Discovery of Mirror Neurons Changes Our Understanding of Human Nature*. Sydney: Social Brain Press, Kindle Edition.
King, Geoff. 2000. *Spectacular Narratives: Hollywood in the Age of the Blockbuster*. London: I.B. Tauris.
Kiss, Miklós, & Steven Willemsen. 2017. *Impossible Puzzles: A Cognitive Approach to Contemporary Complex Cinema*. Edinburgh: Edinburgh University Press.
Koffka, Kurt. 1935. *Principles of Gestalt Psychology*. New York: Harcourt Brace.
Kohler, Ivo. 1964. 'The Formation and Transformation of the Perceptual World'. *Psychological Issues* 3 (4, Monogr. 12): 1-173. DOI:10.1016/0042-6989(64)90016-1.
Kracauer, Siegrefied. 1960. *Theory of Film: The Redemption of Physical Reality*. New York: Oxford University Press.
Lackner, James R. 1988. 'Some Proprioceptive Influences on the Perceptual Representation of Body Shape and Orientation'. *Brain*. 111 (2): 281-297. DOI:10.1093/brain/111.2.281.
Lackner, James R. 1992. 'Spatial Orientation in Weightless Environments'. *Perception*. 21 (6): 803-812. DOI:10.1068/p210803.
Lackner, James R., & Ashton Graybiel. 1979. 'Parabolic Flight: Loss of Sense of Orientation'. *Science*. 206 (4422): 1105-1508. DOI:10.1126/science.493998.

Lackner, James R., & Ashton Graybiel. 1983. 'Perceived Orientation in Free-Fall Depends on Visual, Postural, and Architectural Factors'. *Aviation Space and Environmental Medicine*. 54 (1): 47-51.

Lacroix, Michel. 2001. *Le culte de l'émotion*. Paris: Flammarion.

Lakoff, George, & Mark Johnson. 1999. *Philosophy in the Flesh: The Embodied Mind and Its Challenge to Western Thought*. New York: Basic Books.

Lanzoni, Susan. 2012. 'Empathy in Translation: Movement and Image in the Psychological Laboratory'. *Science in Context*. 25 (3): 329-353. DOI:10.1017/S0269889712000154.

Lee, Ashley. 2015. 'NYFF: How 'The Walk' Director Robert Zemeckis Shot Joseph Gordon-Levitt's "Painful" High-Wire Scenes'. September 26. http://www.hollywoodreporter.com/news/nyff-how-walk-director-robert-827442.

Lewin, Kurt. 1926. 'Vorsatz, Wille und Bedürfnis, mit über die Vorbemerkungen psychischen Kräfte und Energien und die Struktur der Seele'. *Psychologische Forschung*. 7 (4): 294-385.

Lewin, Kurt. 1936. *Principles of Topological Psychology*. Translated by Fritz and Grace Heider. New York: McGraw Hill.

Linden, David E.J., Ulrich Kallenbach, Armin Heinecke, Wolf Singer, & Rainer Goebel. 1999. 'The Myth of Upright Vision. A Psychophysical and Functional Imaging Study of Adaptation to Inverting Spectacles'. *Perception*. 28 (4): 469-481. DOI:10.1068/p2820.

Lipps, Theodor. 1903. *Grundlegung der Ästhetik*. Hamburg/Leipzig: Voss Verlag.

Lipps, Theodor. 1965. 'Empathy and Aesthetic Pleasure'. In *Aesthetic Theories: Studies in the Philosophy of Art*. Edited by Karl Aschenbrenner & Arnold Isenberg. Englewood Cliffs, NJ: Prentice Hall.

Lipps, Theodor. 1979. 'Empathy, Inner Imitation and Sense-Feelings'. In *A Modern Book of Esthetics*. New York: Holt, Rinehart and Winston.

Locke, John. 1960. *An Essay Concerning Human Understanding*. London: The Buffet.

Lux, Vanessa, & Sigrid Weigel, eds. 2017. *Empathy: Epistemic Problems and Cultural-Historical Perspectives of a Cross-Disciplinary Concept*. New York: Palgrave MacMillan.

Lyng, Stephen, ed. 2005. *Edgework: The Sociology of Risk-Taking*. New York: Routledge.

Macauley, David. 2010. *Elemental Philosophy: Earth, Air, Fire, and Water as Environmental Ideas*. Albany: SUNY Press.

MacDougall, David. 2006. *The Corporeal Image: Film, Ethnography, and the Senses*. Princeton: Princeton University Press.

Mach, Erms. 1875. *Grundlinien der Lehre von den Bewegungsempfindungen*. Leipzig: W. Engelmann.

Mallgrave, Henry F., Eleftherios Ikonomou, & Robert Vischer, eds. 1994. *Empathy, Form, and Space: Problems in German Aesthetics, 1873-1893*. Santa Monica: Getty Center for the History of Art and Humanities.

Mauss, Marcel. 1973. 'Techniques of the Body'. *Economy and Society*. 2 (1): 70-88.

Merleau-Ponty, Maurice. 1964. 'Eye and Mind'. In *The Primacy of Perception*. Edited by James E. Edie. Translated by Carleton Dallery, 159-190. Evanston, IL: Northwestern University Press.

Merleau-Ponty, Maurice. 1967. *The Structure of Behavior*. Translated by Alden Fisher. Boston: Beacon Press.

Merleau-Ponty, Maurice. 1968. 'The Film and the New Psychology'. In *Sense and Non-Sense*. Translated by Hubert L. Dreyfus & Patricia Dreyfus, 48-59. Evanston, Ill.: Northwestern University Press.

Merleau-Ponty, Maurice. 2002. *Phenomenology of Perception*. New York: Humanities Press/London: Routledge & Kegan Paul.

Metz Christian. 1982. *The Imaginary Signifier: Psychoanalysis and the Cinema*. Bloomington/Indianapolis: Indiana University Press.

Michelson, Annette. 1969. 'Bodies in Space: Film as "Carnal Knowledge"'. *Artforum VII* (6): 53-64.

Michotte, Albert, Georges Thinès, & Geneviève Crabbé. 1967. *Les complements amodaux des structures perceptives*. Louvain: Publications Universitaires de Louvain.

Michotte, Albert. 1950. 'On Phenomenal Permanence: Facts and Theories'. *Acta Psychologica*. 7: 293-322.

Michotte, Albert. 1963. *The Perception of Causality*. New York: Basic Books.

Michotte, Albert. 1991a. 'The Emotional Involvement of the Spectator in the Action Represented in a Film: Toward a Theory'. Translated by Alan Costall. In Thinès, Costall & Butterworth, eds., 209-217.

Michotte, Albert. 1991b. 'The Emotions Regarded as Functional Connections'. In Thinès, Costall, & Butterworth, eds., 103-116.

Montani, Pietro. 2010. *L'immaginazione intermediale. Perlustrare, rifigurare, testimoniare il mondo inema*. Roma/Bari: Laterza.

Moran, Dermont. 2004. 'The Problem of Empathy: Lipps, Scheler, Husserl and Stein'. In *Amor Amicitiae: On the Love that is Friendship. Essays in Medieval Thought and Beyond in Honor of the Rev. Professor James McEvoy*. Edited by Thomas A.F. Kelly & Phillip W. Rosemann, 269-312. Leuven/Dudley, MA: Peeters

Morin, Edgar. 2005. *The Cinema, or The Imaginary Man*. Translated by Lorraine Mortimer. Minneapolis/London: University of Minnesota Press.

Morris, David. 2004. *The Sense of Space*. Albany: SUNY.

Mukamel, Roy, Arne D. Ekstrom, Jonas Kaplan, Marco Iacoboni, & Itzhak Fried. 2010. 'Single-neuron Responses in Humans during Execution and Observation of Actions'. *Current Biology*. 20 (8): 750-756. DOI:10.1016/j.cub.2010.02.045.

Mullarkey, John. 2009. *Refractions of Reality: Philosophy and the Moving Image*. Houndmills: Palgrave Macmillan.

Münsterberg, Hugo. 2002. *Hugo Münsterberg on Film:* The Photoplay: A Psychological Study *and Other Writings*. Edited by Allan Langdale. New York/London: Routledge.

Murata, Akira, Luciano Fadiga, Leonardo Fogassi, Vittorio Gallese, Vassilis Raos, & Giacomo Rizzolatti. 1997. 'Object Representation in the Ventral Premotor Cortex (Area F5) of the Monkey'. *Journal of Neurophysiology*. 78 (4): 2226-2230. DOI:10.1152/jn.1997.78.4.2226.

Murata, Akira, Vittorio Gallese, Giuseppe Luppino, Masakazu Kaseda, & Hideo Sakata. 2000. 'Selectivity for the Shape, Size and Orientation of Objects in the Hand-Manipulation-Related Neurons in the Anterior Intraparietal (AIP) Area of the Macaque'. *Journal of Neurophysiology*. 83 (5): 2580-2601. DOI:10.1152/jn.2000.83.5.2580.

Murch, Walter. 2001. *In the Blink of an Eye: A Perspective on Film Editing* (2nd ed.) Los Angeles: Silman-James Press.

Nannicelli, Ted, & Paul Taberham. 2014. *Cognitive Media Theory*. New York/London: Routledge.

Neill, Alex. 1996. 'Empathy and (Film) Fiction'. In Bordwell & Carroll, eds., 175-194.

Noë, Alva. 2004. *Action in Perception*. Cambridge, MA: The MIT Press.

Noë, Alva. 2005. 'Real Presence'. *Philosophical Topics*. 33 (1): 235-264. DOI:10.5840/philtopics20053319.

Noë, Alva. 2009. *Out of Our Heads: Why You Are Not Your Brain and Other Lessons from the Biology of Consciousness*. New York: Hill & Wang.

Palmisano, Stephen, Robert S. Allison, Mark M. Schira, & Robert J. Barry. 2015. 'Future challenges for vection research: definitions, functional significance, measures, and neural bases'. *Front Psychol.* 6 (193). DOI:10.3389/fpsyg.2015.00193.

Perrett, David, Mark Harries, Amanda J. Mistlin, & Andrew J. Chitty. 1990. 'Three Stages in the Classification of Body Movements by Visual Neurons'. In *Images and Understanding*. Edited by Horace Barlow, Colin Blakemore, & Miranda Weston-Smith, 94-107. Cambridge: Cambridge University Press.

Petitot, Jean, Francisco J. Varela, Bernard Pachoud, & Jean-Michel Roy, eds. 1999. *Naturalizing Phenomenology: Issues in Contemporary Phenomenology and Cognitive Science*. Stanford: Stanford University Press.

Pinotti, Andrea, & Massimo Salgaro. 2019. 'Empathy or Empathies? Uncertainties in the Interdisciplinary Discussion'. *Gestalt Theory*. 41 (2): 141-158.

Pinotti, Andrea. 2016. *L'empathie: Histoire d'une idée de Platon au posthumain*. Paris: Vrin.

Pisters, Patricia. 2009. 'Illusionary Perception and Cinema: Experimental Thoughts on Film Theory and Neuroscience'. In *Deleuze and New Technology*. Edited by Mark Poster & David Savat, 224-240. Edinburgh: Edinburgh University Press.

Pisters, Patricia. 2012. *The Neuro-Image: A Deleuzian Film-Philosophy of Digital Screen Culture*. Stanford: Stanford University Press.

Plantinga, Carl, & Greg M. Smith, eds. 1999. *Passionate Views: Film, Cognition and Emotion*. Baltimore: Johns Hopkins University Press.

Plantinga, Carl. 1999. 'The Scene of Empathy and the Human Face on Film'. In Plantinga & Smith, eds., 239-255.

Plantinga, Carl. 2009. *Moving Viewers: American Film and the Spectator's Experience*. Berkeley/Los Angeles: University of California Press.

Plantinga, Carl. 2018. *Screen Stories: Emotion and the Ethics of Engagement*. New York: Oxford University Press.

Poulaki, Maria. 2019. 'Between Distancing and Immersion: The Body in Complex Narrative'. In Grishakova & Poulaki, eds., 291-313.

Preston, Stephanie D., & Frans B.M. de Waal. 2001. 'Empathy: Its Ultimate and Proximate Bases'. *Behavioral and Brain Sciences*. 25 (1): 1-20. DOI:10.1017/S0140525X02000018.

Propp, Vladímir J. 1958. *Morphology of the Folktale*. Bloomington: Indiana University Press.

Purves, Dale, George J. Augustine, David Fitzpatrick, William C. Hall, Anthony-Samuel LaMantia, James O. McNamara, & S. Mark Williams, eds. 2010. *Neuroscience* (5th ed.). Sunderland: Sinauer Associates.

Ramachandran, Vilayanur S., & Stuart M. Anstis. 1986. 'The Perception of Apparent Motion'. *Scientific American*. 254 (6): 102-109. DOI:10.1038/scientificamerican0686-102.

Rancière, Jacques. 2014. *Figures of History*. Translated by Julie Rose. Cambridge: Polity Press.

Raos, Vassilis, Maria Alessandra Umiltà, Akira Murata, Leonardo Fogassi, & Vittorio Gallese. 2006. 'Functional Properties of Grasping-Related Neurons in the Ventral Premotor Area F5 of the Macaque Monkey'. *Journal of Neurophysiology*. 95: 709-729. DOI:10.1152/jn.00463.2005.

Reynolds, Dee, & Matthew Reason, eds. 2012. *Kinesthetic Empathy in Creative and Cultural Practices*. Bristol/Chicago: Intellect.

Richmond, Scott C. 2016. *Cinema's Bodily Illusions. Flying, Floating and Hallucinating*. Minneapolis/London: University of Minnesota Press.

Richter, Hans O., S. Magnusson, Kazuyuki Imamura, Mats Fredrikson, Masaaki Okura, & Yasuyoshi Watanabe. 2002. 'Long-Term Adaptation to Prism-Induced Inversion of the Retinal Images'. *Experimental Brain Research*. 144 (4): 445-457. DOI:10.1007/s00221-002-1097-6.

Rizzolatti, Giacomo, & Corrado Sinigaglia. 2007a. *Mirrors in the Brain: How our Minds Share Actions, Emotions, and Experience*. Translated by Frances Anderson. New York: Oxford University Press.

Rizzolatti, Giacomo, & Corrado Sinigaglia. 2007b. 'Mirror Neurons and Motor Intentionality'. *Functional neurology*. 22 (4): 205-210.

Rizzolatti, Giacomo, & Corrado Sinigaglia. 2010. 'The functional role of the parieto-frontal mirror circuit: Interpretations and misinterpretations'. *Nature Reviews: Neuroscience*. 11 (4): 264-274. DOI:10.1038/nrn2805.

Rizzolatti, Giacomo, & Giuseppe Luppino. 2001. 'The cortical motor system'. *Neuron*. 31 (6): 889-901. DOI:10.1016/s0896-6273(01)00423-8.

Rizzolatti, Giacomo, & Laila Craighero. 2004. 'The Mirror-Neuron System'. *Annual Review of Neurosciences*. 27: 169-192. DOI:10.1146/annurev.neuro.27.070203.144230.

Rizzolatti, Giacomo, & Luciano Fadiga. 1998. 'Grasping Objects and Grasping Action Meanings: the Dual Role of Monkey Rostroventral Premotor Cortex (Area F5)'. *Novartis Found Symp*. 218: 81-95; discussion 95-103. DOI:10.1002/9780470515563.ch6.

Rizzolatti, Giacomo, Leonardo Fogassi, & Vittorio Gallese. 2001. 'Neurophysiological Mechanisms Underlying the Understanding and Imitation of Action'. *Nature Reviews: Neuroscience*. 2: 661-670. DOI:10.1038/35090060.

Rizzolatti, Giacomo, Luciano Fadiga, Vittorio Gallese, & Leonardo Fogassi. 1996. 'Premotor Cortex and the Recognition of Motor Actions'. *Brain Research: Cognitive Brain Research*. 3: 131-141. DOI:10.1016/0926-6410(95)00038-0.

Rizzolatti, Giacomo, Luciano Fogassi, & Vittorio Gallese. 1999. 'Cortical Mechanisms Subserving Object Grasping. A New View on the Cortical Motor Functions'. In *The Cognitive Neurosciences*. Edited by Michael S. Gazzaniga, 539-552. Cambridge, MA: MIT Press.

Rizzolatti, Giacomo. 2005. 'The Mirror Neuron System and its Function in Humans'. *Anat. Embryol.* 210 (5-6): 419-421. DOI:10.1007/s00429-005-0039-z.

Robin, Charles. 1853. *Traité de chimie anatomique et physiologique normal et pathologique, ou Des principes immédiats normaux morbides qui constituent et le corps de l'homme et des mammifères, Vol. 1*. Paris: J.-B. Baillière.

Rocha Antunes, Luis. 2016. *The Multisensory Film Experience: A Cognitive Model of Experiential Film Aesthetics*. Chicago/Bristol: Intellect.

Rock, Irvin. 1966. *The Nature of Perceptual Adaptation*. New York: Basic Books.

Rodowick, David N. 2007. 'An Elegy for Theory'. *October*. 122 (1): 91-109.

Rodowick, David N. 2014. *Elegy for Theory*. Cambridge, MA: Harvard University Press.

Rogers, Sheena. 2013 'Truth, Lies, and Meaning in Slow Motion Images'. In Shimamura, ed., 149-164.

Roques, Mario. 1954. 'Introduction'. *Revue internationale de filmologie*. 16: 3-6.

Scheler, Max. 2017. *The Nature of Sympathy*. Translated by Peter Heath. New York: Routledge.

Schnupp, Jan, Israel Nelken, & Andrew J. King. 2011. *Auditory Neuroscience Making Sense of Sound*. Cambridge, MA: The MIT Press.
Shaviro, Steven. 1993. *The Cinematic Body*. Minneapolis: University of Minnesota Press.
Shaviro, Steven. 2008. 'The Cinematic Body Redux'. *Parallax*. 14 (1): 48-54. DOI:10.1080/13534640701781370.
Shaviro, Steven. 2015. *No Speed Limit*. Minneapolis: University of Minnesota Press.
Shaw, Dan. 2016. 'Mirror Neurons and Simulation Theory. A Neurophysiological Foundation for Cinematic Empathy'. In *Current Controversies in Philosophy of Film*. Edited by Katherine Thomson-Jones, 148-162. New York/London: Routledge.
Shimamura, Arthur P., ed. 2013. *Psychocinematics: Exploring Cognition at the Movies*. New York: Oxford University Press.
Simondon, Gilbert. 1964. *L'individu et sa genèse physico-biologique*. Paris: Presses Universitaires de France.
Sinnerbrink, Robert. 2011. *New Philosophies of Film: Thinking Images*. London/New York: Continuum.
Sinnerbrink, Robert. 2019. 'Phenomenology Encounters Cognitivism'. *Projections*. 13 (2): 1-19. DOI:10:3167/proj.2019.130201.
Slugan, Mario. 2020. 'Film Studies and the Experimental Method'. *NECSUS*. European Journal of Media Studies. Autumn. https://necsus-ejms.org/film-studies-and-the-experimental-method.
Smith, Adam. 2002. *The Theory of Moral Sentiments*. Cambridge: Cambridge University Press.
Smith, Karl U., & William K. Smith. 1962. *Perception and Motion. An Analysis of Space-structured Behavior*. Philadelphia: Saunders.
Smith, Murray. 1995. *Engaging Characters: Fiction, Emotion, and the Cinema*. Oxford: Clarendon Press.
Smith, Murray. 2017. *Film, Art, and the Third Culture: A Naturalized Aesthetics of Film*. New York: Oxford University Press.
Smith, Tim. 2012. 'The Attentional Theory of Cinematic Continuity'. *Projections*. 6 (1): 1-27. DOI:10.3167/proj.2012.060102.
Sobchack, Vivian. 1982. 'Toward Inhabited Space: The Semiotic Structure of Camera Movement in the Cinema'. *Semiotica*. 41 (1-4): 317-335.
Sobchack, Vivian. 1987. *Screening Space: The American Science Fiction Film*. New York: Ungar Press.
Sobchack, Vivian. 1992. *The Address of the Eye: A Phenomenology of Film Experience*. Princeton: Princeton University Press.
Sobchack, Vivian. 2004. *Carnal Thoughts: Embodiment and Moving Image Culture*. Berkeley: University of California Press.
Sontag, Susan. 2003. *Regarding the Pain of Others*. New York: Macmillan.
Souriau, Étienne. 1953. *L'univers filmique*. Paris: Flammarion.

Stadler, Jane. 2017. 'Empathy in Film'. In *The Routledge Handbook of Philosophy of Empathy*. Edited by Heidi L. Maibom, 317-326. New York: Routledge. DOI:10.4324/9781315282015.

Stein, Edith. 1964. *On the Problem of Empathy*. Translated by W. Stein. The Hague: Nijhoff.

Stein, Edith. 1991. 'Einführung in die Philosophie'. In *Edith Steins Werke. Vol. XIII*. Freiburg im Breisgau, Basel/Wien: Herder.

Stewart, John, Olivier Gapenne, & Ezequiel A. Di Paolo, eds. 2010. *Enaction: Toward a New Paradigm for Cognitive Science*. Cambridge, MA: The MIT Press.

Stratton, George M. 1896. 'Some Preliminary Experiments on Vision without Inversion of the Retinal Image'. *Psychological Review*. 3 (6): 611-617. DOI:10.1037/h0072918.

Stratton, George M. 1897a. 'Upright Vision and the Retinal Image'. *Psychological Review*. 4 (2): 182-187. DOI:10.1037/h0064110.

Stratton, George M. 1897b. 'Vision Without Inversion of the Retinal Image'. *Psychological Review*. 4 (5): 463-481. DOI:10.1037/h0071173.

Strauven, Wanda, ed. 2006. *The Cinema of Attractions Reloaded*. Amsterdam: Amsterdam University Press.

Stuart Mill, John. 1867. *An Examination of Sir William Hamilton's Philosophy and of the Principal Philosophical Questions Discussed in His Writings*. London: Longmans, Green, and Co.

Stueber, Karsten. 2006. ***Rediscovering Empathy: Agency, Folk Psychology, and the Human Sciences***. Cambridge, MA: The MIT Press.

Tallis, Raymond. 2011. *Aping Mankind: Neuromania, Darwinitis, and the Misrepresentation of Humanity*. Acumen: Durham.

Tan, Ed. 1996. *Emotion and the Structure of Narrative Film: Film as an Emotion Machine*. Mahwah, NJ: Erlbaum.

Tan, Ed. 2013. 'The Empathic Animal Meets the Inquisitive Animal in the Cinema: Notes on a Psychocinematics of Mind Reading'. In Shimamura, ed., 337-367.

Tapley, Kristpoher. 2009. 'The Top 10 Shots of 2008'. February 25. http://maibaap123.blogspot.com/2011/02/top-10-shots-of-2008-kristopher-tapley.html.

Taylor, James G. 1962. *The Behavioral basis of Perception*. New Haven: Yale University Press.

Thinès, Georges, Alan Costall, & George Butterworth, eds. 1991. *Michotte's Experimental Phenomenology of Perception*. Hillsdale, NJ: Erlbaum.

Thompson, Kristin. 2013a. '*Gravity*, Part 1: Two Characters Adrift in an Experimental Film'. *Observations on Film Art*, November 7. http://www.davidbordwell.net/blog/2013/11/07/gravity-part-1-two-characters-adrift-in-an-experimental-film.

Thompson, Kristin. 2013b. '*Gravity*, Part 2: Thinking inside the Box'. *Observations on Film Art*, November 12. http://www.davidbordwell.net/blog/2013/11/12/gravity-part-2-thinking-inside-the-box.

Tikka, Pia. 2008. *Enactive Cinema: Simulatorium Eisensteinense*. Helsinki: University of Art and Design.

Titchener, Edward B. 1909. *Lectures on the Experimental Psychology of the Thought-Processes*. New York: Macmillan.

Turvey, Malcom. 2020. 'Mirror Neurons and Film Studies. A Cautionary Tale from a Serious Pessimist'. *Projections*. 14 (3): 21-46. DOI:10.3167/proj.2020.140303.

Umiltà, Maria Alessandra, Evelyne Kohler, Vittorio Gallese, Leonardo Fogassi, Luciano Fadiga, Christian Keysers, & Giacomo Rizzolatti. 2001. 'I Know What You Are Doing. A Neurophysiological Study'. *Neuron*. 31 (1): 155-165. DOI:10.1016/S0896-6273(01)00337-3.

Vaage, Margrethe Bruun. 2010. 'Fiction Film and the Varieties of Empathic Engagement'. *Midwest Studies in Philosophy*. 1: 158-179. DOI:10.1111/j.1475-4975.2010.00200.x.

Vaage, Margrethe Bruun. 2016. *The Antihero in American Television*. New York/London: Routledge.

Varela, Francisco J. 1995. 'Neurophenomenology: A Methodological Remedy for the Hard Problem'. *Journal of Consciousness Studies*. 4 (3): 330-349.

Varela, Francisco J., Evan Thompson, & Eleanor Rosch. 1991. *The Embodied Mind: Cognitive Science and Human Experience*. Cambridge, MA: The MIT Press.

Vischer, Robert. 1873. *Über das optische Formgefühl: ein Beitrag zur Ästhetik*. Leipzig: Credner.

Vischer, Robert. 1927. *Drei Schriften zum ästhetischen Formproblem*. Halle: Niemeyer.

Voss, Christiane. 2011. 'Film Experience and the Formation of Illusion: The Spectator as "Surrogate Body" for the Cinema'. *Cinema Journal*. 50 (4): 136-150. DOI:10.1353/cj.2011.0052.

Wallon, Henri. 1947. 'De quelques inemas psycho-physiologiques que pose le inema'. *Revue internationale de filmologie*. 1 (1): 15-18.

Wallon, Henri. 1953. 'L'acte perceptif et le inema'. *Revue internationale de filmologie*. 4 (13): 97-110.

Walton, Kendall L. 1990. *Mimesis as Make-Believe: On the Foundations of the Representational Arts*. Cambridge, MA: Harvard University Press.

Warburg, Aby. 1893. *Sandro Botticellis 'Geburt der Venus' und 'Frühling': Eine Untersuchung Über die Vorstellungen von der Antike in den Italienischen Frührenaissance*. Hamburg: Leopold Voss. Then in 1932: *Gesammelte Schriften*. Leipzig/Berlin: B.G. Teubner.

Welch, Robert B. 1978. *Perceptual Modification: Adapting to Altered Sensory Environments*. New York: Academic Press.

Wertheimer, Max. 1961. 'Experimental Studies on the Seeing of Motion'. In *Classics in Psychology*. Edited by Thorne Shipley, 1032-1089. New York: Philosophical Library.

Williams, Linda. 1991. 'Film Bodies: Gender, Genre, and Excess'. *Film Quarterly*. 44 (4): 2-13.

Williams, Linda. 2000. 'Discipline and Fun: Psycho and Postmodern Cinema'. In *Reinventing film studies*. Edited by Linda Williams & Christine Gledhill, 351-378. London: Arnold.

Wölfflin, Heinrich. 1886. *Prolegomena zu einer Psychologie der Architektur*. Berlin: W. Hertz.

Wollheim, Richard. 1996. *The Thread of Life*. Cambridge: Harvard University Press.

Wood, R.W. 1895. 'The "Haunted Swing" illusion'. *Psychological Review*. 2 (3): 277-278. DOI:10.1037/h0073333.

Yoshimura, Hirokazu. 2002. 'Re-acquisition of Upright Vision While Wearing Visually Left-Right Reversing Goggles'. *Japanese Psychological Research*. 44 (4): 228-233. DOI:10.1111/1468-5884.t01-1-00024.

Zahavi, Dan. 2014. *Self and Other Exploring Subjectivity, Empathy, and Shame*. Oxford University Press: Oxford.

Zillman, Dolf. 2006. 'Empathy: Affect From Bearing Witness to the Emotion of Others'. In *Psychology of Entertainment*. Edited by Jennings Bryant & Peter Vorderer, 151-181. Mahwaw, NJ: Erlbaum.

Žižek, Slavoj. 2022. *Welcome to the Desert of the Real: Five Essays on September 11 and Related Dates*. London: Verso.

Filmography

11'09"01 – September 11 (Alejandro González Iñárritu, Mexico, 2002)
127 Hours (Danny Boyle, USA/UK, 2011)
2001: A Space Odyssey (Stanley Kubrick, USA/UK, 1968)
2010: The Year We Make Contact (Peter Hyams, USA, 1984)
Alice in Wonderland (Tim Burton, USA, 2010)
American Gigolo (Paul Schrader, USA, 1980)
Cape Fear (Martin Scorsese, USA, 1991)
City of Angels (Brad Silberling, USA, 1998)
Clockwork Orange, A (Stanley Kubrick, USA/UK, 1971)
Dark Knight, The (Christopher Nolan, USA/UK, 2008)
Departed, The (Martin Scorsese, USA, 2006)
Dr. Strangelove or: How I Learned to Stop Worrying and Love the Bomb (Stanley Kubrick, USA/UK, 1964)
Fahrenheit 9/11 (Michael Moore, USA, 2004)
Fall of the House of Usher, The (*La chute de la maison Usher*, Jean Epstein, France, 1928)
Fifth Element, The (*Le cinquième élément*, Luc Besson, France/USA, 1997)
Fish Called Wanda, A (Charles Crichton, USA/UK, 1988)
Germany, Year Zero (*Germania anno zero*, Roberto Rossellini, Italy/Germany/France, 1948)
Graveyard of Honor (*Jingi no hakaba*, Kinji Fukasaku, Japan, 1975)
Graveyard of Honor (*Shin Jingi no hakaba*, Takashi Miike, Japan, 2002)
Gravity (Alfonso Cuarón, USA/UK, 2013)
Great Dictator, The (Charlie Chaplin, USA, 1940)
Happening, The (M. Night Shyamalan, USA, 2008)
Hours, The (Stephen Daldry, USA, 2002)
Hudsucker Proxy, The (Joel & Ethan Coen, USA/UK/Germany, 1994)
Inception (Christopher Nolan, USA/UK, 2010)
Interstellar (Christopher Nolan, USA/UK, 2014)
Jurassic Park (Steven Spielberg, USA, 1993)
Lethal Weapon (Richard Donner, USA, 1987)
Magnolia (Paul T. Anderson, USA, 1999)
Martian, The (Ridley Scott, USA/UK, 2015)
Matrix, The (Larry & Lilly Wachowski, USA/Australia, 1999)
Maybe Not (Oliver Pietsch, Germany, 2005)
Million Dollar Hotel, The (Wim Wenders, Germany/UK/USA, 2000)
Mission to Mars (Brian De Palma, USA, 2000)
Oldboy (Park Chan-wook, South Korea, 2003)

Open Your Eyes (*Abre los ojos*, Alejandro Amenábar, Spain/France/Italy, 1997)
Outland (Peter Hyams, UK, 1981)
Psycho (Alfred Hitchcock, USA, 1960)
Région Centrale, La (Michael Snow, Canada, 1971)
Royal Wedding (Stanley Donen, USA, 1951)
Sea Inside, The (*Mar adentro*, Alejandro Amenábar, Spain/France/Italy, 2004)
Spider-Man (Sam Raimi, USA, 2002)
Spider-Man 2 (Sam Raimi, USA, 2004)
Star Trek (J.J. Abrams, USA, 2009)
Stealth (Rob Cohen, USA, 2005)
Strange Days (Kathryn Bigelow, USA, 1995)
Titanic (James Cameron, USA, 1997)
Trapeze (Carol Reed, USA, 1956)
Untouchables, The (Brian De Palma, USA, 1987)
Vanilla Sky (Cameron Crowe, USA, 2001)
Vertical Limit (Martin Campbell, USA/Germany, 2000)
Vertigo (Alfred Hitchcock, USA, 1958)
Walk, The (Robert Zemeckis, USA/UK, 2020)
Who Framed Roger Rabbit (Robert Zemeckis, USA, 1988)
Wings of Desire (Wim Wenders, West Germany/France, 1987)

Index

For Product Safety Concerns and Information please contact our EU
representative GPSR@taylorandfrancis.com
Taylor & Francis Verlag GmbH, Kaufingerstraße 24, 80331 München, Germany

www.ingramcontent.com/pod-product-compliance
Ingram Content Group UK Ltd.
Pitfield, Milton Keynes, MK11 3LW, UK
UKHW022134190926
475702UK00013B/1799
9781041183518